The Encyclopedia of Window & Bed Coverings

Charles T. Randall

The Encyclopedia of Window & Bed Coverings
Published in the United States by Charles Randall, Inc.
Orange, CA

Distributed in Great Britain by
Antique Collectors Club Ltd
Woodbridge, Suffolk

The publisher has made every effort to ensure that all instructions given in this book are accurate and safe, but cannot accept liability for any resulting injury, damage or loss to either person or property whether direct or consequential and however arising. The publisher will be grateful for any information that will assist us in keeping future editions up to date.

Internet: www.charlesrandall.com

Illustrations: Patricia Howard, Carlotta Tormey, Burgundy Beam and Ed Pollick

Cover design: Diego Linares

Interior page design by Chemistry Creative, Minneapolis, MN

Library of Congress Cataloging-in-Publication Data

Randall, Charles T.
  The encyclopedia of window & bed coverings / Charles T. Randall. -- 1st [edition]
     pages cm
  ISBN 978-1-890379-18-6
  1. Draperies in interior decoration. 2. Window shades. 3. Bedding. I. Title. II. Title: Encyclopedia of window and bed coverings.
  NK2115.5.D73R355 2012
  747'.3--dc23
                        2011049461

Introduction.

What a fantastic journey the last twenty-five years have been!
In 1986 I wrote the first comprehensive book on window decorating and, honestly, in my wildest dreams did not expect
this book sell more than one million copies.

Over the years several recurring requests have been made by
window decorating professionals; hopefully, this final edition
fulfills a few of those requests. A couple requests stand out:
giving equal weight to black line artwork as well as color; and
adding numbers to the illustrations to help eliminate miscom-
munication between workrooms and designers. The small
numbers that accompany the illustrations have no other function except to help identify the exact treatment specified.
They are not numbers for patterns.

To help you achieve your own perfect window or bedcovering
treatment is the goal of the *Encyclopedia of Window & Bed Coverings*.

Is one picture worth a thousand words? Graphics have always stimulated the creation and
communication of ideas. The uniqueness—and success—of the *Encyclopedia of Window & Bed
Coverings* lies in combining the presentation of 2,000 illustrations with a truly encyclopedic
display of window and bedding treatments. Twenty-five years and one million copies later, this
original publication on window decorating remains the best organized, most effective design
aid available. If your profession is interior design, this new, expanded edition belongs in your
library, on your work table and with you in the field.

Visual definitions of a particular window/bed treatment are immediately effective communication tools. When accompanied by specific yardage requirements, by glossary-supplied perform-
ance summaries of fabric properties and appearance and by alternative approaches to creating
a desired effect, you have all the information necessary to work with your client. Whether a
budget is lavish or modest, the updated and revised edition offers the optimum number of
choices in an individual design situation.

Our book is sure to become an indispensable resource tool in your work. If you are among the
many who own an earlier edition, I extend my sincere appreciation. Without your patronage,
our latest version would not be possible. I know you will find that it continues in the high
tradition you have come to expect from us.

Charles Randall

Charles Randall

Table of contents

Swags & cascades   192

Fabric shades   226

Shades, shutters & blinds   254

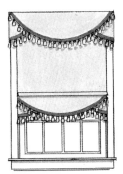

Bed coverings   268

Glossary of decorating terms   309

Glossary of fabric terms   316

Textile fibers & their properties   320

Period style window treatments

The history of window treatments. What book on window treatments could begin without first looking back? Without historical context, we cannot find proper perspective. To begin, look at the adjacent chart. The chart represents the approximate dates of period styles as they relate to art, architecture and interior design. There was some overlapping of dates as styles changed in various regions at different times. For example, the Renaissance began in Italy but it took many years for the style of that period to reach England and France, by which time the Baroque Era had already begun in Italy.

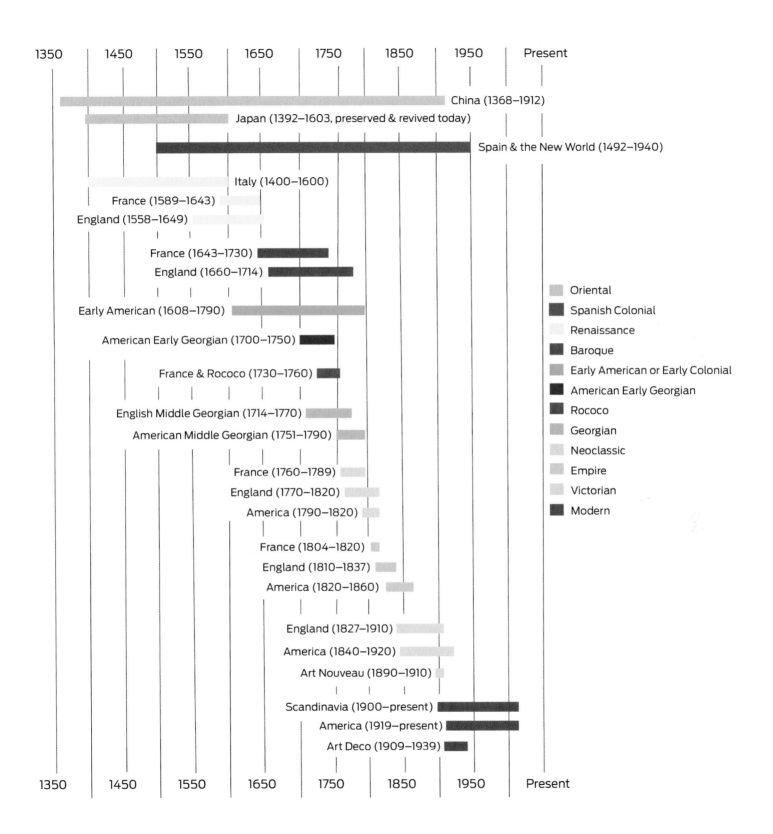

China (1368–1912)
Japan (1392–1603, preserved & revived today)
Spain & the New World (1492–1940)
Italy (1400–1600)
France (1589–1643)
England (1558–1649)
France (1643–1730)
England (1660–1714)
Early American (1608–1790)
American Early Georgian (1700–1750)
France & Rococo (1730–1760)
English Middle Georgian (1714–1770)
American Middle Georgian (1751–1790)
France (1760–1789)
England (1770–1820)
America (1790–1820)
France (1804–1820)
England (1810–1837)
America (1820–1860)
England (1827–1910)
America (1840–1920)
Art Nouveau (1890–1910)
Scandinavia (1900–present)
America (1919–present)
Art Deco (1909–1939)

Oriental
Spanish Colonial
Renaissance
Baroque
Early American or Early Colonial
American Early Georgian
Rococo
Georgian
Neoclassic
Empire
Victorian
Modern

Renaissance, 1440–1649.

The recorded history of interior decoration, as a professional discipline, starts with the Renaissance Era. It was during this time of great change and rebirth in the world of art and architecture that interior design became recognized as a specific art form. The concept of intentionally using one's interior furnishings as decoration, integrating fabrics in a unified and harmonious manner, gained popularity throughout Europe. The values and ideas of "civilized life indoors" began to follow a set of established principles. Thus began the art of interior design and the development of the window covering industry.

Wooden shutters were the primary style of window covering used during the Renaissance period. Mounted on either the interior or exterior of the house, shutters could be closed over the window opening to protect from rain and block out strong sunlight, but did little to provide warmth. Shutters served a purely functional purpose.

The introduction of sheer fabrics allowed for simple, utilitarian curtain making during the sixteenth century. The curtains, most often made of a fine gauze or muslin, provided sun control and some degree of privacy. Hung from iron rods with hooks, usually in single panels, curtains did not become commonplace until after the 1650s.

Although decoration of windows during the Renaissance period was typically simple and understated, bed enclosures and partitions between rooms had curtains that were more elaborate. This allowed for privacy and prevent-

ed drafts and noises from traveling throughout the house. Curtains of this type were called portiere, derived from the French word *porte*, meaning door. The portiere would be hung *ensuite* (within the room). A panel of fabric, perhaps in silk, linen or wool, would be tied to one side during the day and pulled over the door at night for privacy.

During this era, this bed was a person's most cherished possession. Bedrooms of the nobility needed to reflect the importance of their owners. Four-poster beds with canopies were large wooden structures with elaborate hand-carved motifs. Bed hangings were mounted under the canopies to close off the bed. In northern climates, this was to provide warmth and prevent drafts, whereas in the warmer Mediterranean countries, the primary function was to protect from

insects. In fact, the word canopy is believed to be derived from the Greek word *konops*, meaning gnat.

Fabrics at this time were mostly plain weaves of silk, wool or cotton. As new weaving methods were developed, velvets and brocades in rich and vibrant colors became widely used throughout France and Italy. Cotton fabrics now had hand-blocked prints and painted designs in large floral patterns.

Toward the end of the Renaissance, valances began to be incorporated into window treatments. Swags and pelmets, inspired by classical Greek motifs, became the finishing touches to a more elaborate look that flourished during the Baroque era.

Baroque & Early Georgian, 1643–1730.

The Baroque period marked great developments in window dressing. For the first time in history, window curtains became a deliberate and distinctive decorative element to the interior design of a room. New advances in weaving techniques, coupled with increased imports of cotton textiles from India, created new fabrics specifically for use in curtaining.

More "elaborate" and "theatrical" are the most common descriptions of all window coverings of the Baroque era. Cornices and pelmuts gained importance as the preferred method of finishing the top of a window treatment, their primary function being to conceal the rods and workings of the curtains mounted beneath. Cornices were made of wood and usually hand-carved in very

intricate patterns. A pelmut differs from a cornice in that it is usually made of stiffened fabric, shaped and often embellished with hand-made, decorative edgings.

Passementerie, the art of making decorative trims, flourished during the reign of Louis XIV in France. Later the Huguenots, facing religious persecution, fled to Germany, England and the Netherlands, taking with them the skills of their intricate crafts.

The beautiful trimmings initially used to disguise the seams and joins on draperies evolved into decorative details reserved for royalty and nobility. Flat braids, tasseled fringes and soutache made of fine silk yarns adorned the edges of velvets, brocades and damasks during the height of the Baroque era.

Window curtains had previously been simple, single panels of fabric. The innovation of designing them in pairs cre-

ated symmetry at the window. These sets of curtains were usually tied back with a piece of fabric or a metal hold-back during the day and drawn across the window for privacy at night.

Daniel Marot, a French artist and upholsterer of the 17th century, is credited with designing the festoon, a drapery that can be pulled up on the window, creating a swagged effect. From this concept, many varied styles of blinds and valances developed, of which the swag and tail are most notable.

Sashes provided sun control on windows during the day. These were made of very fine, sheer fabric, stretched onto a frame and soaked in oil. The frame was mounted against the window and the oil soaked fabric became translucent, providing a sun barrier.

Bed canopies also became more elaborat-e. The actual wood structure was smaller than during the Renaissance, but the bed hangings and curtains reached new levels of opulence and detailing. Rich embroidered tapestries and silks often were draped from rods mounted under the wood structure.

Early Georgian was the decorative style of England and America during the Baroque period in Europe. While the Early Georgian look was greatly influenced by the French Baroque, it was implemented in a more refined way. Many of the designs that define early Georgian are attributed to Sir Christopher Wren, the Royal Architect of England during the late 1600s.

Late Georgian, 1714–1770.

The most significant concept that developed during the Late Georgian period was the idea of matching window curtains and bed hangings. Previously, these two elements were regarded as unrelated in the interior design of a room. Rich damasks and brocades in gold, blue and red hues were now used for both draperies and bed enclosures. Other colors that dominated interior design during this era included turquoise, teal and coral.

Bed hangings were commonplace throughout Europe by this time, providing warmth and decoration to the stately rooms of the era. Cotton chintz fabrics, block printed in English garden patterns, were more affordable for the

middle class of this time, and increased the popularity of these furnishings. Households of the wealthy would have two sets of bed hangings, a heavy tapestry fabric for winter months and lighter muslin fabric for summer.

Elegantly shaped and elaborately embellished pelmets dominated the silhouette of the Late Georgian period. Appliqué and embroidery techniques further enriched the look of the designs. Billowing festoon blinds, which were pulled up under the pelmets by means of cords, were regarded as the most fashionable look in Europe.

Window treatments during the Late Georgian Era could be described as more fluid. The newest fabrics and designs had a soft flow not previously achieved in window coverings. Adding to this feeling of movement was the

use of ribbons and garlands as motifs on patterned fabrics.

Italian stringing, or reefed curtains, were more popular during this time in England. Thes drapery panels were made to create a festooned look by pulling a string diagonally toward the upper outside corners of the window, causing the curtain fabric to billow and swag gracefully. Interior designers today still use this very elegant method of creating a festoon.

The oil soaked sashes of the Baroque era were still in common use as a means of sun control during this time. Often hand-painted with intricate designs or outdoor scenes, the sashes became the precursor to roller shades,

which were introduced toward the end of this period. Roller blinds were made of natural linen or cotton and used a pulley system to be raised or lowered for sun control and privacy.

Window coverings were becoming more complex as architects began designing window styles and shapes based on the proportions established by sixteenth century Italian architect Andrea Palladio's ideals, called the Palladian principles. These were a specific set of proportions based on the classical architecture of ancient Greece that could be applied to various exterior elements, including windows.

Rococo & Louis XV, 1730–1760.

Upholsterers from the Baroque through the Victorian Eras were solely responsible for the interior design of a home. The finely-made bed hangings and window treatments were the designs of these skilled and influential people who dutifully commissioned and supervised the various trades required to execute their lavish designs. One such person was Thomas Chippendale.

In 1754, Chippendale published a greatly influential pattern book of designs, *The Gentleman and Cabinet-Makers Director*. Chippendale commonly used motifs of Chinese influence as well as the trademark shell design of the Rococo period. These motifs were used in fabric patterns, as well as the richly-carved wooden structure of beds and other furniture.

Window shapes of this era posed many difficulties, as they often do today. The Gothic-peaked window and Palladian-arch window were common throughout Europe and Britain. Chippendale created curved pelmet boards and lambrequins to decorate these windows and then draped them with softly folded swags.

Much of this era took on a lighter approach to draperies and bed hangings, favoring a greater desire for comfort. Lightweight silk taffeta called quinze-seize was the most common fabric for window curtaining and was made in the new lighter hues that typified this period. Colors were more refined; soft pastels in yellow, pink and blue replaced the dark jewel tones of the previous century.

Pull-up curtains, and what were referred to as Roman drapery curtains, were the most fashionable window coverings of the day. Additional fullness was included in the styling of the pull curtains, giving them a softer look. These curtains were paired with draperies of a richer, darker fabric on top or with an embellished pelmet.

Developments in the textile industry during this era allowed for the creation of fabrics that would take on timeless qualities. *Toiles de Jouy* was a printed fabric from the village of Jouy in France. It literally means the work of Jouy and is the origin of fabric that today is known simply as *toile*. Toile was the first fabric to be printed using the copperplate method. This method produced fabrics that had better definition of design and allowed for a larger repeat. Glazing fabrics to produce chintz was also introduced during this time.

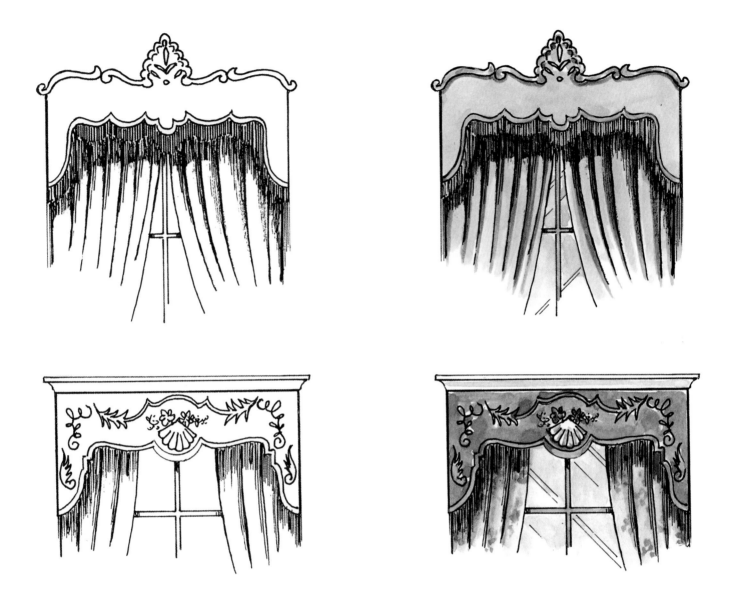

The wooden structure of the bed was redefined in several variations as canopies adopted a lighter look. The half tester was a shorter canopy that projected out from the wall over a portion of the bed rather than the whole length. *Lit a la polonaise* was a domed canopy supported by rods on each of the four corners and distinguished by beautiful silk panels. In France, it had become common to place beds in alcoves and build lambrequins graced with side panels around them.

Cotton and silk replaced heavier fabrics such as velvet and tapestry used for the canopies and bed hangings during the Baroque era. The Rococo period marked a transition from the very ornate, elaborate style in the Baroque era to a refined and classic style that dominated the Neoclassic period of the late eighteenth century.

Neoclassic 1770–1820.

Neoclassicism is an elegant style of design characterized by simple, geometric forms. Ancient Greek and Roman Classical artifacts, found in the excavations at Pompeii and Herculaneum during the 1700s, inspired this styling.

Discoveries at these ruins also inspired popular colors during the Neoclassic Era. A palette of earth tones including clay, terracotta and green were all accented with black. Other influences for decorative colors came from industry rather than history. Wedgwood pottery inspired a range of blue colors that was popular at this time, and the colors used in the tapestry factories Aubusson and Gobelins in France also contributed to the color trends.

The designing of beds and bed canopies became the responsibility of the cabinetmaker rather than the upholsterer at this time. This resulted in less focus on the bed hangings as well as the introduction of coordinated cornices for both the bed and window. One cabinetmaker whose designs were influential in the late 1700s was Thomas Sheraton.

Sheraton was renowned for unique beds and elaborate cornices. The introduction of the Pagoda cornice, with a distinctly Chinese influence, is credited to Sheraton. His designs, published in the 1793 pattern book, *Cabinet-*

maker and Upholsterer's Drawing Book, were carved and gilded with Classical motifs.

Draperies, made in pairs for symmetry, were the most common style of window covering in the Neoclassic Era. This simpler look led to the need to improve the rods used for decorative purposes or functionality. The introduction at this time of the first cord and pulley style rod, now known as a traverse rod, reduced wear and tear on draperies.

These new rods had an overlap in the center that greatly enhanced the finished look of the draperies. In addition, decorative rods with elaborate finials and rings gave interest and balance to the simplicity of the silhouette of this time.

Layers of curtains were added beneath the over drapes as sheers gained popularity. These muslin curtains were

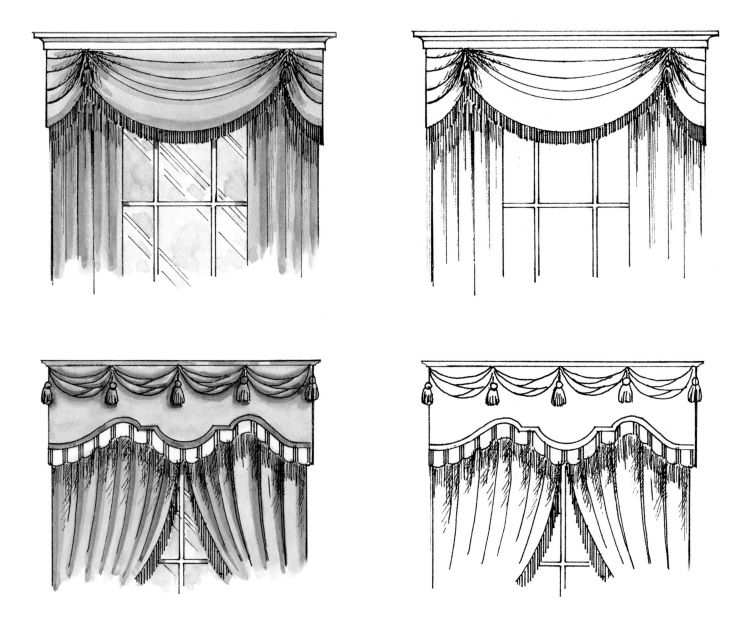

installed onto the window frame to provide added privacy and sun protection in a room.

The biggest technological achievement in the production of decorative textiles in this era was the invention of the Jacquard loom by Joseph Jacquard in 1804.This complex loom allowed the most intricate patterns to be woven into fabric by machine, something that could only be done painstakingly, by hand, in the past. Toward the end of the

Neoclassic period, the sharp symmetry that silhouetted the drapery styling was replaced by an asymmetrical look that was later popularized in the Empire period.

Federal, Empire & Regency 1804–1860.

Once health concerns arose that bed hangings and canopies reduced air circulation and attracted dust, and that wooden structures housed insects, open beds made of iron replaced them. This resulted in a greater emphasis on bed coverings and window treatments during the Empire and Regency Periods.

With the same concerns that saw the demise of the canopy bed, pelmets and cornices also became less important. Window treatments maintained a look of opulence as multiple layers of curtains were now used, often in an asymmetrical styling. It was not uncommon for a window to have four or five individual layers of curtains — an over drape, an

under curtain made of a lighter-weight fabric, a sub curtain and blinds, and possibly a swag valance mounted over the entire ensemble.

The popularity of the sheer sub curtain continued to rise during the Empire period. Made of silk or cotton muslin, these became standard window coverings in neutral hues. Alternatively, glass curtains, also made of muslin, were used in less formal room settings and fitted on the lower half of the window, next to the panes of glass. History suggests that both types of curtain served to protect against unwanted insects entering through open windows and to filter the light from the sun.

The elimination of pelmets and cornices necessitated in refining and designing more intricate drapery headings and rods. French pleats, goblet pleats and smocked headings maintained folds in a more regulated and decorative manner while rods became opulent display pieces. Made of brass or wood, the finials and brackets of these rods took inspiration from classic motifs such as laurel and acanthus leafs, and military ornamentation such as spearheads and eagles.

"Continued drapery," a term used to describe the practice of disguising two or more separate windows as one by means of a continuous valance or rod, easily lent itself to the asymmetrical designs of this era. Each window alone was asymmetrical, but when coupled with the other windows within the arrangement, the mirror image would create a balanced effect.

The popularity of the puddled drapery increased during the Empire period. Designers of the time differed in opinion as to what length was appropriate, from a few inches hanging gracefully on the floor to yards of fabric creating a more dramatic, puddled effect.

Historians also differ in opinion as to the reason for the extra length of fabrics used in what some termed, receptacles for dust. Some believe that the length of draperies represented wealth: the more fabric that person could afford, the wealthier that they were. Others believe that it was purely functional: to stop drafts from the window. This is especially likely since the bed hangings of previous times had been eliminated.

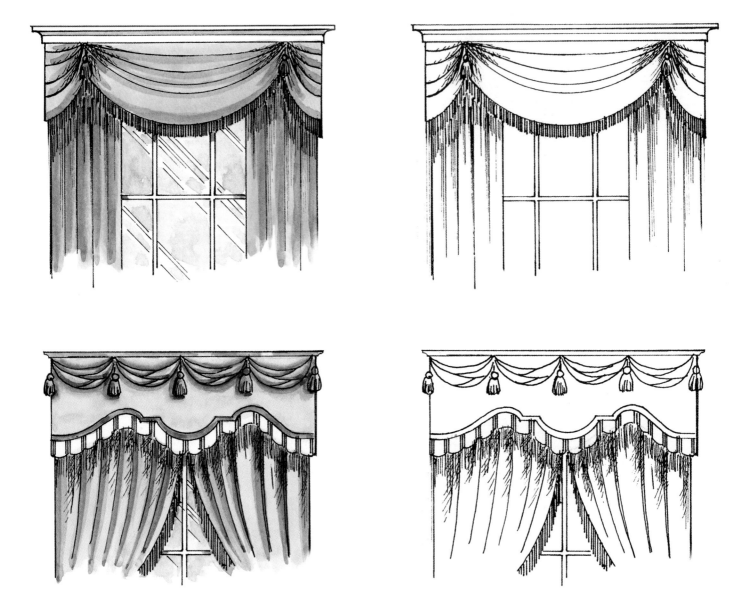

Another decorative detail widely used throughout this time was reverse lining. A secondary fabric could give the effect of an additional layer of drapery, when used as the lining of the main drapery, which was turned back or reversed to reveal the contrast fabric.

Roller blinds added an artistic element to interior design. These became the canvases for landscape paintings and printed designs. Sometimes trimmed with fringe or borders, roller blinds were often an integral part of a window treatment during this period.

Historically, window treatments evolve in cycles of lavishness and opulence to periods of understated simplicity with transitory periods building up to a crescendo. The layered styling of the Empire and Regency periods was the transitory time cresting toward the opulent look of the Victorian Era.

Victorian 1840–1901.

The Victorian Era was a complex period with many different phases defining it. Historians agree, however that it was time of excessiveness and clutter. The multiple layers of curtaining that dominated the silhouette were a reflection of the extravagant look of the Victorian interior. As in the past, it was not unusual for a window treatment to consist of four or five layers of curtains.

Details using fabrics and fringes were the trend. Bands of contrast fabric were often applied to the edges of draperies and valances. The much heavier look of bouillon fringe replaced tassel fringe and braids.

Lace grew in popularity for use as under curtains and glass curtains. Machine-made laces and netting made these fabrics more affordable to the middle class. Lace or sheer panels were gathered onto brass rods and either hung freely at the bottom or attached to the window frame with a second rod at the hem. When used in bedrooms or on doors, these panels would be tied with ribbon, pulling in at the center and creating an hourglass effect.

Respected designers of the time advised their clients on the importance of adding lining and interlining to draperies. Not only would the lining extend the life of the fabric, it would provide thermal qualities and help prevent other furnishings from becoming bleached by the sun.

It was the opinion of noted designer John Loudon that draperies could not perform the function of preventing drafts

unless a cornice valance was used. This wooden box would close off the space at the top of the curtains that could allow cold air to circulate. The cornices used during this era were smaller and less ornate than those of earlier periods, though still gilded and sometimes augmented with brass ornamentation.

Lambrequins, an elongated version of the cornice, which exhibited "legs" extending down the sides of a window, had been in vogue during the Empire and early Victorian eras but became obsolete by the end of the nineteenth century. It was felt that these large structures were too heavy for the interiors of the day and blocked out too much light.

New designs in fabric window shades were evolving. More fabric and fullness were constantly being added to create soft billows. The Austrian shade, with smaller, closely-sewn festoons, was the result of this. Swag and tail valances were

often paired with the Austrian curtain for a refined, elegant look.

Roller shades, now manufactured with spring mechanisms, remained an important window covering for privacy and sun control. Other blinds that became highly developed during this time were the wooden horizontal blind and louvered shutters.

Critics of the excessiveness of the Victorian Era started a reform group advocating more simplicity in styling and a return to Gothic design principles. This came to be known as the Aesthetic Movement. William Morris, a name synonymous with decorative fabrics, was a founder of the Aesthetic Movement in interior design. He and other influential

designers, such as Charles Eastlake, objected to the suffocating, overly-draped look of the high Victorian Era. Their designs were kept simple and functional so as to serve only as a background to the room's interior.

The ideals of the Aesthetic Movement prevailed until the end of the nineteenth century when a revival movement reintroduced the French-influenced styling of draperies, returning once again to elaborate cornices, overdrapes, under-drapes and all the embellishments that typify the window treatments of eras gone by.

Draperies & curtains

Once health concerns arose that bed hangings and canopies reduced air circulation and attracted dust, and that wooden structures housed insects, open beds made of iron replaced them. This resulted in a greater emphasis on bed coverings and window treatments during the Empire and Regency Periods.

With the same concerns that saw the demise of the canopy bed, pelmets and cornices also became less important. Window treatments maintained a look of opulence as multiple layers of curtains were now used, often in an asymmetrical styling. It was not uncommon for a window to have four or five individual layers of curtains — an over drape, an under curtain made of a lighter-weight fabric, a sub curtain and blinds, and possibly a swag valance mounted over the entire ensemble.

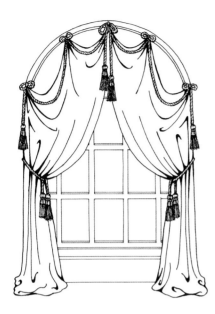

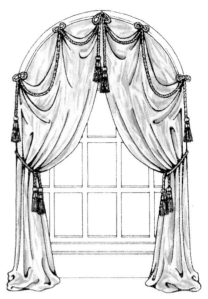

(DR100) Instead of hiding the shape of this grand window, a drapery treatment was chosen to accent its graceful arch. Tassel detailing is an inspired choice.

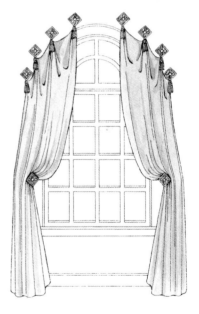

(DR101) Intriguing drapery hardware provides the focal point for this arch top window; drapeable fabric provides the soft accent.

The popularity of the sheer sub curtain continued to rise during the Empire period. Made of silk or cotton muslin, these became standard window coverings in neutral hues. Alternatively, glass curtains, also made of muslin, were used in less formal room settings and fitted on the lower half of the window, next to the panes of glass. History suggests that both types of curtain served to protect against unwanted insects entering through open windows and to filter the light from the sun.

The elimination of pelmets and cornices necessitated in refining and designing more intricate drapery headings and rods. French pleats, goblet pleats and smocked headings maintained folds in a more regulated and decorative manner while rods became opulent display pieces. Made of brass or wood, the finials and brackets of these rods took inspiration

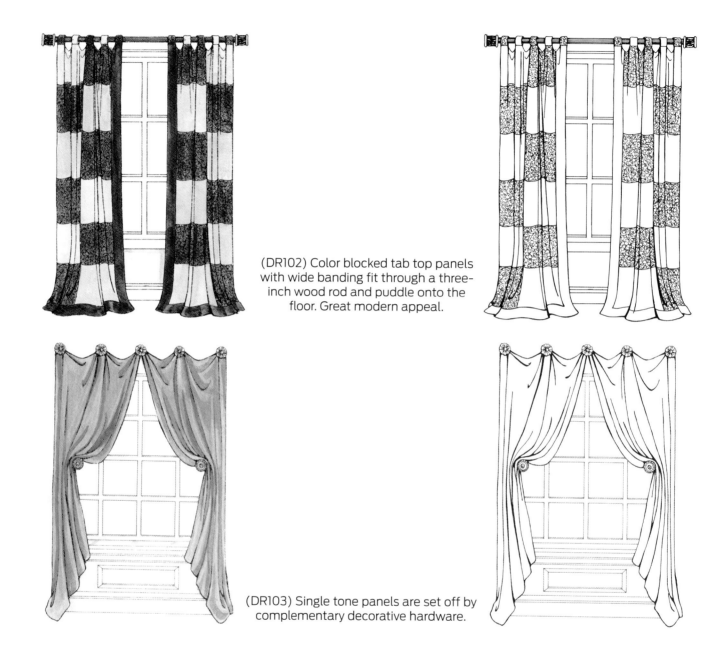

(DR102) Color blocked tab top panels with wide banding fit through a three-inch wood rod and puddle onto the floor. Great modern appeal.

(DR103) Single tone panels are set off by complementary decorative hardware.

from classic motifs such as laurel and acanthus leafs, and military ornamentation such as spearheads and eagles.

"Continued drapery," a term used to describe the practice of disguising two or more separate windows as one by means of a continuous valance or rod, easily lent itself to the asymmetrical designs of this era. Each window alone was asymmetrical, but when coupled with the other windows within the arrangement, the mirror image would create a balanced effect.

The popularity of the puddled drapery increased during the Empire period. Designers of the time differed in opinion as to what length was appropriate, from a few inches hanging gracefully on the floor to yards of fabric creating a more dramatic, puddled effect.

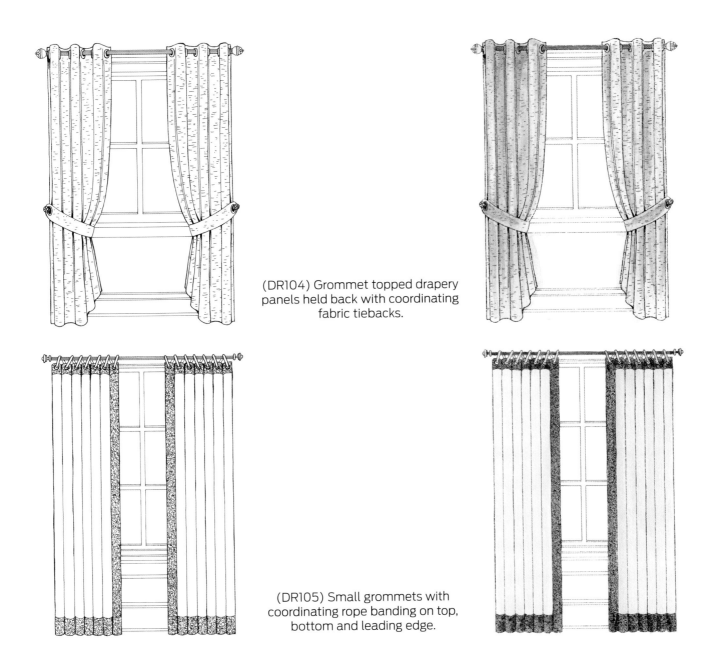

(DR104) Grommet topped drapery panels held back with coordinating fabric tiebacks.

(DR105) Small grommets with coordinating rope banding on top, bottom and leading edge.

Historians also differ in opinion as to the reason for the extra length of fabrics used in what some termed, receptacles for dust. Some believe that the length of draperies represented wealth: the more fabric that a person could afford, the wealthier that they were. Others believe that it was purely functional: to stop drafts from the window. This is especially likely since the bed hangings of previous times had been eliminated.

Another decorative detail widely used throughout this time was reverse lining. A secondary fabric could give the effect of an additional layer of drapery, when used as the lining of the main drapery, which was turned back or reversed to reveal the contrast fabric.

(DR106) Unique string top drapery panels are held back with coordinating fabric tiebacks.

(DR107) Ring top draperies with multiple horizontal banding, finished with bullion fringe.

Roller blinds added an artistic element to interior design. These became the canvases for landscape paintings and printed designs. Sometimes trimmed with fringe or borders, roller blinds were often an integral part of a window treatment during this period.

Historically, window treatments evolve in cycles of lavishness and opulence to periods of understated simplicity with transitory periods building up to a crescendo. The layered styling of the Empire and Regency periods was the transitory time cresting toward the opulent look of the Victorian Era.

The Victorian Era was a complex period with many different phases defining it. Historians agree, however that it was

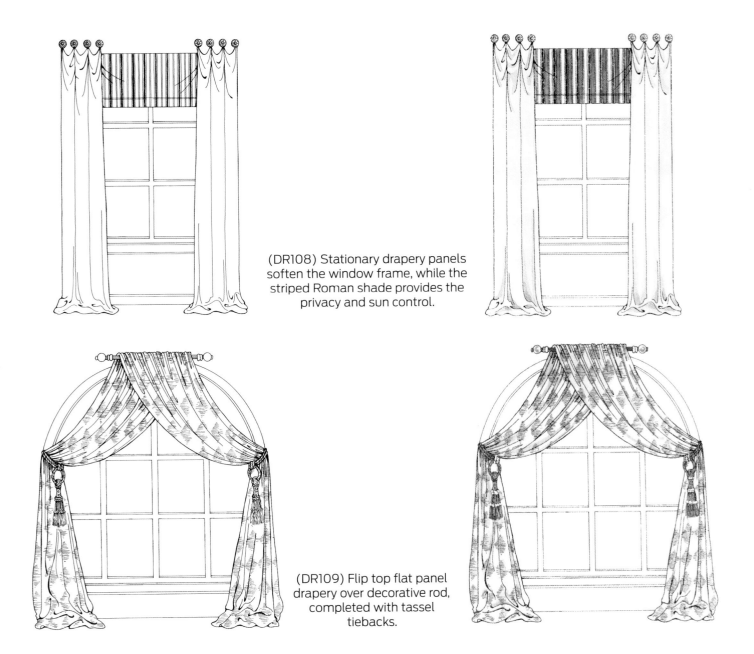

(DR108) Stationary drapery panels soften the window frame, while the striped Roman shade provides the privacy and sun control.

(DR109) Flip top flat panel drapery over decorative rod, completed with tassel tiebacks.

a time of excessiveness and clutter. The multiple layers of curtaining that dominated the silhouette were a reflection of the extravagant look of the Victorian interior. As in the past, it was not unusual for a window treatment to consist of four or five layers of curtains. Details using fabrics and fringes were the trend. Bands of contrast fabric were often applied to the edges of draperies and valances. The much heavier look of bouillon fringe replaced tassel fringe and braids.

Lace grew in popularity for use as under curtains and glass curtains. Machine-made laces and netting made these fabrics more affordable to the middle class. Lace or sheer panels were gathered onto brass rods and either hung freely at the bottom or attached to the window frame with a second rod at the hem. When used in bedrooms or on doors, these

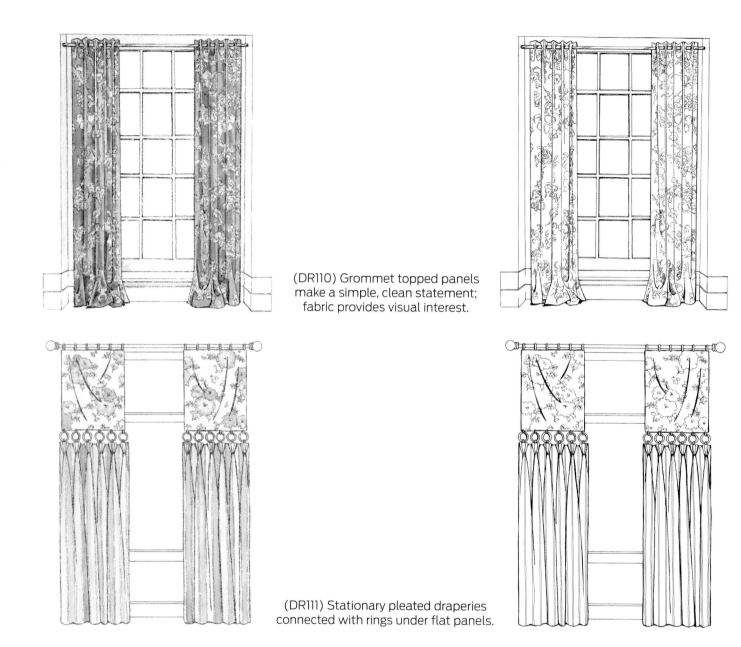

(DR110) Grommet topped panels make a simple, clean statement; fabric provides visual interest.

(DR111) Stationary pleated draperies connected with rings under flat panels.

panels would be tied with ribbon, pulling in at the center and creating an hourglass effect.

Respected designers of the time advised their clients on the importance of adding lining and interlining to draperies. Not only would the lining extend the life of the fabric, it would provide thermal qualities and help prevent other furnishings from becoming bleached by the sun.

It was the opinion of noted designer John Loudon that draperies could not perform the function of preventing drafts unless a cornice valance was used. This wooden box would close off the space at the top of the curtains that could allow cold air to circulate. The cornices used during this era were smaller and less ornate than those of earlier periods, though

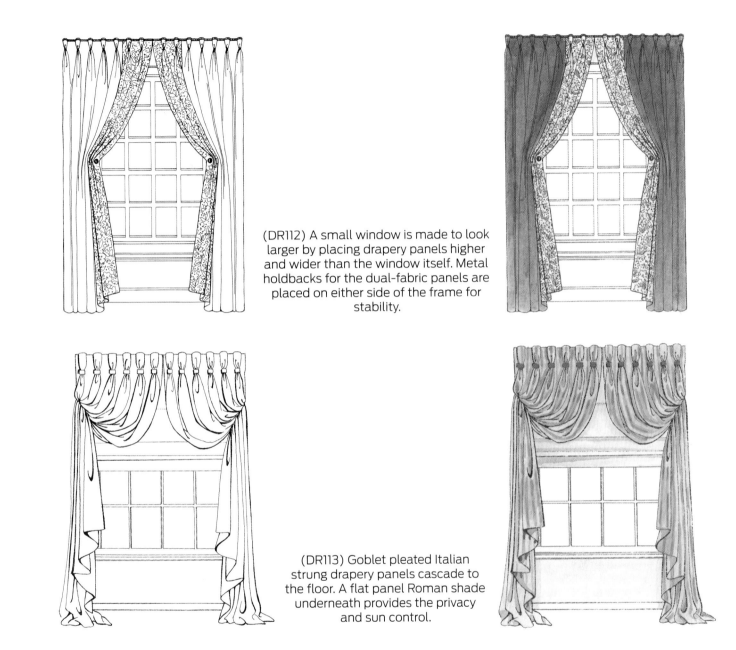

(DR112) A small window is made to look larger by placing drapery panels higher and wider than the window itself. Metal holdbacks for the dual-fabric panels are placed on either side of the frame for stability.

(DR113) Goblet pleated Italian strung drapery panels cascade to the floor. A flat panel Roman shade underneath provides the privacy and sun control.

still gilded and sometimes augmented with brass ornamentation. Lambrequins, an elongated version of the cornice, which exhibited "legs" extending down the sides of a window, had been in vogue during the Empire and early Victorian eras but became obsolete by the end of the nineteenth century. It was felt that these large structures were too heavy for the interiors of the day and blocked out too much light. New designs in fabric window shades were evolving. More fabric and fullness were constantly being added to create soft billows. The Austrian shade, with smaller, closely-sewn festoons, was the result of this. Swag and tail valances were often paired with the Austrian curtain for a refined, elegant look. Roller shades, now manufactured with spring mechanisms, remained an important window covering for privacy

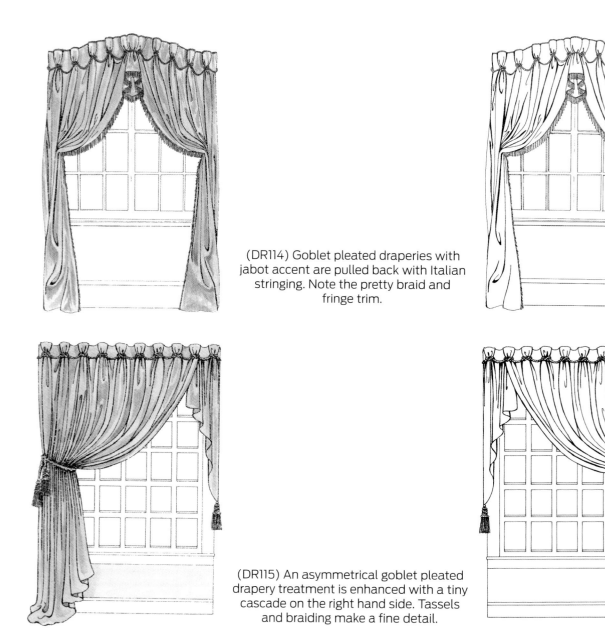

(DR114) Goblet pleated draperies with jabot accent are pulled back with Italian stringing. Note the pretty braid and fringe trim.

(DR115) An asymmetrical goblet pleated drapery treatment is enhanced with a tiny cascade on the right hand side. Tassels and braiding make a fine detail.

and sun control. Other blinds that became highly developed during this time were the wooden horizontal blind and louvered shutters. Critics of the excessiveness of the Victorian Era started a reform group advocating more simplicity in styling and a return to Gothic design principles. This came to be known as the Aesthetic Movement. William Morris, a name synonymous with decorative fabrics, was a founder of the Aesthetic Movement in interior design. He and other influential designers, such as Charles Eastlake, objected to the suffocating, overly-draped look of the high Victorian Era. Their designs were kept simple and functional so as to serve only as a background to the room's interior.

The ideals of the Aesthetic Movement prevailed until the end of the nineteenth century when a revival movement rein-

(DR116) Arched goblet pleated draperies create a dramatic effect. Bishop sleeve effect with rope ties adds to the drama.

(DR117) Fringe-edged goblet pleated drapery panels with jabot accents are contained by fleur de lys holdbacks and tassel ties.

troduced the French-influenced styling of draperies, returning once again to elaborate cornices, over drapes, under drapes and all the embellishments that typify the window treatments of eras gone by.

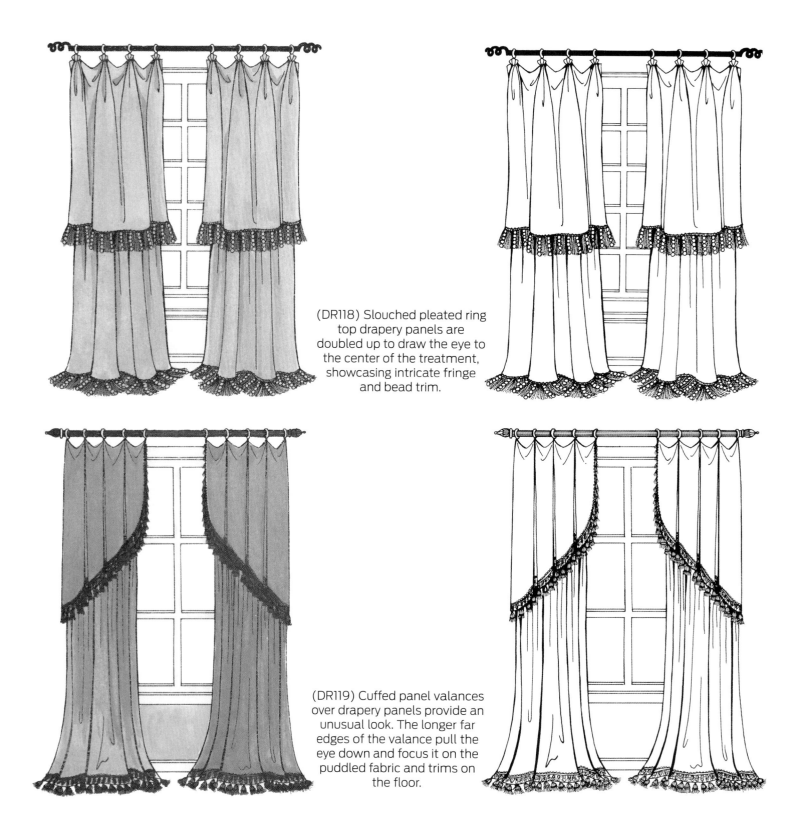

(DR118) Slouched pleated ring top drapery panels are doubled up to draw the eye to the center of the treatment, showcasing intricate fringe and bead trim.

(DR119) Cuffed panel valances over drapery panels provide an unusual look. The longer far edges of the valance pull the eye down and focus it on the puddled fabric and trims on the floor.

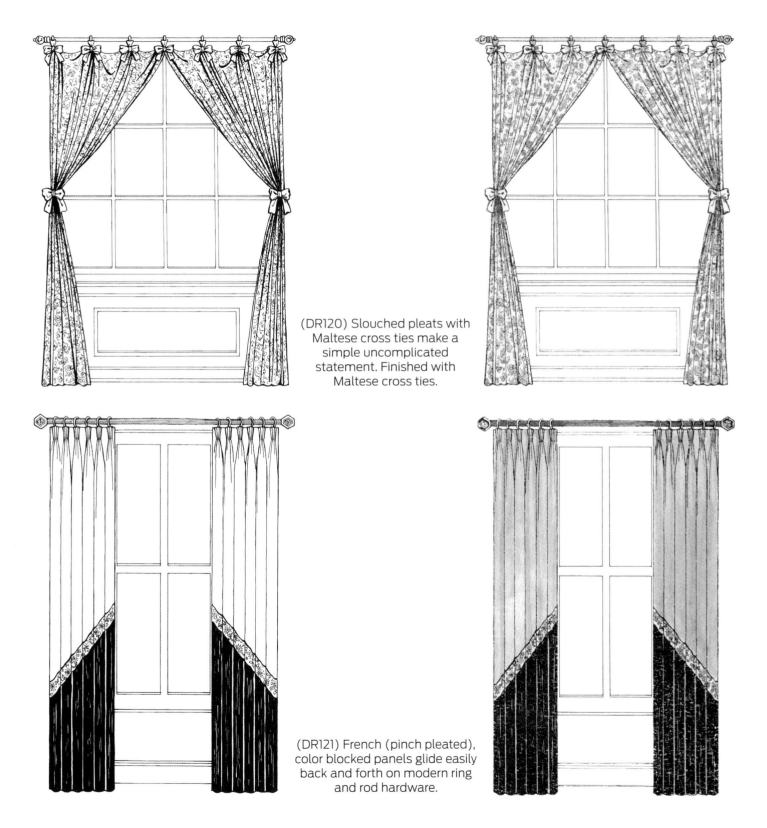

(DR120) Slouched pleats with Maltese cross ties make a simple uncomplicated statement. Finished with Maltese cross ties.

(DR121) French (pinch pleated), color blocked panels glide easily back and forth on modern ring and rod hardware.

(DR122) Goblet pleated drapery panels edged with pompom trim are accented with flags and small jabots with matching ties make a stunning portiere (a drapery hung in a doorway).

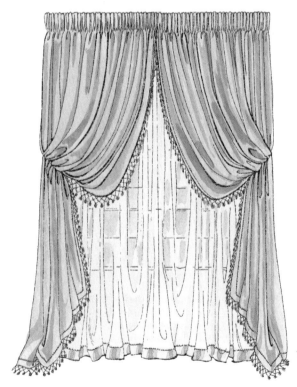

(DR123) Pencil pleated draperies are enhanced with intricate trim and are held back from the window invisibly to reveal a sheer undertreatment.

(DR124) Euro pleated panels with swag flags and jabots on decorative rod. Pleated ties above puddled draperies gives a simple but elegant feeling to this treatment.

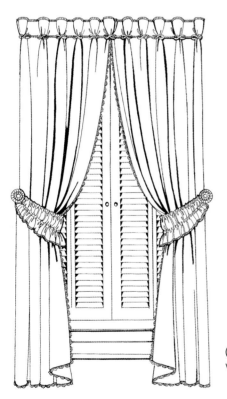

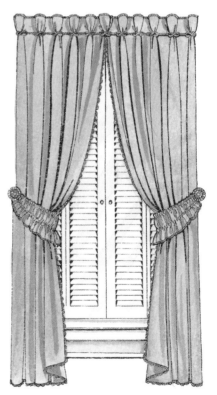

(DR125) Goblet pleated drapery panels with ruffled fabric tiebacks soften hard shutter panels stylishly.

(DR126) This asymmetrical treatment is a beauty with goblet pleats and bullion fringe. Note that the right hand panel has top and middle tassel tiebacks, which balance and enhance its beauty.

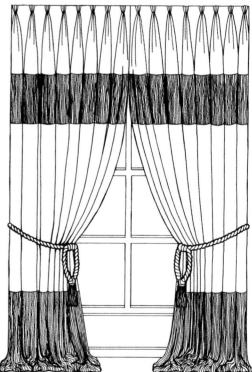

(DR127) Butterfly pleat drapery panels in a color block pattern are dramatic when puddled onto the floor.

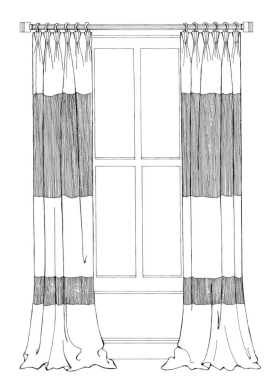

(DR128) Simple French pleated multi-fabric panels on decorative rod are great for a contemporary look. If puddled, stationary panels are adequate, but I recommend non-puddled for traversing draperies.

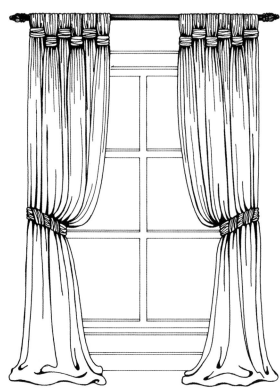

(DR129) Uniquely knotted tab top drapery panels with coordinating tiebacks. This is obviously a stationary treatment.

Rod pocket

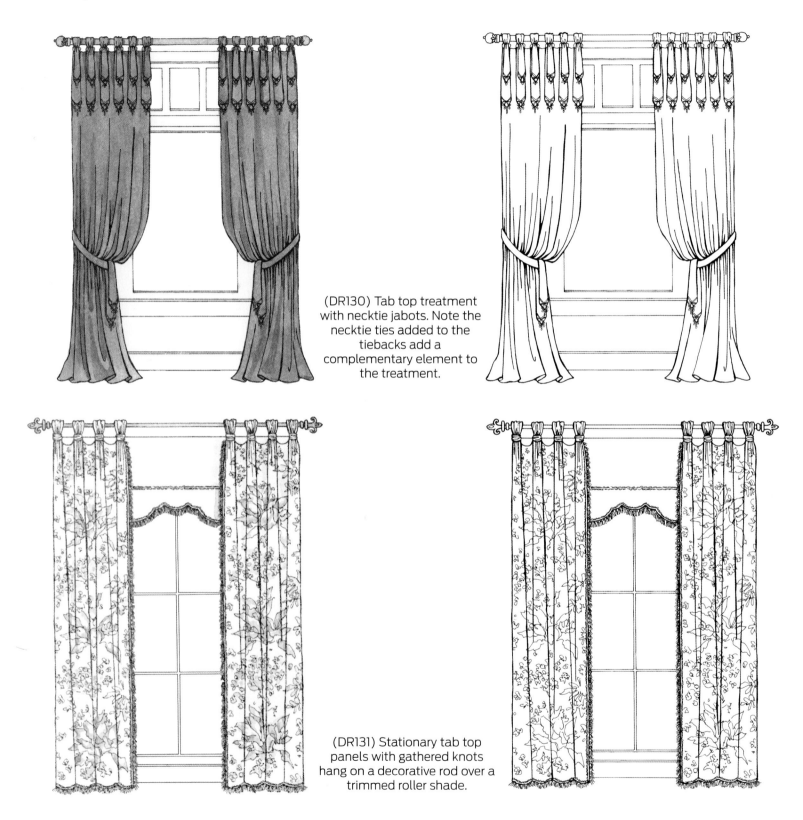

(DR130) Tab top treatment with necktie jabots. Note the necktie ties added to the tiebacks add a complementary element to the treatment.

(DR131) Stationary tab top panels with gathered knots hang on a decorative rod over a trimmed roller shade.

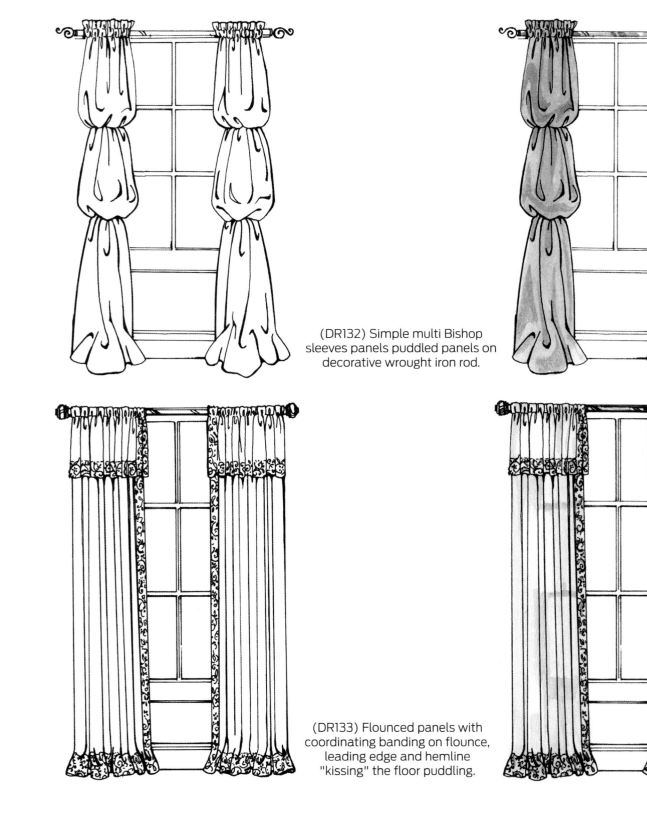

(DR132) Simple multi Bishop sleeves panels puddled panels on decorative wrought iron rod.

(DR133) Flounced panels with coordinating banding on flounce, leading edge and hemline "kissing" the floor puddling.

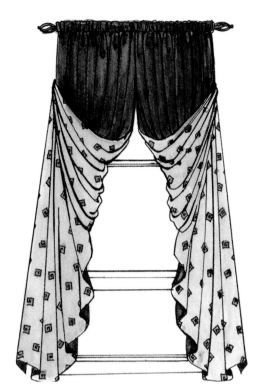

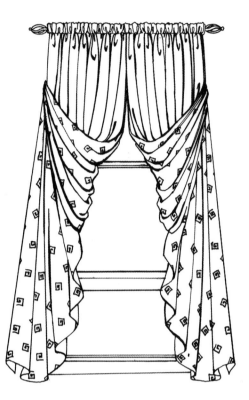

(DR134) Rod pocket tuxedo panels with coordinating lining with high ties on wood rod.

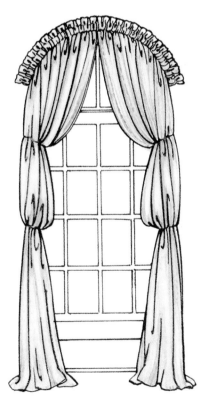

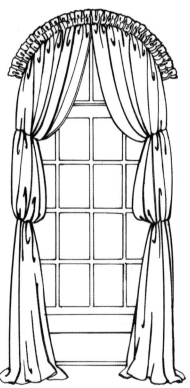

(DR135) Arched rod pocket Bishop sleeve puddled panels.

(DR136) Specialty swinging hardware allow for easy access to French doors. Coordinating fabric add a nice touch. This treatment usually has hidden wands to pull back the panels.

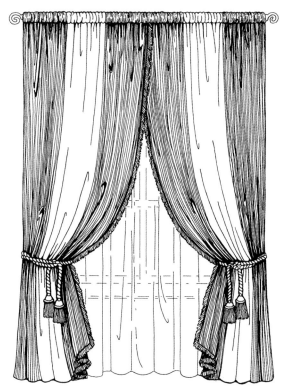

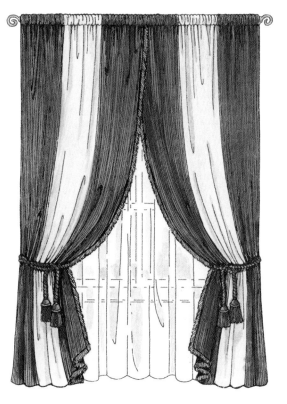

(DR137) Color blocked rod pocket drapery panels with sheer underdraperies are lush and eye-catching.

(DR138) Double rod pocket side panels. The outer panel is on a wood rod, while the back panel is on hidden 1" metal rod. Medallion hold back finishes the treatment nicely.

(DR139) Simple and cost effective rod pocket treatment with 2" stand-up ruffle sleeve over medallion hold backs.

(DR140) Puddled blouson drapery panels hung with rings offer casual elegance.

(DR141) Triple blouson tops on the drapery panels draw the eye with their unique beauty.

(DR142) Multi arched flounced gathered and puddled panels on shepherds crook decorative wrought iron rod.

(DR143) Stationary flounced puddled panel with trim and background gathered swag and cascade on decorative pole offer an asymmetrical look.

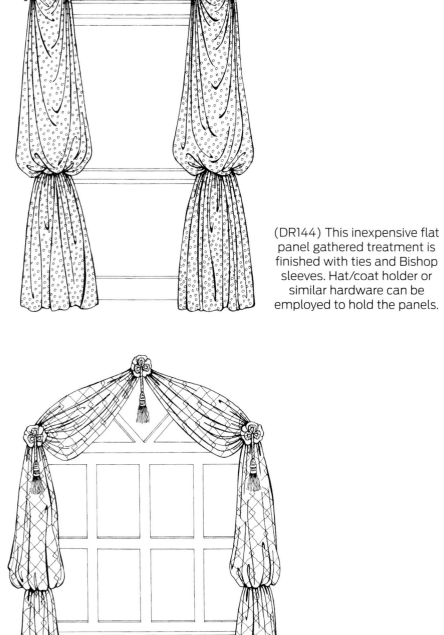

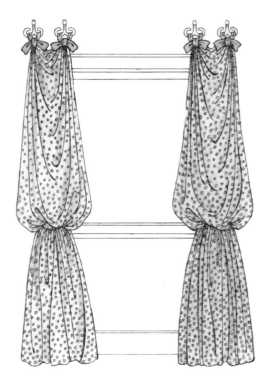

(DR144) This inexpensive flat panel gathered treatment is finished with ties and Bishop sleeves. Hat/coat holder or similar hardware can be employed to hold the panels.

(DR145) Arched Bishop sleeve panels with rosettes and rope tassels.

Curtain styles

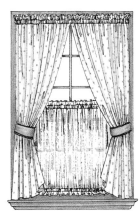

(*Left to right*) Flat rod pocket curtain, tied back; Rod pocket drapery over café curtain with rod pocket top and bottom; Rod pocket tiebacks with ruffles

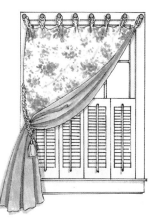
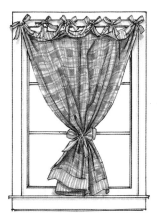

(*Left to right*) Rod pocket valance with rod pocket café curtains; Tabbed curtain over shutters; Tabbed curtain gathered in the middle

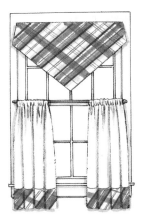

(*Left to right*) Chevron valance over cafe curtains; Curtain on decorative rod with holdback; Sheer lace tied-back curtains with gathered valance

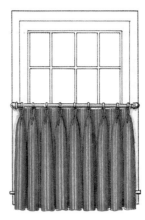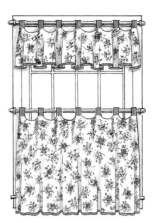

(*Left to right*) Shirred cafe curtain on high res; Cafe curtain with French pleated tops on rings;
Scalloped tab valance over cafe curtains

(*Left to right*) Priscilla curtains with ruffles; Valance on brass decorative rod over tied-back curtains with ruffles;
Rod pocket curtains with high ties and large ruffles

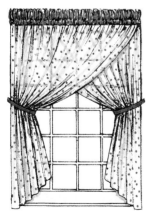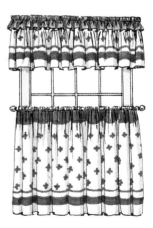

(*Left to right*) Priscilla curtains with rod pocket top; Cafe curtains with arched top and valance;
Cafe curtains on brass rod with gathered valance

(*Left to right*) Traditional swag with mini blind; Pleated tab top cafe curtain on brass rod; Cafe curtain shirred top to bottom between two rods

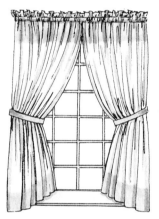

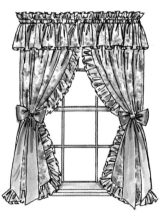

(*Left to right*) Tied-back curtains gathered on a rod; Drapery pleated on a decorative rod and tied back with large bows; Bow tied ruffled tiebacks

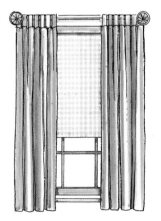

(*Left to right*) Tab top curtains on decorative rod over roller shade; Ruffled tiebacks over balloon shade; Tab top curtains on decorative rod

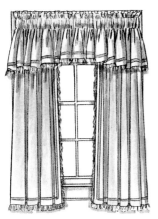  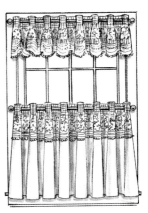

(*Left to right*) Arched rod pocket valance over straight curtains; Ruffled tiebacks over shutters;
Lace curtains and valance threaded on rod

(*Left to right*) Banded tieback curtains; Banded valance over tiebacks; Tab top banded curtains, tied back

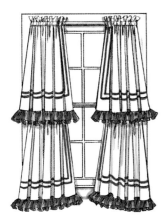 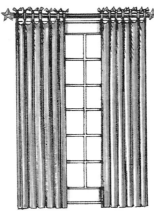 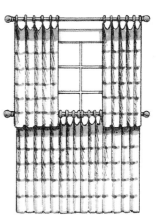

(*Left to right*) Tiered curtains with ribbon banding; Tab tied curtains on brass decorative rod; Double cafe curtains
with scalloped top on brass rod

Additional drapery styles

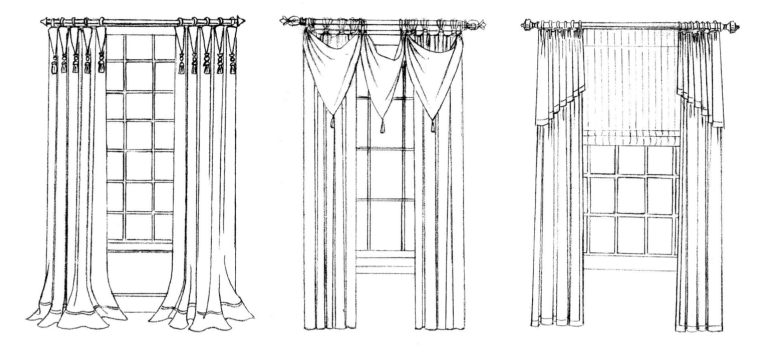

(*Top row, left to right*) Pleated draperies with small flags and tassels; Tab draperies with large flags and tassels;
Pleated asymmetrical flounced draperies on decorative rod over Roman shade
(*Bottom row*, *left to right*) Flat panel draperies with ties on decorator rod with pleated flounced heading and hems;
Flounced French pleated panels with banding and braided rope tiebacks

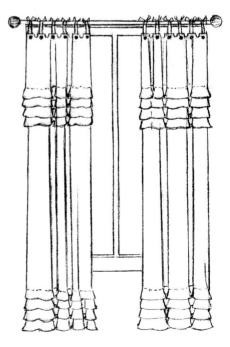

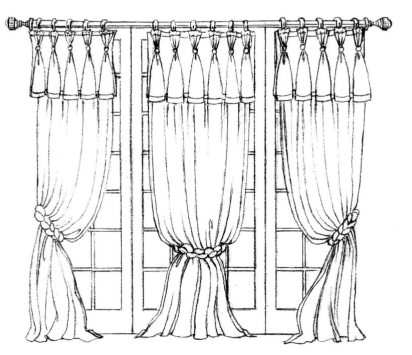

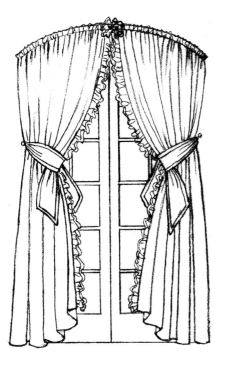
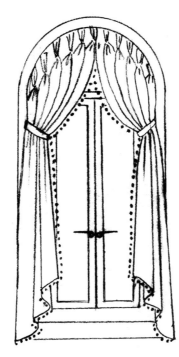
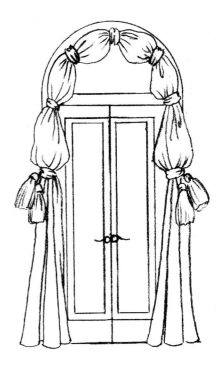

(*Top row, left to right*) Arched rod pocket draperies with ruffle banding and high ties; Arched French pleated draperies with high tiebacks; Arched flat panel draperies with Bishop sleeves and large tassels
(*Bottom row, left to right*) Arched rod pocket drapery; Arched knotted swag drapery; Arched gathered drapery with tiebacks and large tassels

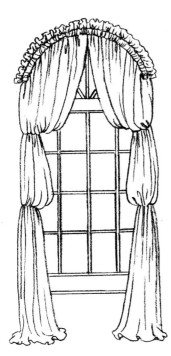

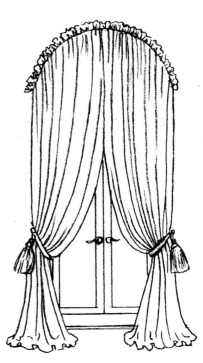

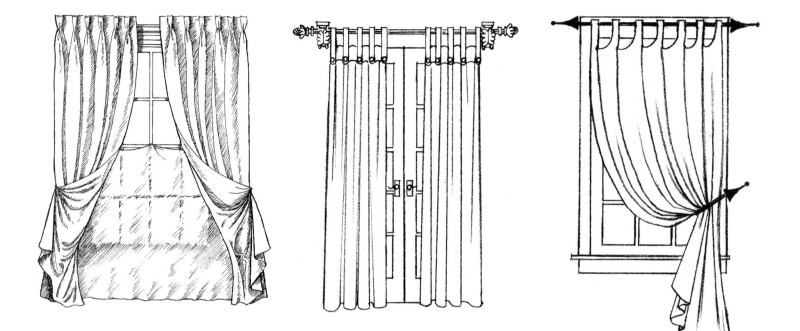

(*Top row, left to right*) French pleated draperies over flat panel sheers; Tab draperies on decorative rod with sconces; Tab drapery on decorative rod with matching holdback
(*Bottom row, left to right*) Tab draperies on decorative rod with matching holdbacks; Double tab draperies on decorative rod with matching holdbacks; Flounce tab top draperies

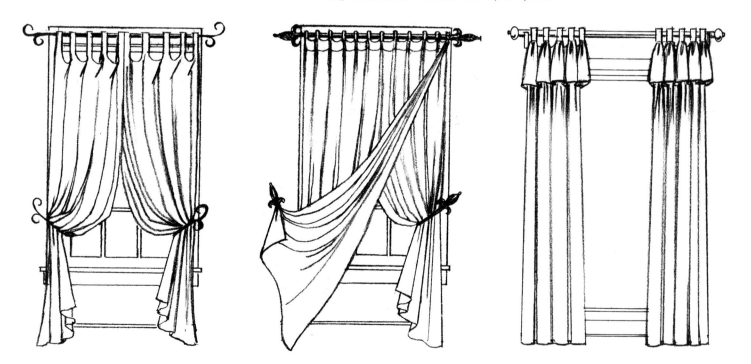

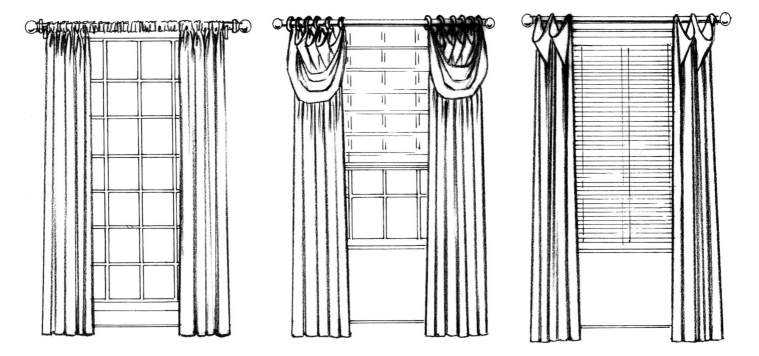

(*Top row, left to right*) Rod pocket draperies with gathered fabric covering rod; Flat panel draperies with swag flags on decorator rod over Roman shade; Flat panel draperies on decorator rod over horizontal blind
(*Bottom row, left to right*) Double rod pocket draperies with tuxedo style hold backs; Tabbed drapery with bows and tieback; Tabbed drapery with tieback

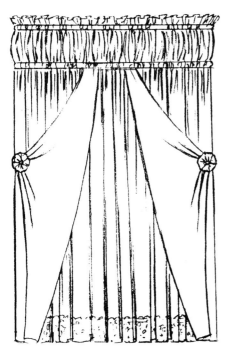

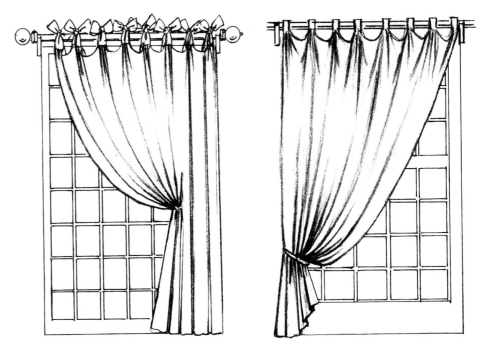

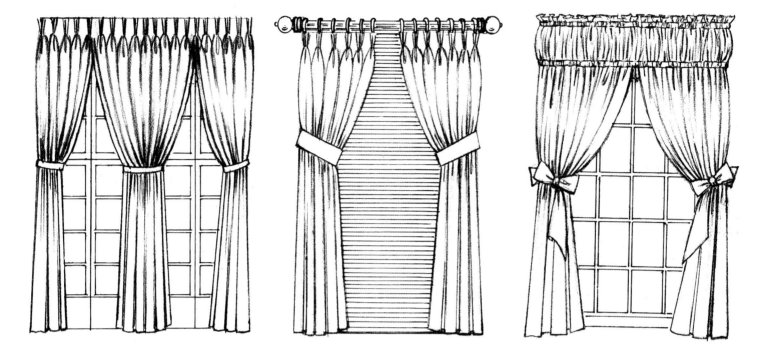

(*Top row, left to right*) Pleated draperies with tiebacks; Pleated tieback draperies over horizontal blinds; Double rod pocket draperies with large bow ties (*Bottom row, left to right*) Double rod pocket draperies with tiebacks; Stationary rod pocket draperies with 3" stand-up and fabric covered rod; Tied-back stationary draperies on decorative rod with fabric covered rod and holdbacks

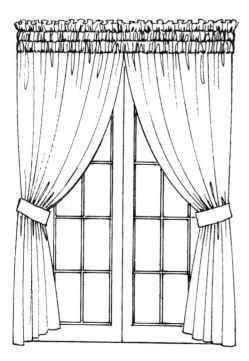

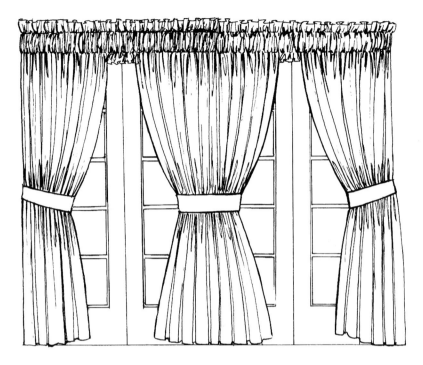
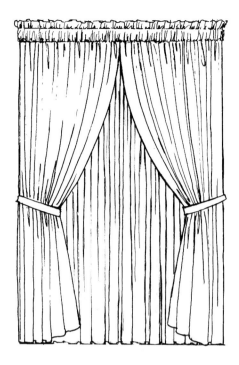

(*Top row, left to right*) Rod pocket drapery panels with fabric covered rod (fabric sleeve);
Rod pocket drapery over sheers
(*Bottom row, left to right*) Rod pocket drapery with center sleeve and tiebacks; Rod top draperies

(*Top row, left to right*) Bow-tied Bishop sleeve draperies gathered on decorative rod; Stationary rod pocket draperies on decorative pole with sleeve in middle; French pleated draperies over cloud shade
(*Bottom row, left to right*) Tab draperies over cafe curtain; Rod pocket draperies with matching valance on same rod over wood blinds with cloth tapes; Draperies gathered on decorative rod over Austrian shade

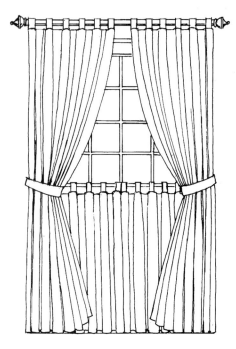  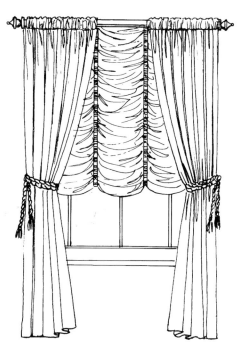

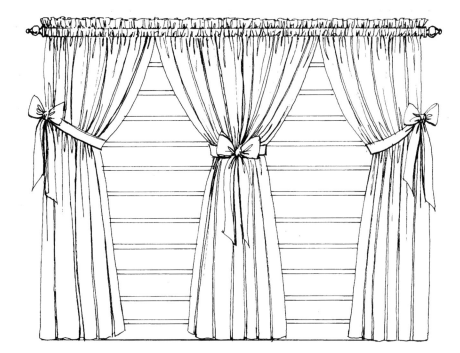

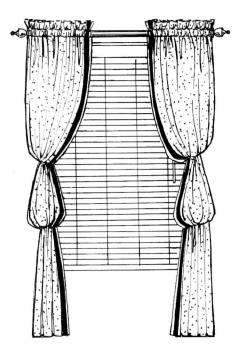

(*Top row, left to right*) Rod pocket draperies with multiple bowties over Roman shades;
Banded stationary Bishop sleeve panels over mini blinds
(*Bottom row, left to right*) Flip top draperies over horizontal blind; Flat rod pocket draperies and
cafe curtain with ties; Rod pocket draperies with banding and ties

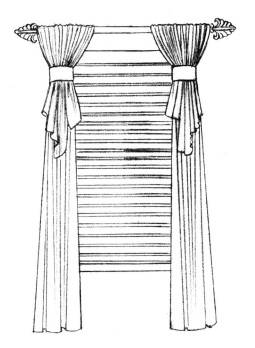

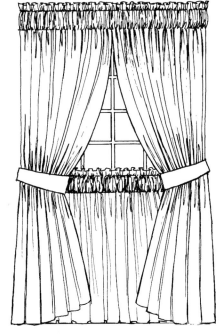

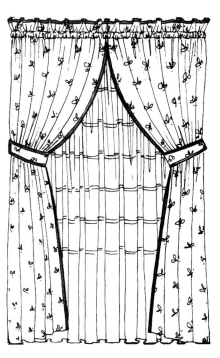

Custom draperies

Standard custom workmanship & quality features
- Double wrapped headings
- 4" or 5" permanent buckram headings (unless "slouched, no buckram" heading requested)
- Pleating is custom tacked with extra thread
- All seems serged and overlocked
- All draperies perfectly matched & table sized
- Blind stitched bottom and side hems. Chain weights may be necessary to prevent billowing in lightweight fabrics.
- Double wrapped 4" or 5" bottom hems and .5" double side hems
- All draperies weighted at corners and seams.
- Multiple width draperies are placed so that joining seams are hidden behind pleats

Drapery terminology
- *Width* is one strip of material of any length that can be pleated to a finished dimension across the TOP of between 16" and 24". For example, using a 48" wide material, a width that finishes to 24" is considered double fullness, or 2 to 1; a 16" finished width is considered triple fullness, or 3 to 1. Any number of widths can be joined together to properly cover the window area.
- *Panel* is a single drapery unit of one or more widths which is used specifically for one way (o/w) draw, stack left or stack right and/or stationary units.
- *Pair* is two equal panels that cover a desired area — unless an offset pair is necessary.
- *Return* is the measurement from the rod to the wall; in other words, the projection.
- *Overlap* is the measurement, when draperies are fully closed, of the right leading edge and the left leading edge overlapping each other. This helps balance the pleats and reduce light seepage.

Options available on draperies
(*see appendices for more options*):
- Pinch pleated with 4" or 5" buckram
- Box pleated or box pleated with tabs for rod. Add diameter of rod to finished length. For flat tab draperies use 2 to 1 fullness.
- Rod pocket, gathered (shirred), goblet, flounced, blouson or cuffed.
- Self-lined, interlined or lined with polyester-cotton, black-out or thermal suede.

Pleat spacing
Pleat spacing varies according to the widths of material used to achieve a specified finished width. For example, three widths of material pleated to 59" to the pair will not have the same pleat spacing as three widths of material pleated to 72" to the pair. If the pleats and pleat spacing are to look alike on draperies of different widths, you should specify "comparable fullness" when you order custom draperies. Vertically striped fabrics will not fabricate to allow an identical stripe to fall between pleats.

Ordering custom draperies
Since "made-to-measure" draperies are to your exact specifications, measurements must be made with the greatest care and with a steel tape only. Double check all measurements for accuracy — it is often more expensive to remake draperies than make new ones! Measure each window separately even if they appear to be the same size. If length varies, use the shortest length, especially for ceiling to floor length. If this rule is not followed a portion of the drapery may drag on the floor.

Drapery Width (see page 85 for more details)
- Measure width of drapery rod from end to end.
- Add 12" to this figure to include the allowance for standard traverse rod returns and overlap.
- Standard returns are 3" in depth. For over-draperies allow for 6" clearance of under-treatment..
- When ordering panels that draw o/w (one-way), specify which direction: left or right.

Drapery Length
- Measure from top of rod, to floor, to carpet.
- Undertreatment should be at least .5" shorter than overtreatment.
- When floor-length draperies are used, it is best to measure the length at each side and in the center. Use the shortest figure for your measurements (as mentioned above).
- Rod should be placed a minimum of 4" above the window so that hooks and pleats will not be visible from the outside.
- If sill-length, allow 4" below sill so that the bottom hem will not be visible from the outside.
- When using pole rings, measure length from bottom of rings.

Yardage chart for 4" or 5" heading FL (finished length) plus 20", plain fabrics only
Total number of widths per pair or panel

Finished length

	2W	3W	4W	5W	6W	7W	8W	9W	10W	11W	12W	13W	14W	15W
36"	3¼	4¾	6¼	7¾	9¼	10¾	12¼	13¾	15¼	16¾	18¼	19¾	21¼	22¾
40"	3½	5	6½	8	9½	11	12½	14	15½	17	18½	20	21½	23
44"	3¾	5½	7¼	9	10¾	12½	14¼	16	17¾	19½	21¼	23	24¾	26½
48"	4	5¾	7½	9¼	11	12¾	14½	16¼	18	19¾	21½	23¼	25	26¾
52"	4	6	8	10	12	14	16	18	20	22	24	26	28	30
56"	4¼	6½	8½	10¾	12¾	15	16¾	19	21¼	23¼	25½	27½	29¾	31¾
60"	4½	6¾	9	11¼	13½	15¾	18	20	22¼	24½	26¾	29	31¼	33½
64"	4¾	7	9½	11¾	14	16½	18¾	21	23½	25¾	28	30½	32¾	35
68"	5	7½	10	12¼	14¾	17¼	19¾	22	24½	27	29½	32	34¼	36¾
72"	5¼	7¾	10¼	13	15½	18	20½	23	25¾	28¼	30¾	33¼	36	38½
76"	5½	8	10¾	13½	16	18¾	21½	24	26¾	29½	32	34¾	37½	40
80"	5¾	8½	11¼	14	16¾	19½	22¼	25	28	30¾	33½	36¼	39	41¾
84"	6	8¾	11¾	14½	17½	20¼	23¼	26	29	32	34¾	37¾	40½	43½
88"	6	9	12	15	18	21	24	27	30	33	36	39	42	45
92"	6¼	9½	12½	15¾	18¾	22	25	28	31¼	34¼	37½	40½	43¾	46¾
96"	6½	9¾	13	16¼	19½	22¾	26	29	32¼	35½	38¾	42	45¼	48½
100"	6¾	10	13½	16¾	20	23½	26¾	30	33½	36¾	40	43½	46¾	50
104"	7	10½	14	17¼	20¾	24¼	27¾	31	34½	38	41½	45	48¼	51¾
108"	7¼	10¾	14¼	18	21½	25	28½	32	35¾	39¼	42¾	46¼	50	53½

Pleat-to-fullness chart

(48" fabric) 2½ times fullness

Pleat to	19	38	57	76	95	114	133	152	171	190	209	228	247	266	285
Widths	1	2	3	4	5	6	7	8	9	10	11	12	13	14	15

(48" fabric) 3 times fullness

Pleat to	15	30	45	60	75	90	105	120	135	150	165	180	195	210	225
Widths	1	2	3	4	5	6	7	8	9	10	11	12	13	14	15

(54" fabric) 2½ times fullness

Pleat to	21	42	63	84	105	126	147	168	189	210	231	254	273	294	315
Widths	1	2	3	4	5	6	7	8	9	10	11	12	13	14	15

(54" fabric) 3 times fullness

Pleat to	17	34	51	68	85	102	119	136	153	170	187	204	221	238	255
Widths	1	2	3	4	5	6	7	8	9	10	11	12	13	14	15

Calculating yardages

General calculations
(for detailed terms and information see next page)
With drapery calculations, one must consider the following: width and length of window, area to be covered, amount of fullness desired, width and type of fabric, allowances for hems and headings, and pattern repeat, if applicable. And after obtaining accurate measurements proceed with the following steps.

Step 1:
Determine the number of the fabric widths required. This is calculated by multiplying the width of the area to be covered by the given fullness factor (listed on the drapery treatment page). Divide this by the by the width of the fabric being used. The result is the number of widths of fabric that are required to achieve the desired fullness. Since fabric suppliers will not sell a part of the width, this figure must be a whole number.

Step 2a:
Calculate the yardage. Add to the length of the treatment, the allowances for hems, headings and where applicable, styling allowances, such as cuffs or blouson tops (such as image below). These allowances are listed on the item page under the corresponding yardage calculation. Next, multiply these amounts by the number of widths required and divide by 36 to obtain the number of yards. This calculation applies only to solid fabrics or to fabrics that have a pattern repeat of less than six inches. (*Or, to calculate the yardage for a fabric with a pattern repeat of more than six inches.*)

Step 2b:
Add the length and applicable allowances together and divide by the pattern repeat. This figure is the number of pattern repeats that are required to achieve the desired length. If this number is a fraction it must be rounded upward to the nearest whole number.

Step 2c:
Determine the cut length—this is the actual length that the workroom will cut the fabric after allowing for pattern repeats, hems cuffs, puddling, etc. Multiply the number of repeats required by the size of the pattern repeat. This number is the cut length.

Step 2d:
Multiply the number of widths required, as calculated in Step 1, by the cut length. Divide by 36 to obtain the total yardage required for a pattern repeat.

Special note:
Every attempt has been made to ensure the accuracy of the calculations and yardage charts of the items in this book; however, variations in fabrics or workroom specifications may require certain modifications to the yardage calculations. For complex or elaborate style treatments such as swags, cascades and arched treatments please consult a designer or professional drapery workroom.

Please also note that the photographs and illustrations accompanying each set of yardage calculations are not for the images shown. These images are for illustrative purposes only.

Puddled blouson drapery panels hung with rings offer casual elegance.

Bishop's Sleeve Minimum length = Add 15" to 20" per pouf.

CD = Cascade Drop. Length of cascades. Usually 3/5 of the undertreatment is most visually pleasing.

CL = Cut Length. The length of fabric to be cut, including allowance for headings, hems and specialty items such as bishop sleeves or cuffs.

C/O = Center opening drapery.

F = Fullness. Fullness after pleating or gathering of drapery; usually 2x for flat panel or tabbed draperies, 2.5x for pinch or box pleated and 3x for sheers

FL = Finished Length. The length of pairs or panels before adding for headings and hems (what the finished length of the drapery will be after fabrication).

Fullness Minimum = To be considered "custom" draperies usually need $2\frac{1}{2}$ to 3x fullness. Sheers require triple fullness.

FW = Finished Width. The total width of a pair or panel of draperies including returns and overlap.

HH = Heading and Hem allowance. Custom draperies require doubling wrapping the heading and hems. Therefore, you must add 16" for a drapery with 4" headings and hems and 20" for a drapery with 5" heading and hem.

OL = Overlap(s). 6" per pair of single hung (no sheers) draperies and 3.5x" for single hung panel.

O/W = Single panel, one-way drapery.

Puddle panels = Add 6" to 18" to the FL (finished length)

R = Repeat. The total inches before a pattern repeats itself.

RFW = Rod Face Width, the total rod width, not including return to the wall.

RT = Return(s). Rod projection from wall. Add 6" (3" for each side) for standard single hung draperies and 12" for double hung (over sheers) draperies. Example: A 102" Rod (RFW) single hung pair of draperies would require an additional 12". 6" for returns to the wall and 6" for overlap. A double hung pair of draperies would require an additional 18". 12" for returns to wall and 6" for OL.

SB = Stack-back. The amount fabric that stacks back when you open the pair or panel of draperies, usually one-third of the rod face.

SBGC = Stack-back with full glass clearance = rod face x 1.5.

SD = Swag Drop. Using the rule of fifths (ratios of 5 or 6 are more pleasing to the eye), swag drop should equal about one-fifth of the length of the undertreatment.

TW = Total Width. The total width of drapery fabric required after multiplying the fabric widths required.

TY = Total Yardage. Total yardage required.

Try it! = Calculate based on a 70" RFW (rod face width) and 84" FL (finished length) single hung, center opening drapery.
70" RFW + 12" for RT & OL (returns and overlap) = 82" FW (finished width). 82 x 2.5 = 205 TW (total width). 205 ÷ 54 (width of fabric used) = 3.79. Round to the next whole number because fabric stores do not sell half widths of fabric.

Now figure the length. 84" FL + 16" HH (heading and hem allowance) = 100" CL (cut length).

Now multiply 4 (fabrics widths required) x 100" (CL) for a total of 400". 400" ÷ 36 = 11.1 (total yards required). Always round this number up to the next whole number, in this case 12. It's always good for the workroom to have a little extra fabric to work with.

Refer back to this page when using calculations on the succeeding pages.

Pinch pleated specifications

This very traditional panel drapery is topped with a series of narrow, "pinched" folds. Also called "French" pleats, this type of drapery requires a good bit of stackback space, as pinching the top of the fabric results in a greater fabric fullness at the bottom.

Yardage (including pinch pleat, goblet, cartridge, bell, euro and fan pleated)

Step 1 – RFW (rod face width) + 12" for RT & OL (returns and overlap) x 2.5 or 3.0 ÷ width of fabric = number of widths required (round up to whole number) Three times fullness is recommended for very light weight fabrics such as silk.

Step 2a – FL (finished length) + 16" for HH (headings and hems) x widths required ÷ 36 = yardage (round up to whole number) without pattern repeat

—or—

Step 2b – FL (finished length) + 16" for HH ÷ pattern repeat = number of repeats required (round up to whole number)

Step 2c – Number of repeats x pattern repeat = CL (cut length)

Step 2d – Number of widths x CL (cut length) ÷ 36 = yardage with pattern repeat (round up to whole number)

Things to consider
- Alternate lining color
- Center opening or one way panel
- What type of rod?
- Tiebacks required?

Special notes
1. A check measure is recommended for all full length draperies.
2. See page 85 for detailed calculating terms.

This very attractive heading exhibits even gathers across the width of the curtain or drape to great feminine appeal.

Yardage (including pencil, smocked accordion and shirred cuff)

Step 1 – RFW (rod face width) + 6" for RT (returns) x 2.5 or 3.0 ÷ width of fabric = number of widths required (round up to whole number) Three times fullness recommended for very light weight fabrics such as silks and sheers

Step 2a – FL (finished length) + 16" for HH (headings and hems) x widths required ÷ 36 = yardage (round up to whole number) without pattern repeat

—or—

Step 2b – FL (finished length) + 16" for HH ÷ pattern repeat = number of repeats required (round up to whole number)

Step 2c – Number of repeats required x pattern repeat = cut length

Step 2d – Number of widths x CL (cut length) ÷ 36 = yardage with pattern repeat (round up to whole number)

Things to consider
- Alternate lining color
- Tiebacks required?
- Center opening or one way panel

Special notes
1. A check measure is recommended for all full length draperies.
2. Smocked treatments should stay stationary due to the nature of the header.
3. See page 85 for detailed calculating terms

Box pleated specifications

Crisp folds that resemble the corners of a box are the hall-mark of this tailored drapery treatment.

Yardage (including box pleated, inverted box pleat)

Step 1 – RFW (rod face width) + 12" for RT and OL (returns and overlap) x 2.5 or 3 ÷ width of fabric = number of widths required (round up to whole number) Use 2.5 fullness if using a traverse rod

Step 2a – FL (finished length) + 16" for HH (headings and hems) x widths required ÷ 36 = yardage (round up to whole number) without pattern repeat

—or—

Step 2b – FL (finished length) + 16" for HH ÷ pattern repeat = number of repeats required (round up to whole number)

Step 2c – Number of repeats x pattern repeat = CL (cut length)

Step 2d – Number of widths x CL (cut length) ÷ 36 = yardage with pattern repeat (round up to whole number)

Things to consider
- Alternate lining color
- Center opening or one way panel
- What type of rod, if any? This treatment can also be mounted on a board
- Tiebacks required?

Special notes
1. A check measure is recommended for all full length draperies.
2. Reduce fullness to 2.5 if using a traverse rod.
3. See page 85 for detailed calculating terms

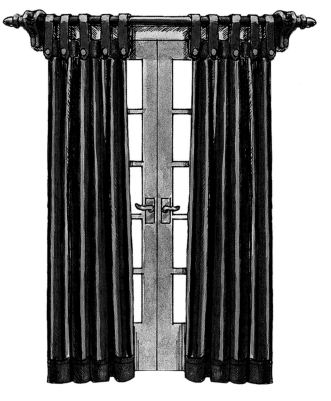

This simple style has been popular for many years, as it has many options for decoration and also celebrates the beauty of the rod that it hangs from.

Yardage (including tab, gathered tab, pleated tab and ties)

Step 1 – RFW (rod face width) + 6" for RT (returns) x 2 ÷ width of fabric = number of widths required (round up to whole number) Two and a half times fullness is recommended for very light weight fabrics such as silks and sheers

Step 2a – FL (finished length) + 20" for HH (headings and hems) x widths required ÷ 36 = yardage (round up to whole number) without pattern repeat

—or—

Step 2b – FL (finished length) + 20" for HH ÷ pattern repeat = number of repeats required (round up to whole number)

Step 2c – Number of repeats x pattern repeat = CL (cut length)

Step 2d – Number of widths x CL (cut length) ÷ 36 = yardage with pattern repeat (round up to whole number)

Things to consider
• Alternate lining color
• What type of rod?
• Center opening or one way panel

Special notes
1. Yardage calculations include tabs.
2. Only 2 times fullness is required on this treatment to obtain the proper effect.
3. See page 85 for detailed calculating terms

Athena specifications

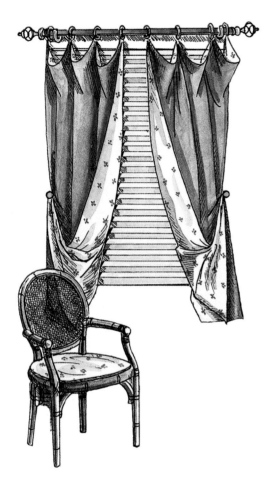

This type of treatment is created from a simple flat panel with generously-spaced rings or clips to attach it to the rod, as well as offer an almost swagged effect at the heading. This type of treatment usually puddles.

Yardage (including athena, flat panel)

Step 1 – RFW (rod face width) + 12" for RT (returns) x 2 or 2.5 ÷ width of fabric = number of widths required (round up to whole number) Two and one half fullness is recommended for very light weight fabrics such as silks and sheers

Step 2a – FL (finished length) + 16" for HH (headings and hems) x widths required ÷ 36 = yardage (round up to whole number) without pattern repeat

—or—

Step 2b – FL + 16" for HH ÷ pattern repeat = number of repeats required (round up to whole number)

Step 2c – Number of repeats x pattern repeat = CL (cut length)

Step 2d – Number of widths x CL (cut length) ÷ 36 = yardage with pattern repeat (round up to whole number)

Things to consider
- Alternate lining color
- What type of rod, ring and clip?
- Center opening or one way panel?

Special notes
1. A puddle of 6" has been allowed in the yardage. If more is desired, add to length + allowance.
2. Soft, drapeable fabrics are recommended.
3. For self or contrast facing, allow 1/4 yard per width
4. Lining or contrast lining equals drapery yardage
5. See page 85 for detailed calculating terms

This treatment has a pocket at the top through which a rod for hanging is inserted. It can be dressed with a ruffle above the rod and also, depending upon the amount of fabric used, create a "shirred" effect.

Yardage (including rod pocket, double rod pocket, rod pocket with standup and rod pocket with belt loops)

Step 1 – RFW (rod face width) + 6" for RT (returns, if used) x 2.5 or 3.0 ÷ width of fabric = number of widths required (round up to whole number). 3x fullness is recommended for very light weight fabrics such as silks and sheers ÷ 36 = yardage without pattern repeat

Step 2a – FL (finished length) + 16" for HH (headings and hems) x widths required ÷ 36 = yardage (round up to whole number) without pattern repeat

—or—

Step 2b – FL + 16" for HH ÷ pattern repeat = number of repeats required (round up to whole number)

Step 2c – Number of repeats x pattern repeat = CL (cut length)

Step 2d – Number of widths x CL (cut length) ÷ 36 = yardage with pattern repeat (round up to whole number)

Things to consider
- Alternate lining color
- Center opening or one way panel
- What type of rod and tiebacks?
- Ruffle or frill needed on top of treatment?

Special notes
1. This is a stationary treatment but can be moved with some difficulty — not recommended.
2. This treatment cannot be used when the treatment underneath is mounted up at the ceiling.
3. See page 85 for detailed calculating terms

Tuxedo specifications

A tuxedo drapery is more about the mid-section of the treatment than the header as its most recognizable aspect is the way it folds back to reveal a contrast lining.

Yardage (including tuxedo, tent fold and stationary flat panel)

Step 1 – RFW (rod face width) + 10" for RT and OL (returns and overlap, if used) ÷ width of fabric = number of widths required (round up to whole number)

Step 2a – FL (finished length) + 12" for HH (headings and hems) x widths required ÷ 36 = yardage (round up to whole number) without pattern repeat
—or—

Step 2b – FL (+ 12" for HH ÷ pattern repeat = number of repeats required (round up to whole number)

Step 2c – Number of repeats x pattern repeat = CL (cut length)

Step 2d – Number of widths x CL (cut length) ÷ 36 = yardage with pattern repeat (round up to whole number)

Step 3 – Calculate with same formula for contrast lining

Step 4 – Allow 1/2 yard for ties; 1 yard for larger sash ties

Things to consider
- Alternate lining color
- What type of rod?
- Center opening or one way panel

Special notes
1. Large returns are not recommended.
2. Tuxedo draperies limit the amount of light entering the room.
3. Not recommended for windows that are proportionately wider than high.
4. See page 85 for detailed calculating terms

A drape where the fabric is stretched between two rods creating an all-over shirred effect. An excellent treatment if privacy is required or if working with a narrower window. Add a collar tieback to create a decorative hourglass shape.

Yardage

Step 1 – Width of area to be covered x 2.5 ÷ width of fabric = number of widths

Step 2a – Number of widths x (length of area + 16") ÷ 36 = yardage without pattern repeat

—or—

Step 2b – Length + 16" ÷ pattern repeat = number of repeats required (round upward to nearest whole number)

Step 2c – Number of repeats required x pattern repeat = cut length

Step 2d – Number of widths x cut length ÷ 36 = yardage with pattern repeat

Things to consider
- Width
- Length
- Color of lining
- Size of rods being used
- Inside or outside mounts
- Frill size top and bottom of rod

Special notes
1. Stationary treatment.
2. Not recommended for windows larger than 48".
3. A frill is recommended for this treatment to conceal hardware.
4. See page 85 for detailed calculating terms

Window types

 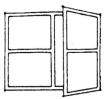  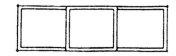

Double hung; In-swinging casement

Out-swinging casement; Ranch

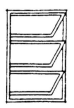 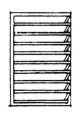 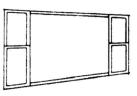 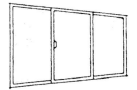

Awning; Jalousie

Picture; Sliding glass doors

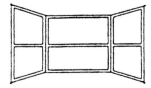 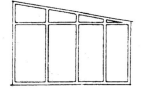 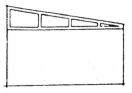 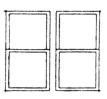

Bay; Clerestory

Slant; Double

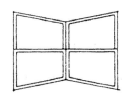 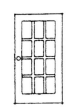 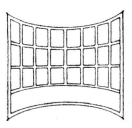

Corner; French door

Bow; Dormer

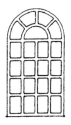 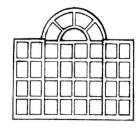  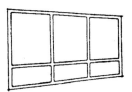

Arched; Palladian

Transom; Glass wall

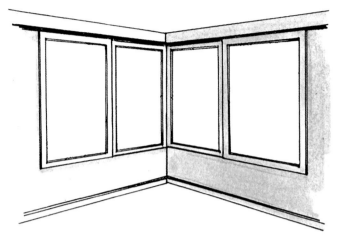

(*Above*) Corner gliding window with structural beam on top

(*Below*) Two solutions

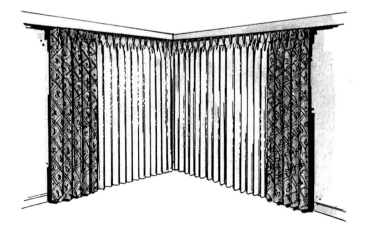

(*Above*) Door with window and skylights

(*Below*) Two solutions

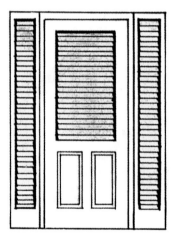

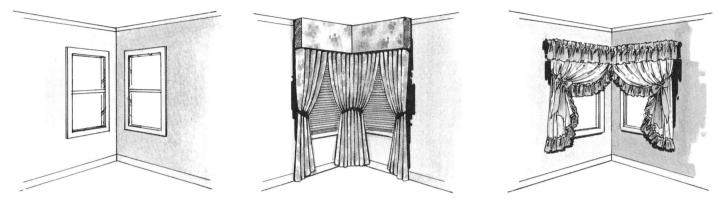

(*Above*) Corner windows; (*Following*) Five solutions

(*Below left*) Clerestory window; (*Following*) One solution

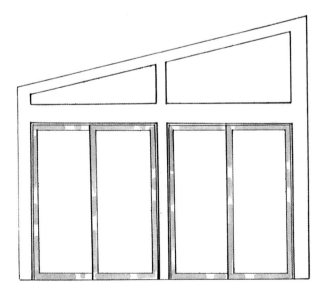

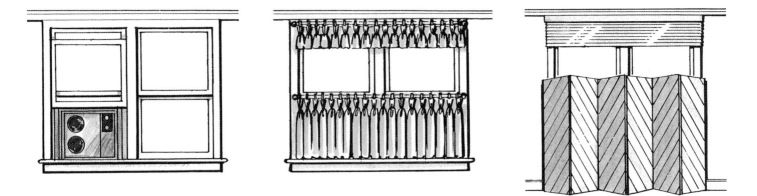

(*Above*) Air conditioner in a double hung window; (*Following*) Two solutions

(*Below left*) Picture window with baseboard heater; (*Following*) Two solutions

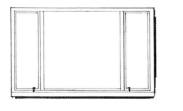
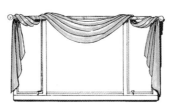
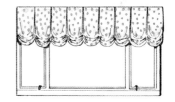

(*Below left*) French doors; (*Following*) Two solutions

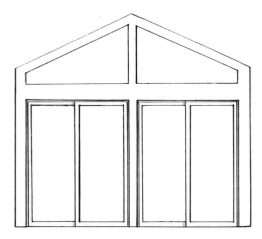

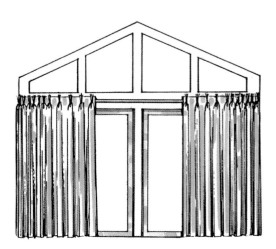

(*Above*) Sliding glass doors and cathedral windows

(*Below and adjacent*) Five solutions

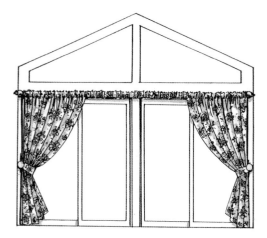

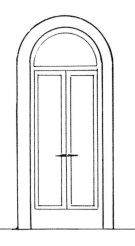

(*Above*) Arch top windows

(*Below and adjacent*) Five solutions

(*Above*) Triple double hung windows

(*Below and adjacent*) Two solutions

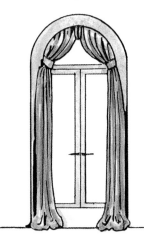

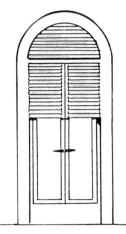

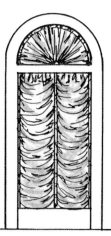

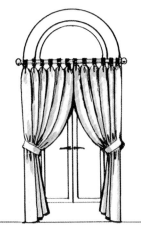

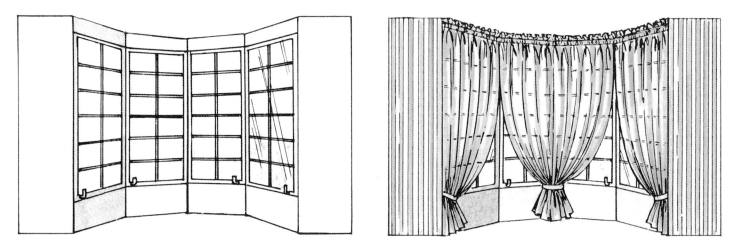

(*Above*) Bay with casement windows; (*Following*) Three solutions

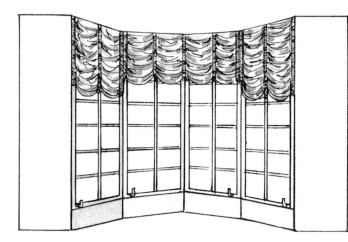

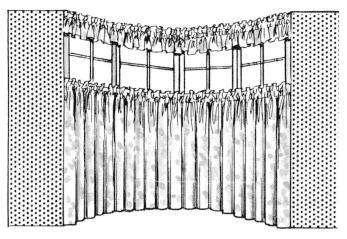

(*Below left*) Bay with double hung windows; (*Following*) Three solutions

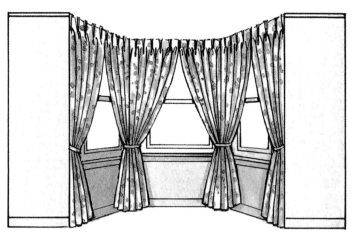

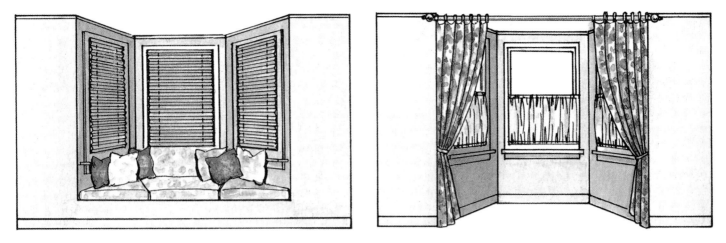

(*Below left*) Jalousie windows and doors; (*Following*) Three solutions

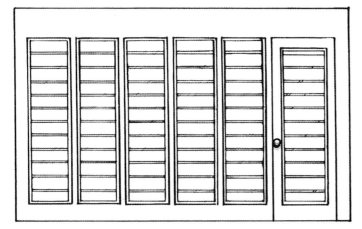

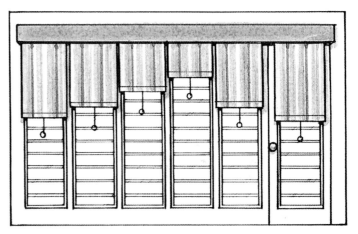

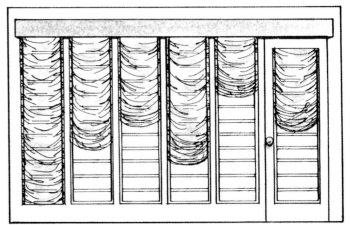

Hemlines & embellishments

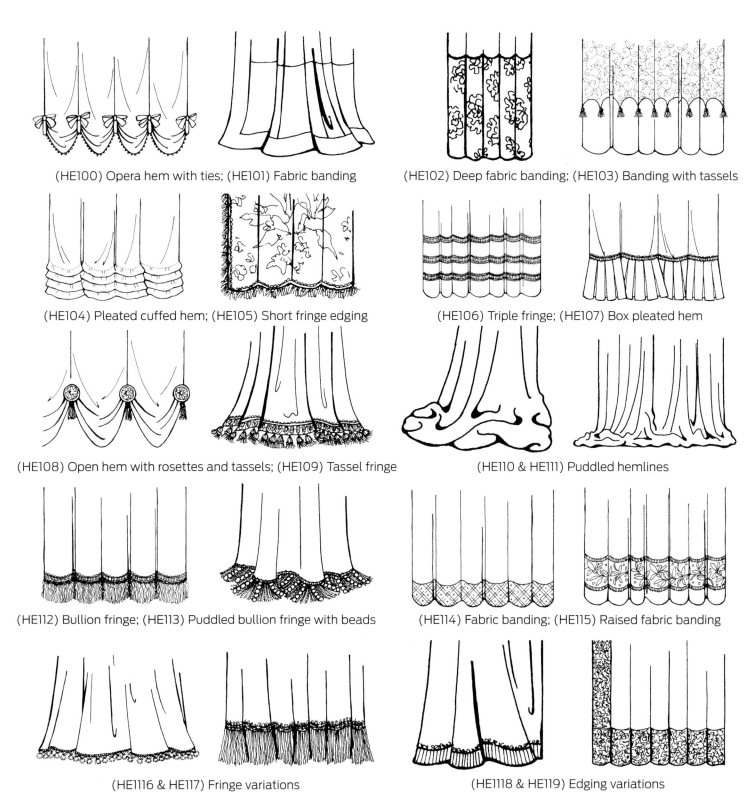

(HE100) Opera hem with ties; (HE101) Fabric banding

(HE102) Deep fabric banding; (HE103) Banding with tassels

(HE104) Pleated cuffed hem; (HE105) Short fringe edging

(HE106) Triple fringe; (HE107) Box pleated hem

(HE108) Open hem with rosettes and tassels; (HE109) Tassel fringe

(HE110 & HE111) Puddled hemlines

(HE112) Bullion fringe; (HE113) Puddled bullion fringe with beads

(HE114) Fabric banding; (HE115) Raised fabric banding

(HE1116 & HE117) Fringe variations

(HE1118 & HE119) Edging variations

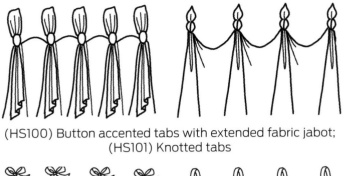

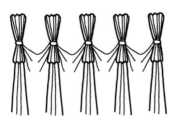

(HS100) Button accented tabs with extended fabric jabot; (HS101) Knotted tabs

(HS102) Hourglass gathered tabs; (HS103) Flat panel drapery with switchback loops

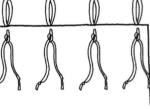

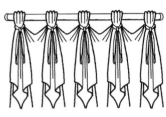

(HS104) Tab panel with decorative bows on individual hardware pieces; (HS105) Buttonhole panel w/looped skinny tabs

(HS106) Flip over rod jabot tab header; (HS107) Waterfall-style gathered tab with swags

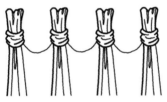

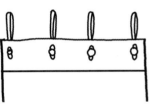

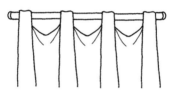

(HS108) Gathered tabs with contrast fabric sleeves; (HS109) Looped tab top

(HS110) Looped tab top; (HS111) Tab top variation

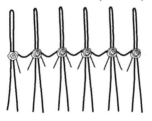

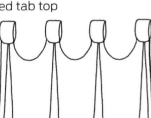

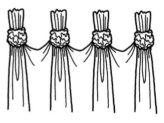

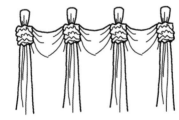

(HS112) Extended tab loop panel with rosette detail; (HS113) Tab top variation

(HS114) Gathered tabs; (HS115) Ruched tabs with swag detailing on panel

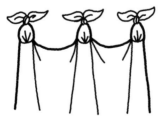

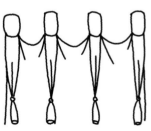

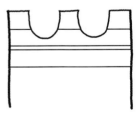

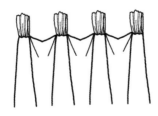

(HS116) Tied top; (HS117) Tab top variation

(HS118) Tab top variation; (HS119) Triple pleat gathered tabs

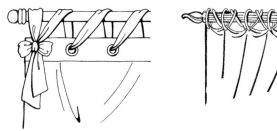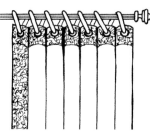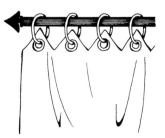

(HS120) Grommet & tie top; (HS121) Crisscrossed string top   (HS122) String top w/grommets; (HS123) Grommet top w/rings

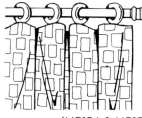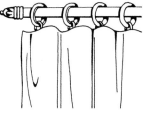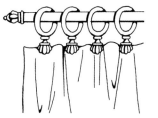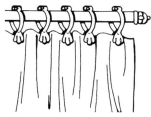

(HS124 & HS125) Ring top variations   (HS126 & HS127) Ring top variations

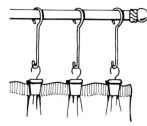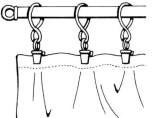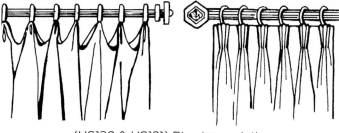

(HS128) Ring top variation; (HS129) Clip with ring top   (HS130 & HS131) Ring top variations

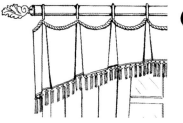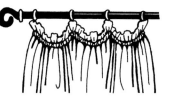

(HS132 & HS133) Ring top variations   (HS134 & HS135) Ring top variations

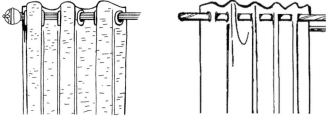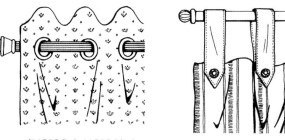

(HS136 & HS137) Traditional grommet top variations   (HS138 & HS139) Grommet top variation; Tab top

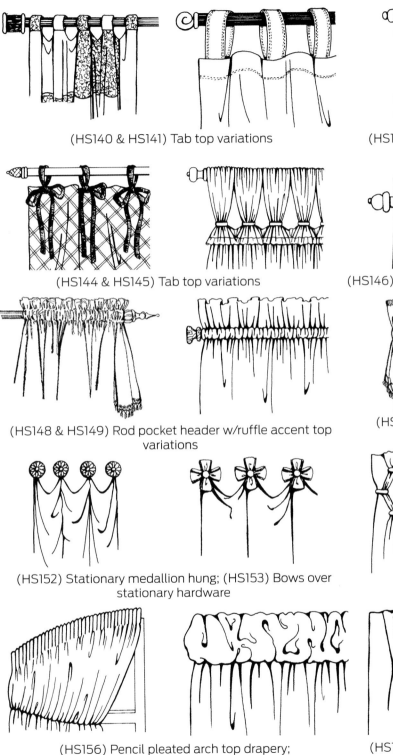
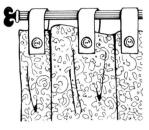
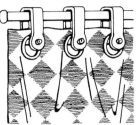

(HS140 & HS141) Tab top variations

(HS142) Specialty hardware w/grommets: (HS143) Tab top

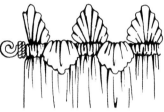
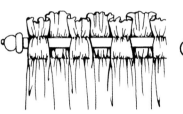

(HS144 & HS145) Tab top variations

(HS146) Rod pocket tab top: (HS147) Rod pocket w/fan stand-ups

(HS148 & HS149) Rod pocket header w/ruffle accent top variations

(HS150) Goblet pleated top; (HS151) Goblet pleats on arch top window

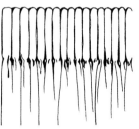

(HS152) Stationary medallion hung; (HS153) Bows over stationary hardware

(HS154) Smocked tape; (HS155) Pencil pleated

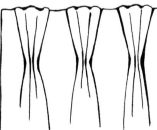
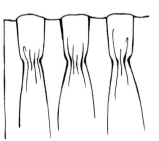

(HS156) Pencil pleated arch top drapery; (HS157) Blouson top

(HS158) Butterfly pleated drapery; (HS159) Slightly gathered cartridge pleats

Rosettes & ties

(RT100) Folded spiral w/ choux;
(RT101)daffodil rosette

(RT102) Petal rosette;
(RT103) accordion fan

(RT104) Bunched fan;
(RT105) peacock

(RT106) Choux; (RT107) shirred
spiral

(RT108) Double choux; (RT109)
knot

(RT110) Shirred pouf;
(RT111) twisted knot

(RT112) Pleated rosette; (RT113)
pleated double rosette

(RT114) Shirred rosette; (RT115)
Maltese Cross

(RT116) Padded Maltese cross;
(RT117) Maltese cross w/rosette

(RT118) Pointed petal rosette;
(RT119) accordion bow

(RT120) Multi-ribbon bow;
(RT121) ruched square

(RT122) Ruched doughnut;
(RT123) bow tie

(RT124) Straight ribbon bow;
(RT125) hanging ribbon bow

(RT126) Shirred bow; (RT127)
triple petal bow

(RT128) Bow with rosette; (RT129)
thin ribbon bow

(RT130) Double Maltese cross;
(RT131) trefoil

(RT132) Pointed trefoil; (RT133)
flame trefoil

(RT134) Pointed cross; (RT135)
pointed petal cross

(RT136) Wired ribbon bow;
(RT137) knotted tie

(RT138) Single pointed tie; (RT139)
double clipped tie

(RT140) Double angled tie;
(RT141) pointed tie

(FG100) Triangle rod pocket flag with tassel; (FG101) Triangle flag with ties and tassels; (FG102) Custom shaped flag with banding and tassel; (FG103) Triangle flag with hooks and tassel; (FG104) Triangle flag with rings and tassel

(FG105) Tab top triangle flag with flounce; (FG106) Square flag with hooks and fringe; (FG107) Chevron flag with hooks and tassel fringe; (FG108) Flared flag with hooks; (FG109) Cascade flag

  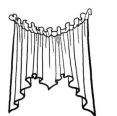  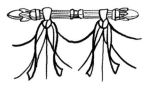

(FG110) Chevron flag with hooks, banding; (FG111) Custom shaped flag with ties, fringe; (FG112) Custom shaped flag with rings, applique; (FG113) Square flag with scalloped hem; fringe on medallions; (FG114) Tab top custom shaped flag with scalloped hem

 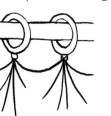 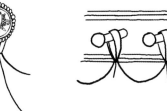 

(FG115) Austrian shaped flag with knife edge banding; (FG116) Asymmetrical flag with tassel and rope; (FG117) Arched gathered flag; (FG118) Tab top Chevron flag with jabots and banding; Tab top with ties on designer wood pole

Ceiling hung panel with ties; Flat panel with sewn rings; Tab top on medallion; Tab top wall mounted pegs; Ceiling mounted hook with tassel

Tiebacks

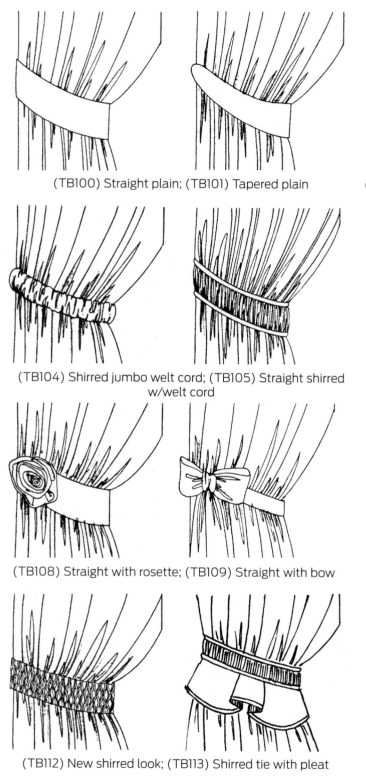

(TB100) Straight plain; (TB101) Tapered plain

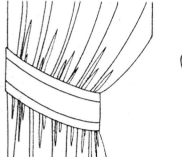
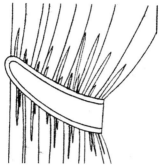

(TB102) Straight with banding; (TB103) Tapered with welt cord

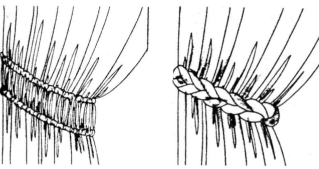

(TB104) Shirred jumbo welt cord; (TB105) Straight shirred w/welt cord

(TB106) Straight shirred; (TB107) Braided

(TB108) Straight with rosette; (TB109) Straight with bow

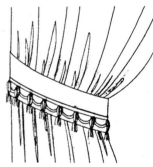
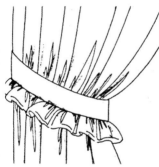

(TB110) Straight with fringe; (TB111) Straight with ruffle

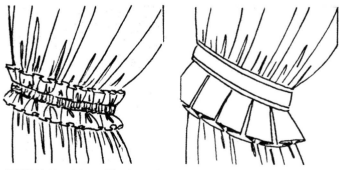

(TB112) New shirred look; (TB113) Shirred tie with pleat

(TB114) Double ruffled tie; (TB115) Box pleated tie with welt

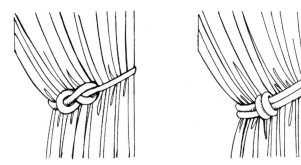

(TB116) 1" welting tied into knot; (TB117) Double 1" welting with bands

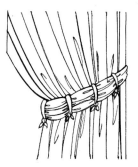

(TB118) Scalloped with welting; (TB119) 4" ruched with ties

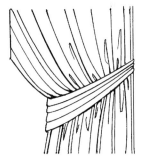 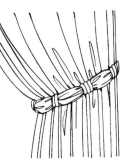

(TB120) Tapered and pleated; (TB121) 2" ruched with welted bands

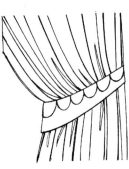 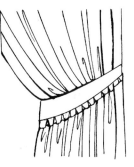

(TB122) Tapered and scalloped; (TB123) Tapered with box pleated ruffle

A decorative accent by which draperies and curtains are held back from the window panes. The various styles give a personal touch to the window treatment.

Yardage
Standard –
 1/2 yard
Standard with piping –
 1/2 yard + 1/2 yard piping
Standard with banding –
 1/2 yard + 1/2 yard banding
Standard with bows –
 1/2 yard + 1 yard bows
Contour –
 3/4 yard
Ruched tieback –
 1 yard
Ruffled tieback –
 1 yard + 1½ yard ruffle
Streamer tieback –
 2 yards

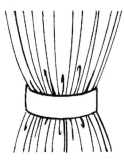 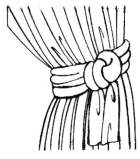

(TB124) 4" center tieback; (TB125) Gathered and tied

Braided tieback –
 1/2 yard each strand (three strands)
Collar with hook & loop fastener –
 1/2 yard

Things to consider
 • Style
 • Fabric (if contrasts are used)

Banding & tieback styles

(TB126) Ruffled banding; (TB127) Banding set back from leading edge; (TB128) banding on leading edge; (TB129) Tassel banding on leading edge

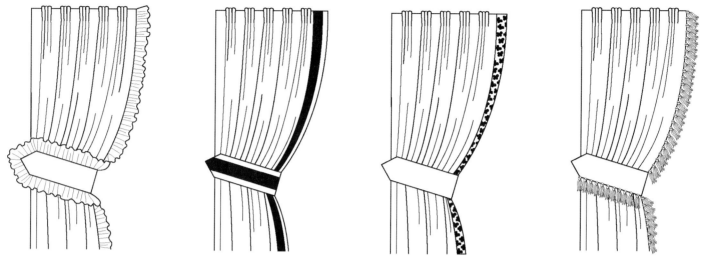

Various tieback styles

There are many details that may be added to personalize a window treatment. Ruffles add charm and romance to the look of a room. Use on draperies, tiebacks, cushions or comforters for a country-style look.

Inset banding adds dramatic contrast to a window treatment. A band of two inches or more is sewn inset from the edges.

Reverse lining is a decorative facing sewn to the lining, then folded outward to reveal the contrast and held in place with tiebacks.

Fringe and braids used decoratively on a window treatment echo the elegance of past eras.

Yardage
Ruffles –
 1/4 yard for each 24" ruffles
Inset banding –
 Length + hem allowances
Reverse lining –
 Length + hem allowances
Fringe & braids –
 Length + additional 10%

Things to consider
 • Treatment
 • Fabrics

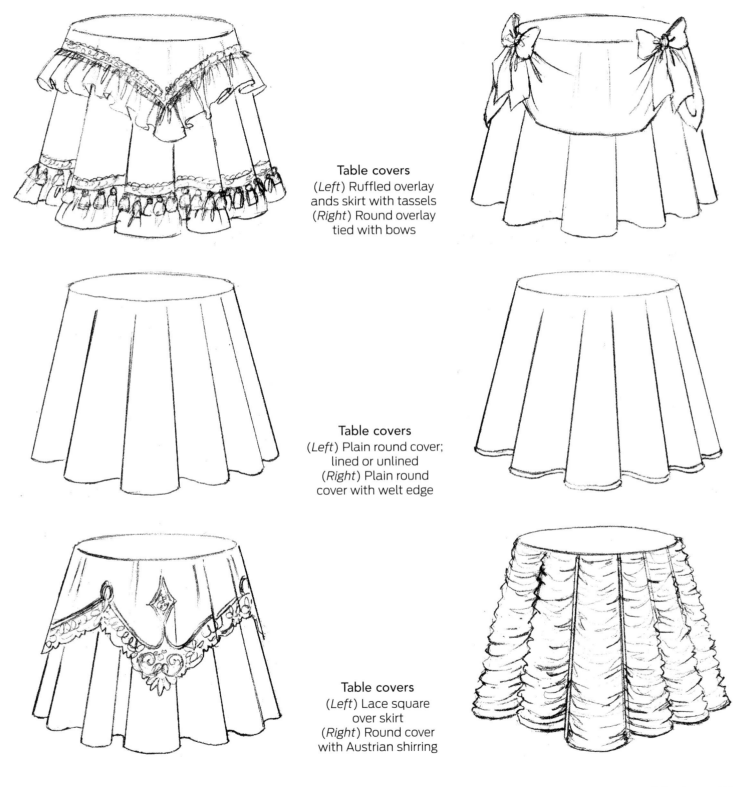

Table covers
(*Left*) Ruffled overlay
ands skirt with tassels
(*Right*) Round overlay
tied with bows

Table covers
(*Left*) Plain round cover;
lined or unlined
(*Right*) Plain round
cover with welt edge

Table covers
(*Left*) Lace square
over skirt
(*Right*) Round cover
with Austrian shirring

Sunbursts & dressing tables

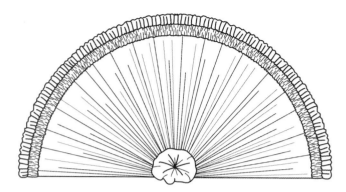

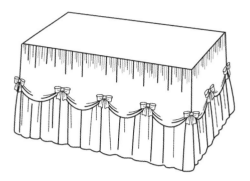

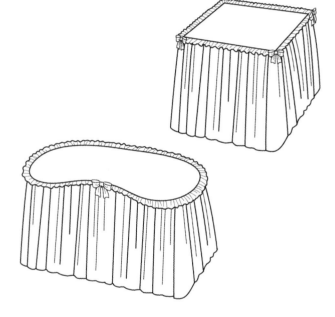

Sunburst

A decorative accent for an arched window. The sunburst is softly gathered into the center and is usually made in a sheer or lace fabric to enhance (rather than block) the window and filter the light. A rosette may be added.

Yardage
- For 118" sheer or lace: 1½ yards
- For 48" lace: 3½ yards
- Windows up to 48" diameter

Things to consider
- Specify fabric
- Specify if a rosette is desired
- A template of the window should be provided

Dressing tables & stools

A romantic detail to add to the most feminine bedroom. The separate cover is gathered in two styles, balloon or ruffled. Upholstered stools coordinate with either style.

Yardage
Balloon style:
- Top and balloon skirt: 7 yards
- Underskirt: 5 yards
- Bows: 2 yards

Ruffled style:
- Skirt: 10 yards
- Contrast bow: 1/2 yard

Stool:
- Skirt: 3½ yards
- Bows: 1/2 yard (for two)

Things to consider
- Style of table
- Fabric details

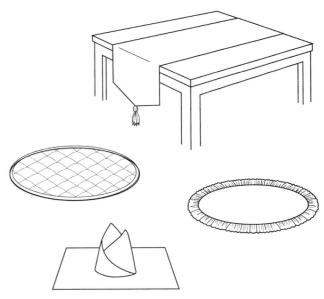

Tablecloths & toppers

Decorative tablecloths and toppers can complement any room décor. The tablecloth is finished with piping at the bottom and may have jumbo piping, ruched or ruffles added. Table toppers complete the look in a basic square handkerchief, stylish Austrian or box pleated.

Yardage: See chart, below

Round tablecloth with:	Up to 74" diameter	Up to 90" diameter
Regular piping	4¾ yards	6 yards
Jumbo piping	add 1½ yards	add 1½ yards
Ruched band	add 2½ yards	add 3 yards
Ruffle	add 4 yards	add 5 yards
Square handkerchief		
Topper (50")	1½ yards	1½ yards
Austrian topper	2¾ yards	3½ yards
Pleated topper	2¾ yards	3½ yards

Things to consider
- Diameter of table
- Drop measurement to the floor
- Style of tablecloth or topper
- Fabric details

Napkins, placemats & runners

Quilted placemats can be custom made to your color scheme and may be finished with piping or a one-inch ruffle. Coordinating 18" square dinner napkins are double hemmed and stitched. Runners add a decorative touch and display a fine wood or glass table to its best advantage.

Yardage
Placemats:
- Print fabrics: 18–27" pattern repeat; allow 1 repeat per placemat
- Plain or small prints: allow 1/2 yard per placemat
- For ruffle, add 1/4 yard per placemat

Napkins
- Print fabrics: 18–27" pattern repeat
- 1½ yards = 4 napkins
- Plain or small print: 1¼ yards = 4

Runners
- Length of table + 24" ÷ 36 = number of yards

Things to consider
- Fabric details
- Sizes

Upholstered rods & fabric framed mirrors

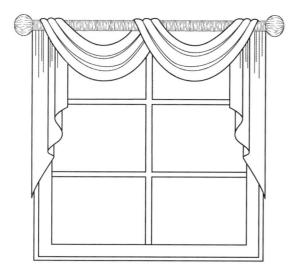

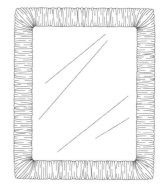

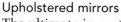

Upholstered mirrors

The ultimate in custom décor — fully upholstered mirrors. Fabric may be ruched onto a frame or pulled flat and finished around the edges with matching piping or ruffles.

Yardage
Ruched:
- 2 yards

Flat:
- 1¼ yards

Piping:
- add 1/2 yard

Ruffle:
- add 1¼ yards

Things to consider
- Style of mirror
- Size of mirror
- Fabric details

Covered rods

For a truly customized window treatment, fabric-covered wood rods and finials add decorative flare. A swag casually draped over a rod or drapes on café rings are excellent ways in which this treatment can be used.

Yardage
For rod & finial:
- Up to 60" wide: allow 1 yard
- Up to 108" wide: allow 1½ yards
- Up to 144" wide: allow 2 yards

Things to consider
- Size and diameter of rod
- Fabric details

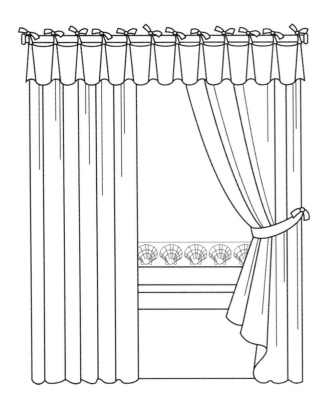

From practical to stylish to extravagant, the shower curtain can often be the focal point of a bathroom. Swags, installed at the ceiling level, can provide added opulence. Ornamental tiebacks also add elegance. For a more personalized look, replacing ordinary curtain rings with ribbons, grommets or decorative rings can add a hint of flair.

Yardage
- 54" fabric, 27" repeat, 11 yards
- 48" fabric, no repeat, 13 yards

Standard shower curtain, 72" x 72" requires:
- Solid fabric or small print: 5 yards
- Large print: 5½ yards

Things to consider
- Fabric details

Special note
Mock curtains using shirred or pleated heading and tiebacks may also be used by installing into ceiling.

Valances

Top treatments, such as the versatile valance, have the wonderful capability to be infinitely casual and also completely elegant. Take the breezy scarf valance, for example: it will step into a supporting role alongside an elegant set of draperies or a modest vertical blind. Other styles will command a room, drawing the spotlight upon themselves so all may enjoy their stand-alone beauty. From the most petite bathroom window to a large picture window, a soft valance may be the answer to any window dressing question.

(VAL100) Tassel fringed Kingston valance with rosettes over tieback draperies.

(VAL101) An open Kingston valance works perfectly with flanking, stationary drapery panels.

(VAL102) Sheer underdraperies are flanked with bullion trimmed side panels and an Empire valance top treatment with decorative trimmings.

(VAL103) Arched wide Austrian valance with rosettes and jabot accents. Simple side panels with bullion fringe along the hemline keeps the eye focused on the beauty of the arch.

(VAL104) Gracefully arched soft cornice valance with accenting welting and cascades over puddled tieback draperies with rosettes.

(VAL105) Arched wide Austrian valance with swags, center jabot and rosettes French pleated draperies.

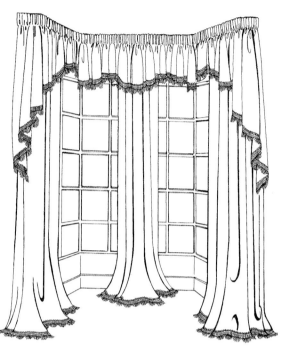

(VAL106) A scalloped flat rod pocket valance enhances the shape of the bay window and hides the hardware for the stationary drapery panels.

(VAL107) Double arched gathered valance with decorative rope and ties and coordinating trim make a simple but elegant treatment.

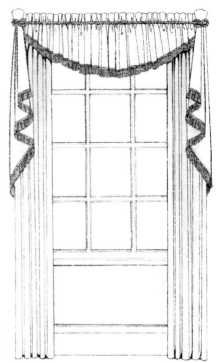

(VAL108) A rod pocket valance with cascades top simply pleated, traversing drapery panels. Brush fringe is a terrific, eye-catching accent.

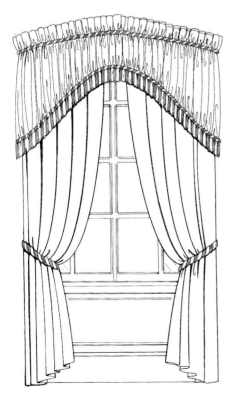

(VAL109) A classic arched valance creates a comfortable country style window treatment.

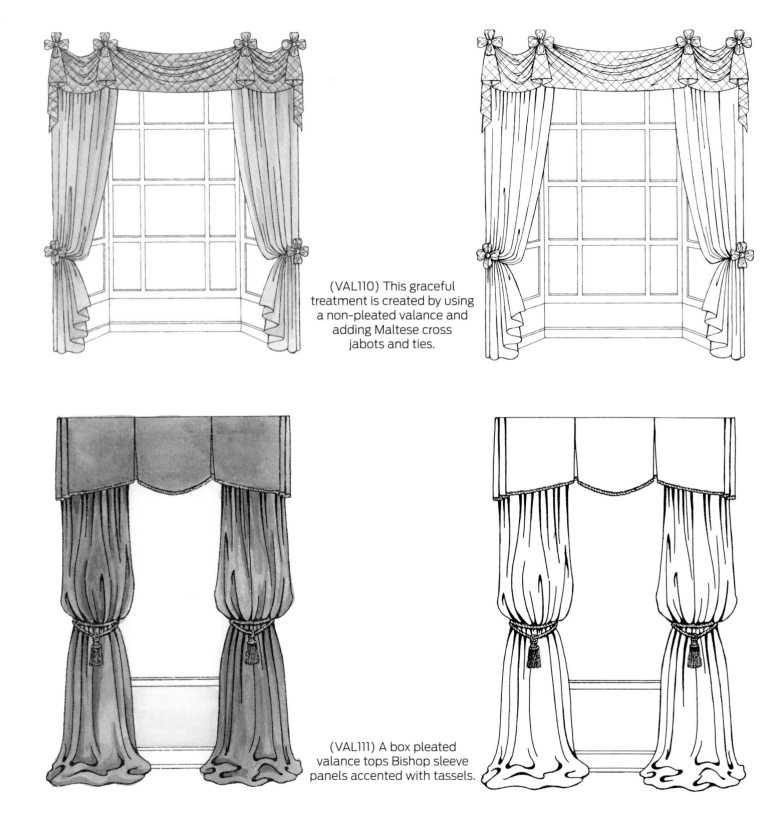

(VAL110) This graceful treatment is created by using a non-pleated valance and adding Maltese cross jabots and ties.

(VAL111) A box pleated valance tops Bishop sleeve panels accented with tassels.

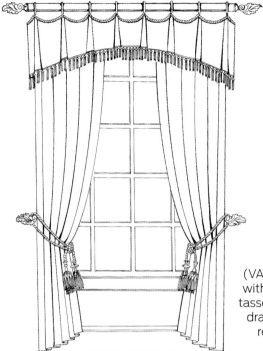

(VAL112) A scalloped ring top valance with inverted box pleats, edged in tiny tassel fringe, complements the pleated drapery panels—which can easily be released from their holdbacks to provide privacy.

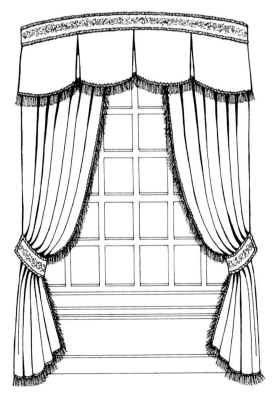

(VAL113) An arched box pleated valance edged with brush fringe, paired with pleated, matching drapery panels.

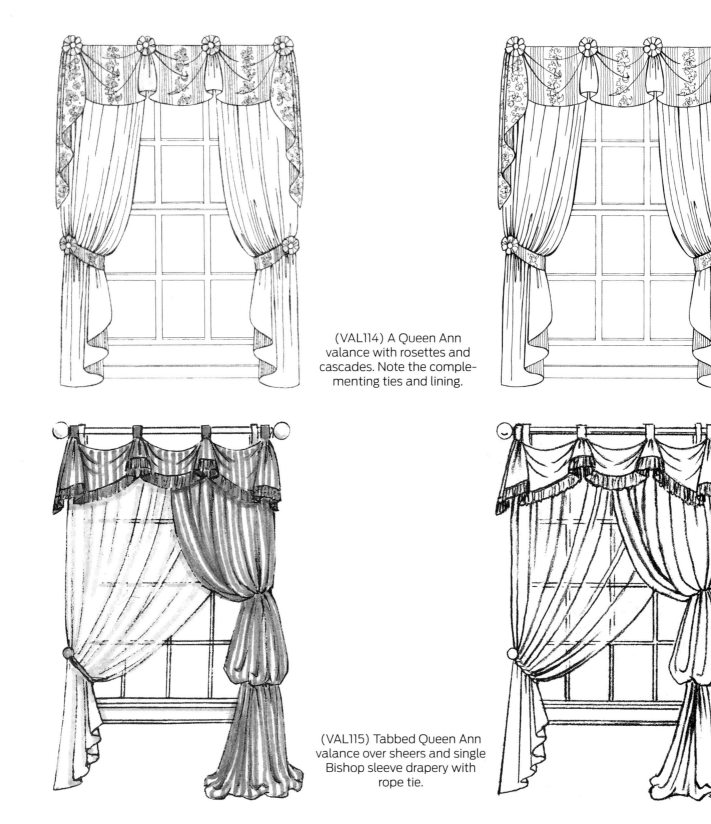

(VAL114) A Queen Ann valance with rosettes and cascades. Note the complementing ties and lining.

(VAL115) Tabbed Queen Ann valance over sheers and single Bishop sleeve drapery with rope tie.

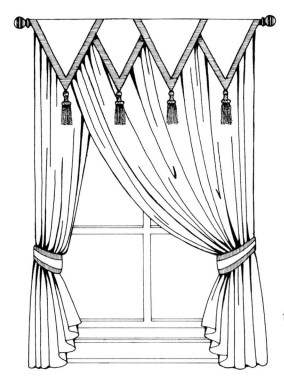

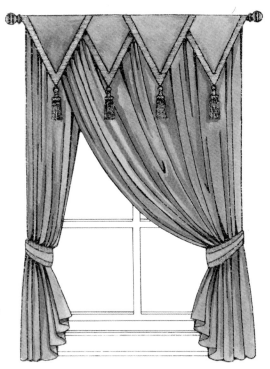

(VAL116) Triangle flags with flip top triangle valances with oversized tassels balance this otherwise asymmetrical drapery panel treatment.

(VAL117) Pointed box pleated valance is is a dainty accent to the larger and more powerful pleated and puddled drapery panels.

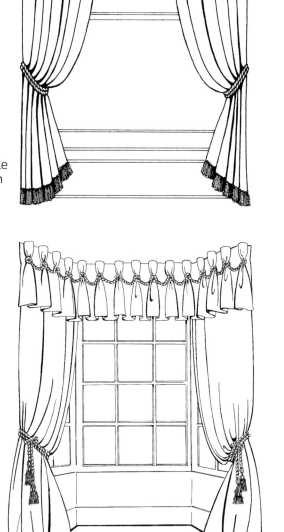

(VAL118) A soft cornice with simple side pleats enhanced with bullion fringe and tiebacks.

(VAL119) A deep goblet pleated top treatment works perfectly in this bay window with flanking, stationary drapery panels.

(VAL120) This unique rod pocket valance was created by gathering fabric vertically on decorative wood poles. Two complimentary fabrics on the side panels finish the ensemble nicely.

Patterns Plus Design:
www.patternsplus.com

(VAL121) Color blocked drapery panels with button accents complements the inverted box pleated valance.

(VAL122) A handkerchief soft valance creates visual interest at the top of the window. Drapery panels with matching fabric tiebacks on either side add softness.

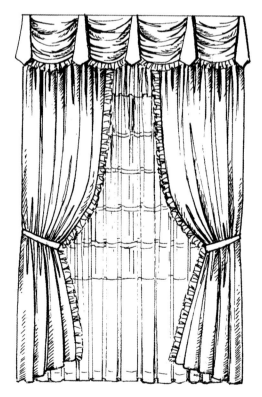

(VAL123) Austrian valance with jabots over sheers and tied back pleated draperies trimmed with knife edge banding.

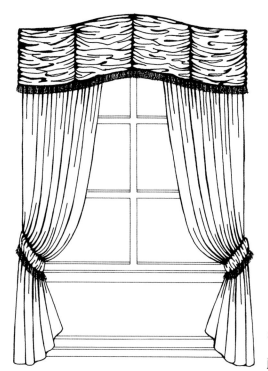

(VAL124) An arched Austrian valance with brush fringe and stationary drapery panels with matching tiebacks could be just right in a master bedroom.

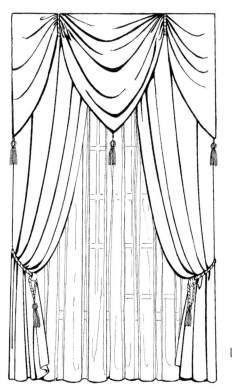

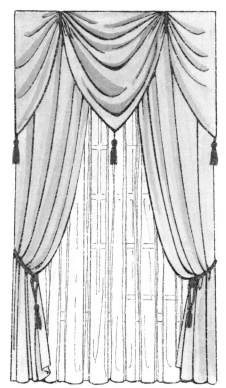

(VAL125) A triangle handkerchief valance with tassel accent is the top layer in this three layer treatment with sheer underdraperies and full side panels.

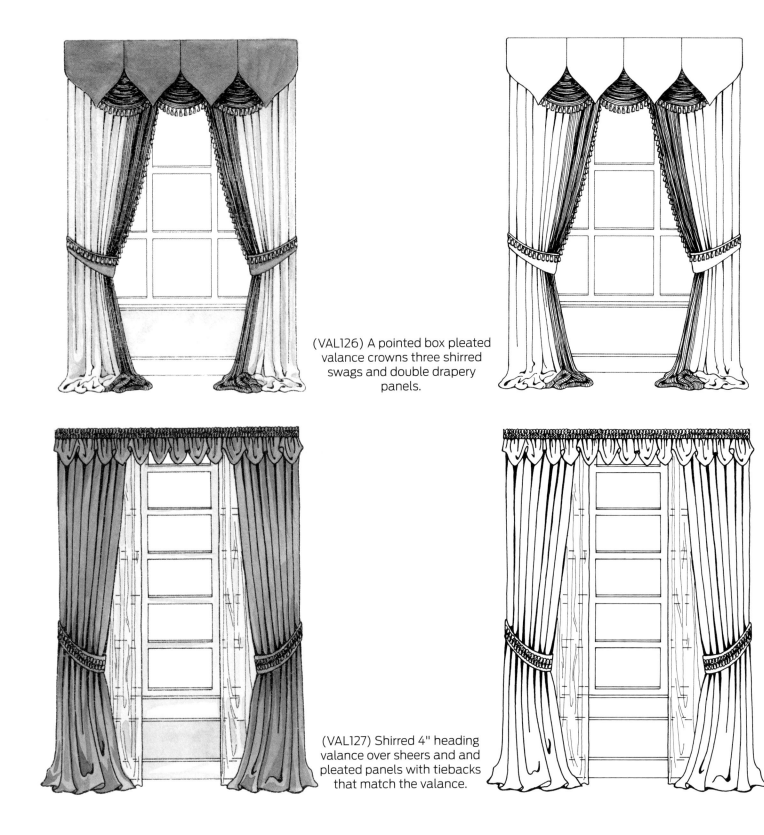

(VAL126) A pointed box pleated valance crowns three shirred swags and double drapery panels.

(VAL127) Shirred 4" heading valance over sheers and and pleated panels with tiebacks that match the valance.

(VAL128) A soft cornice with flags pull the eye up with the contrast fabric. Note that the drapery panels have matching contrast fabric tiebacks.

(VAL129) An offset arched non-pleated valance with offset triangle flag is an unusual twist. Pleated stationary panels complete the treatment.

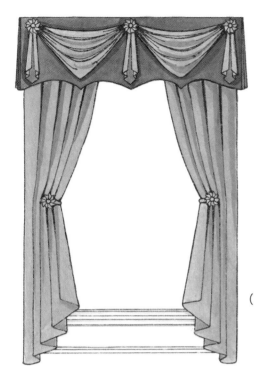

(VAL130) Soft shaped non-pleated valance with swag flags, rosettes and jabots. Drapery panels with medallion hold backs finish this elegant treatment.

(VAL131) A scalloped soft cornice frames crisply pleated drapery panels.

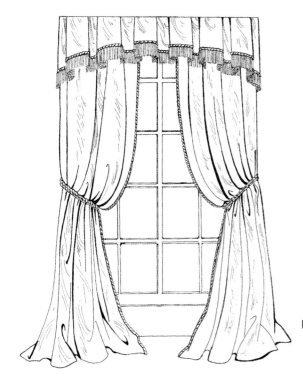

(VAL132) An arched box pleated valance with bullion fringe over tied back draperies with rope ties.

(VAL133) A gathered valance with small triangle flags and side cascades over tied back stationary draperies with complementing fabric ties.

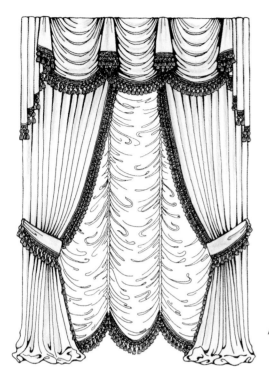

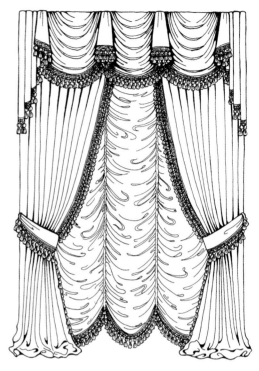

(VAL134) Does this treatment look expansive? It is! This is a Kingston valance with heavy tassel fringe over an Austrian shade. Kingston valances and Austrian shades are two of the most labor intensive drapery treatments.

(VAL135) An Austrian valance with buttoned jabots hangs from a plain wood cornice. Drapery panels with matching fabric tiebacks puddle onto the floor.

(VAL136) Kingston valance with 1" coordinating welting and simple tassel tieback puddled French pleated draperies.

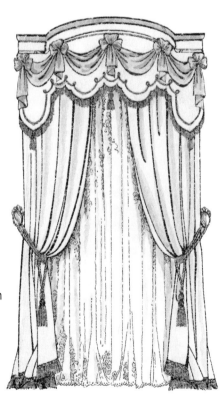

(VAL137) An arched scalloped Kingston valance with Maltese crosses and bullion fringe also complement the hemline, showcasing sheer lace underdraperies flanked with bullion fringe-trimmed side panels and tassel ties.

Valance styles

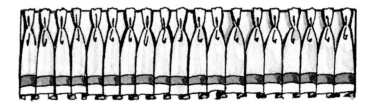

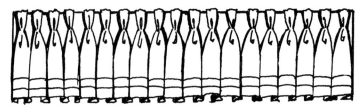

(VAL138) French pleated valance

(VAL139) Double pinch pleat

(VAL140) Space pleated valance

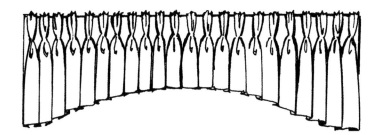

(VAL141) Pleated arched valance

(VAL142) Queen Ann valance with unique scallops

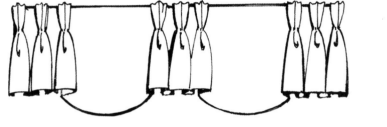

(VAL143) Space pleated Queen Ann valance

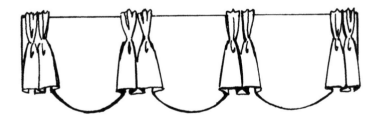

(VAL144) Double pleat Queen Ann

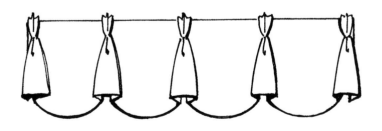

(VAL145) Queen Ann valance

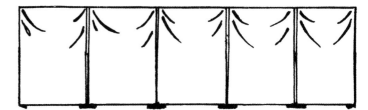

(VAL146) Inverted box pleat

(VAL147) Tapered box pleated valance with banding

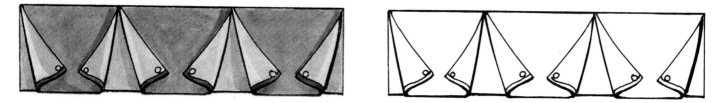

(VAL148) Box pleated valance with buttons

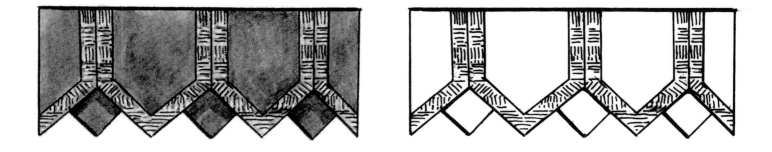

(VAL149) Box pleated valance with points and banding

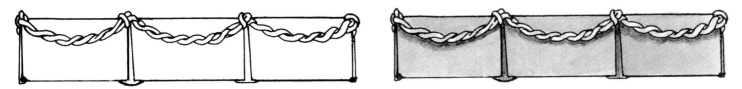

(VAL150) Inverted box pleated valance with twisted cording

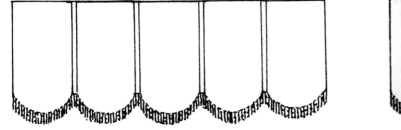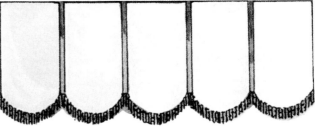

(VAL151) Scalloped inverted box valance with fringed edge

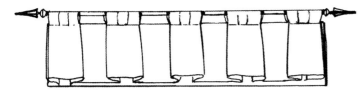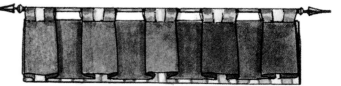

(VAL152) Tabbed box pleated valance with tabs

(VAL153) Arched box pleated valance with heading

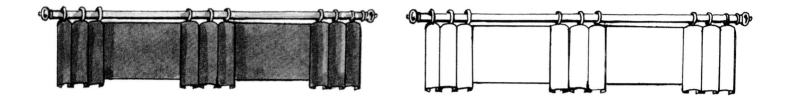

(VAL154) Triple cone pleated valance on decorative rod

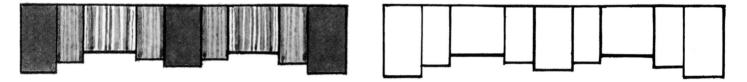

(VAL155) Multi-level box pleated valance

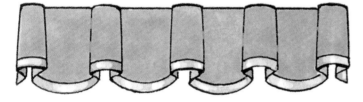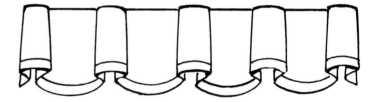

(VAL156) Regal valance

(VAL157) Arched pleated valance

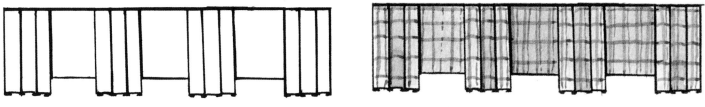

(VAL158) Asymmetrical box pleated valance

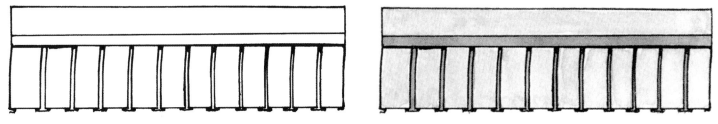

(VAL159) Inverted box pleated valance with banding and heading

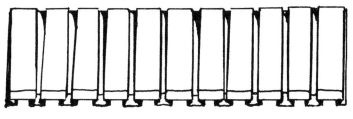
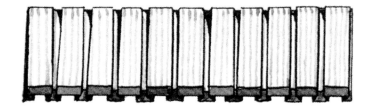

(VAL160) Box pleat with banding

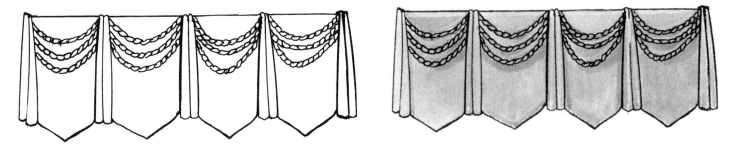

(VAL161) Pointed box pleated valance with rope accent

(VAL162) Gathered valance on flat rod with decorative rods at top and bottom

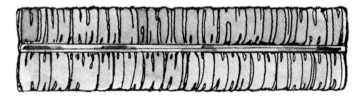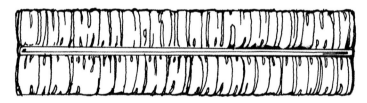

(VAL163) Double rod pocket valance with brass rod in middle.

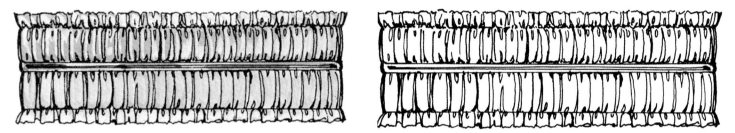

(VAL164) Two gathered valances on flat rods with decorative rod in middle

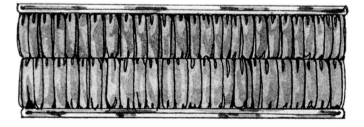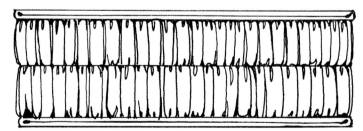

(VAL165) Two 4.5" flat rods with decorative rods top and bottom

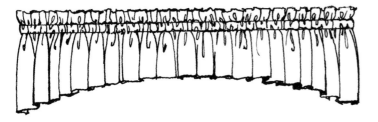
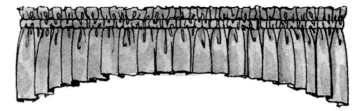

(VAL166) Rod pocket arched valance

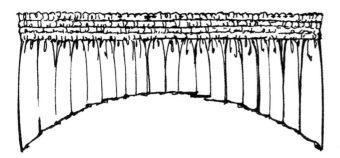
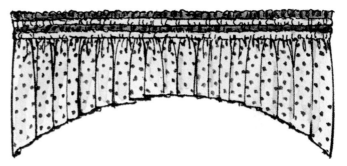

(VAL167) Arched four inch shirred heading

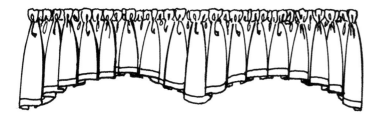

(VAL168) Rod pocket with multiple arched valance

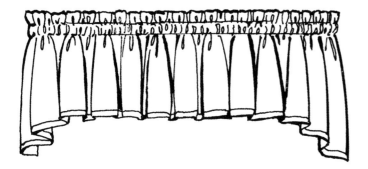

(VAL169) Rod pocket with arched valance

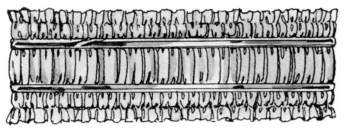 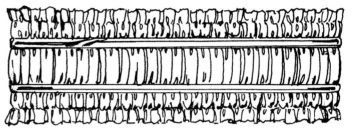

(VAL170) Gathered valance with flat rod in middle and two decorative rods between

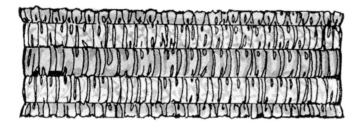 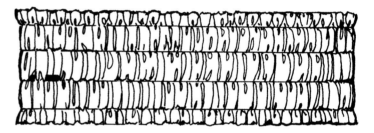

(VAL171) Triple rod pocket with multiple fabrics

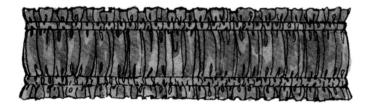 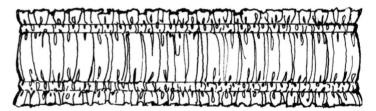

(VAL172) Rod pocket top and bottom valance

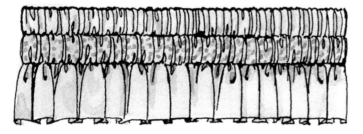 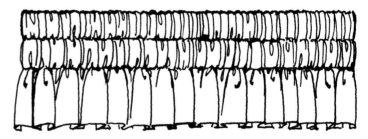

(VAL173) Double rod pocket with no stand up

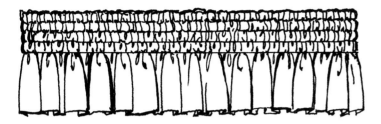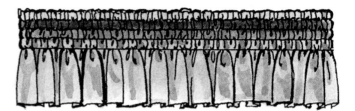

(VAL174) Four inch shirred heading

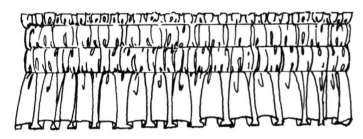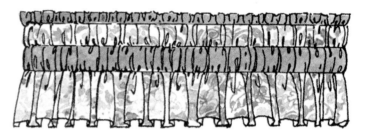

(VAL175) Double rod pocket with stand up top

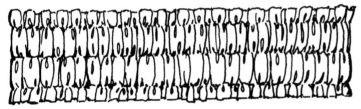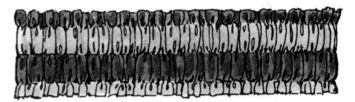

(VAL176) Double rod pocket with stand up top and bottom

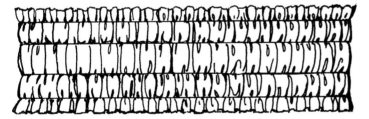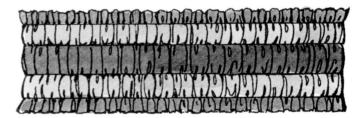

(VAL177) Triple flat rods with gathers at top and bottom

(VAL178) Cloud valance with shirred heading

(VAL179) Double rod pocket with cloud valance

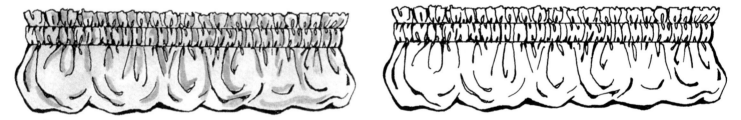

(VAL180) Cloud valance with stand up ruffle

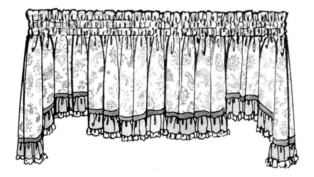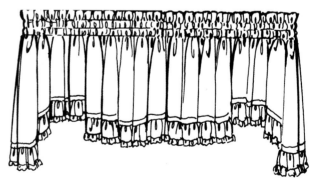

(VAL181) Arched gathered valance with ruffles on narrow double rods

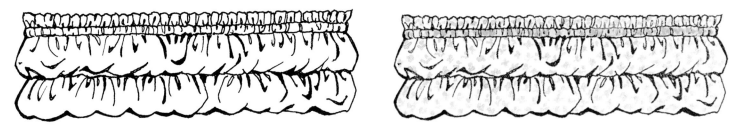

(VAL182) Double rod pocket top and bottom valance

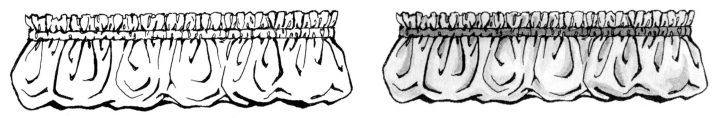

(VAL183) Cloud valance with rod pocket heading

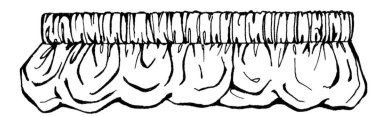
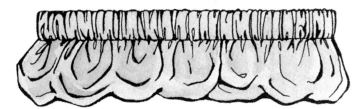

(VAL184) Rod pocket top and bottom valance with lower rod lifted

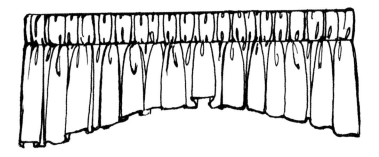
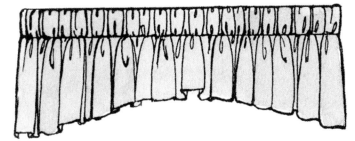

(VAL185) Arched rod pocket

(VAL186) Rod pocket petticoat valance

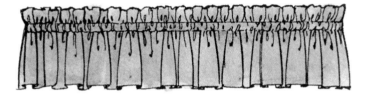

(VAL187) Rod pocket valance

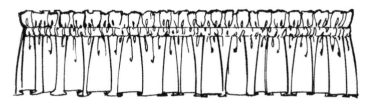

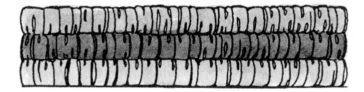

(VAL188) Triple 4.5" gathered flat rod valance

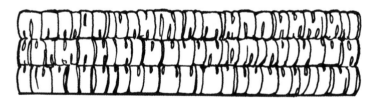

(VAL189) Rod pocket heading with no stand up

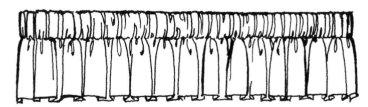

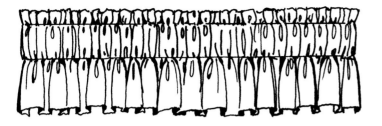 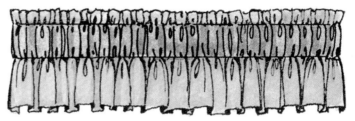

(VAL190) Rod pocket with stand-up ruffle

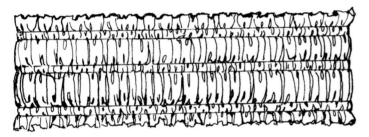 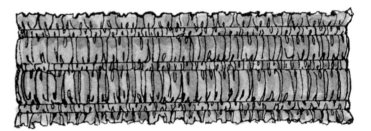

(VAL191) Double rod pocket top and bottom valance

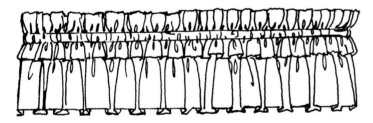 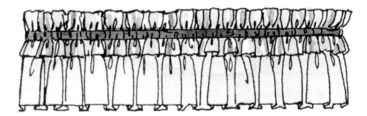

(VAL192) Double ruffled valance shirred on rod

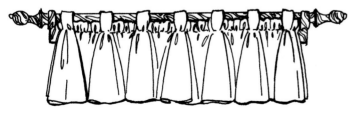 

(VAL193) Tab valance on decorative rod

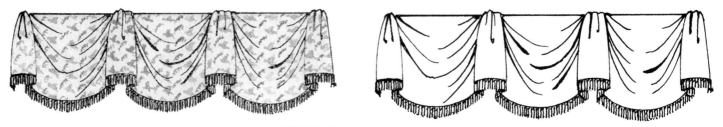

(VAL194) Kingston valance

(VAL195) Open Kingston valance on decorative rod

(VAL196) Louis XV valance

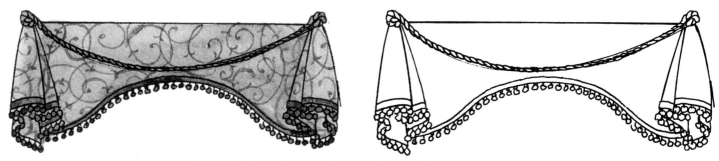

(VAL197) Arched and gathered valance with rope and fringe.
Patterns available for many of these valances: www.patternsplus.com and www.mfay.com

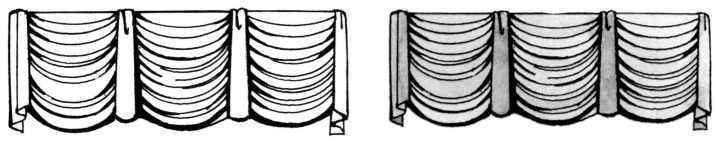

(VAL198) Austrian valance with jabots

(VAL199) Murphy valance

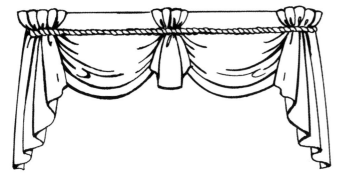
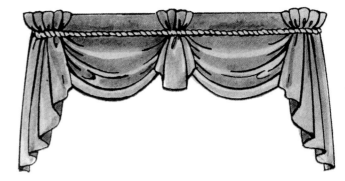

(VAL200) Bordeaux valance

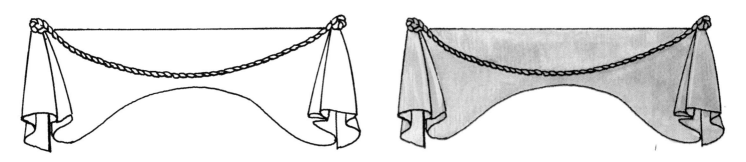

(VAL201) Arched and gathered valance with rope

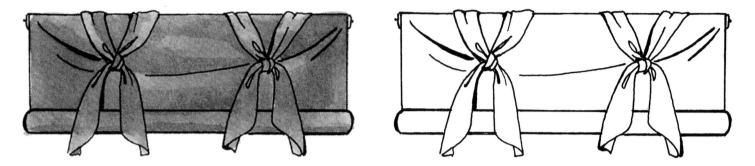

(VAL202) Rolled stagecoach valance with wide knotted tie bands

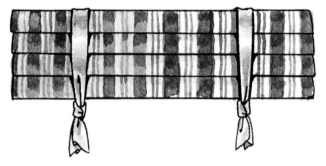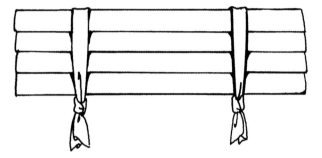

(VAL203) Mock Roman cornice with ties

(VAL204) Rod top and bottom valance with ties

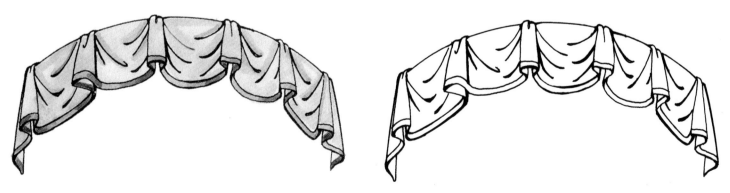

(VAL205) Arched Kingston valance

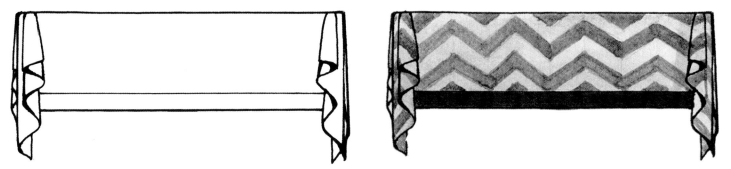

(VAL206) Soft cornice valance with cascades and accent banding

(VAL207) Mock Roman

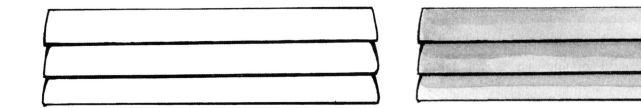

(VAL208) Scalloped tabbed valance with trim

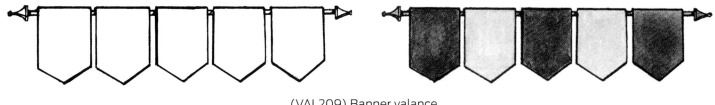

(VAL209) Banner valance

(VAL210) Gathered valance under small soft cornice with ties

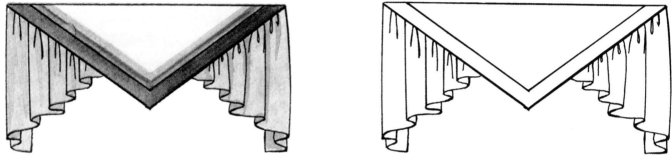

(VAL211) Handkerchief and gathered valance combo

(VAL212) Multiple point valance with edge banding

(VAL213) Swags over gathered valance over soft cornice valance

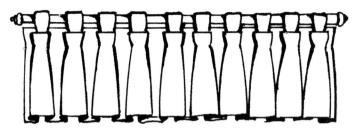

(VAL214) Box pleated tabbed valance

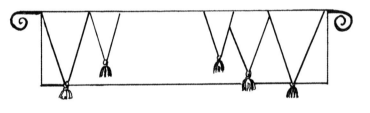

(VAL215) Balloon valance with matching welting

(VAL216) Soft cornice with banners

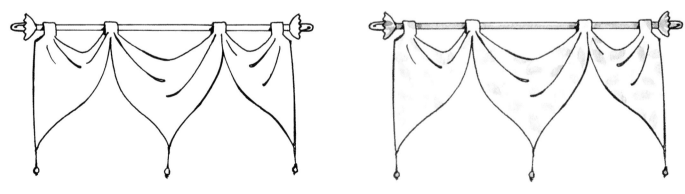

(VAL217) Tear drop valance

Additional valance styles

(*Top row, left to right*) Rod pocket valance with banding; Rod pocket valance with jabots over Austrian shade;
Arched rod pocket valance with brush tassel over café curtain
(*Bottom row, left to right*) Rod pocket valance over tieback panels with scalloped banding; Arched box pleated
scalloped valance with rope accent and tassels; Arched valance with ruffle trim over café curtain

(*Top row, left to right*) Tieback draperies with balloon valance; Triangle valance over tiebacks; Gathered valance over draperies
(*Bottom row, left to right*) Gathered valance over Bishop sleeve draperies with café curtain; Double arched valance over tiebacks and cloud shade; Gathered and swagged valance over tiebacks

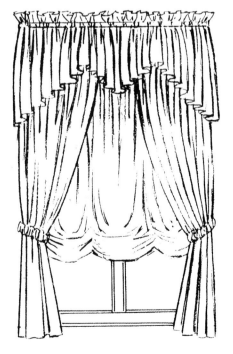

(*Top row, left to right*) Rod pocket valance over Bishop sleeve draperies with bow ties; Pleated arched valance over tiebacks and sheer balloon shade; Bishop sleeve draperies with valance
(*Bottom row, left to right*) Rod top and bottom valance with matching tiebacks over mini blind; Kingston valance over tied back draperies and sheers; Cluster pleated valance with pleated draperies over Roman shade

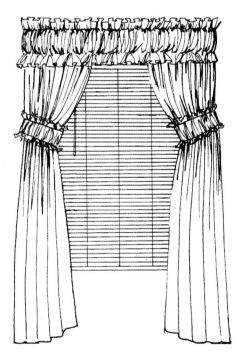

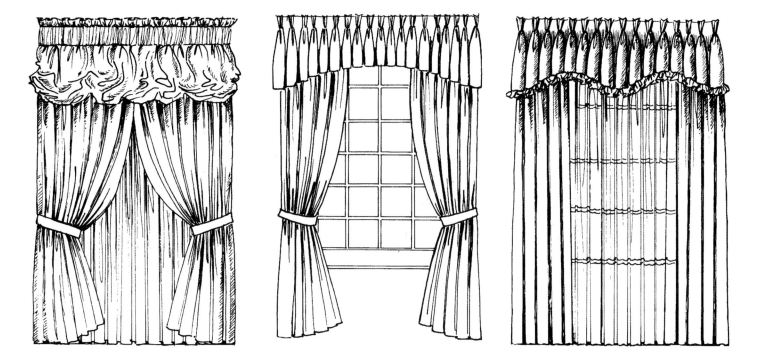

(*Top row, left to right*) Rod pocket cloud valance with tiebacks over sheers; Arched French pleated valance with tiebacks; Multiple arched valance over draperies and sheers

(*Bottom row, left to right*) Tieback draperies with balloon valance over Austrian shade; Space pleated Queen Ann valance with scalloped edge over tiebacks and sheers; Rod pocket drapery with banding

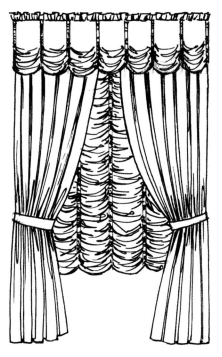
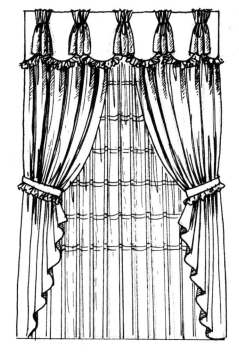
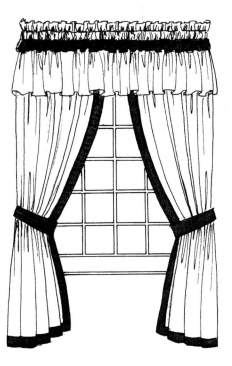

Valance yardage specifications

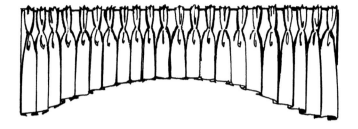

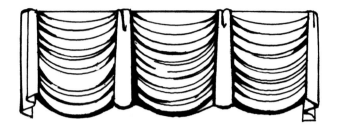

This softly shaped arched pleated valance adds an interesting touch to a window without distorting the view. The heading may be pleated, shirred or tunneled.

Yardage (including French pleated; Rod pocket (including arched); Queen Ann & box pleated)

Step 1 – Width of area to be covered + returns x 2.5 ÷ width of fabric = number of widths

Step 2a – Length to longest point + 16" x number of widths ÷ 36 = yardage without pattern repeat

—or—

Step 2b – Length to longest point + 16" ÷ pattern repeat = number of repeats required (round upward to nearest whole number)

Step 2c – Number of repeats required x pattern repeat = cut length

Step 2d – Number of widths x cut length ÷ 36 = yardage with pattern repeat

Things to consider
- Width
- Returns
- Length to longest point
- Length to shortest point
- Fabric details
- Type of heading

A soft, formal valance created by vertical shirring between scallops. Combine with other treatments to create a complete look.

Yardage: Austrian valance

Step 1 – Width of area to be covered + returns x 1.5 ÷ width of fabric = number of widths (whole numbers only)

Step 2a – Number of widths x (length of valance x 3) ÷ 36 = yardage without pattern repeat

—or—

Step 2b – Length of valance x 3 ÷ pattern repeat = number of repeats required (round upward to nearest whole number)

Step 2c – Number of repeats required x pattern repeat = cut length

Step 2d – Number of widths x cut length ÷ 36 = yardage with pattern repeat

Things to consider
- Width
- Length
- Color of lining
- Inside or outside mount
- Returns

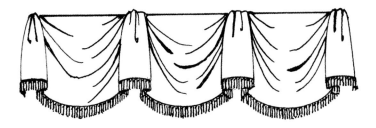

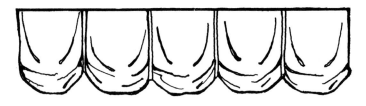

The Kingston is an elaborate valance that gets its fullness from behind the horns, whereas the Empire valance get its fullness from pulling the pleats up to the top of the board.

Yardage (including Empire or Kingston valance)

Step 1 – BF (board face) + 6" for RT (returns, if going over draperies) x 2.5 ÷ width of fabric = number of widths required (round up to whole number)

Step 2a – FL (finished length) x 2 + 10" for HH (headings and hems) x widths required ÷ 36 = yardage (round up to whole number) without pattern repeat

—or—

Step 2b – FL (finished length) x 2 + 10" for HH ÷ pattern repeat = number of repeats required (round up to whole number)

Step 2c – Number of repeats x pattern repeat = CL (cut length)

Step 2d – Number of widths x CL (cut length) ÷ 36 = yardage with pattern repeat (round up to whole number)

Things to consider
• Width and length, color of lining
• Mounting: board or decorative rod

This valance has large, inverted pleats that create a more tailored effect than its counterpart, the cloud valance. Used alone or with an undertreatment, its soft look and pretty poufs add a feminine touch.

Yardage (including Balloon or Cloud valance)

Step 1 – Width of valance + RT (returns) x 2.5 ÷ width of fabric = number of fabric widths required (round up to whole number)

Step 2a – Valance length + 16" for HH (heading and hems) x widths required ÷ 36 = yardage without pattern repeat

—or—

Step 2b – Valance length + 16" for HH ÷ pattern repeat = number of repeats required (round up whole number)

Step 2c – Number of repeats required x pattern repeat = CL (cut length)

Step 2d – Number of widths x CL ÷ 36 = yardage with pattern repeat (round up to whole number)

Things to consider
• Width, length and color of lining
• Placement: inside, outside, or ceiling mounted
• Size of returns and mounting: board or rod

Cornices & lambrequins

Whether alone or as an accompaniment to an existing window treatment, cornices can be a wonderful addition to any home decor.

Though they are a permanent window treatment usually installed snugly next to a window frame, a cornice box is anything but sedentary. Situated atop a tall window, an intricately carved cornice box can transport the room to a time when kings and queens lived in opulence. Conversely, a shaped cornice above a child's window, adorned with a favorite animal or icon, can contribute to a playful theme in a big way.

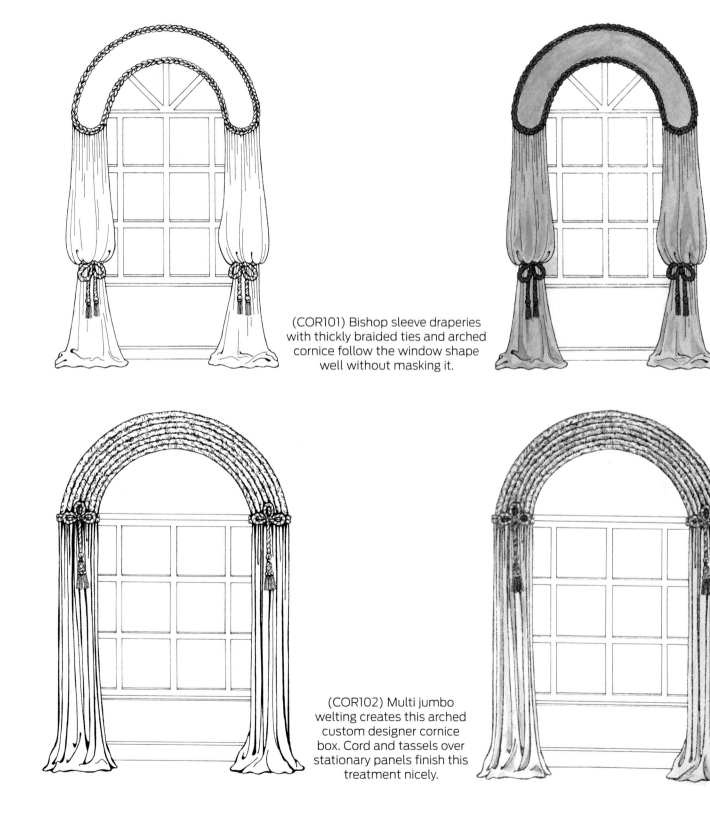

(COR101) Bishop sleeve draperies with thickly braided ties and arched cornice follow the window shape well without masking it.

(COR102) Multi jumbo welting creates this arched custom designer cornice box. Cord and tassels over stationary panels finish this treatment nicely.

(COR103) An arched quilted cornice box is mirrored on the deep bottom hem of the pleated draperies.

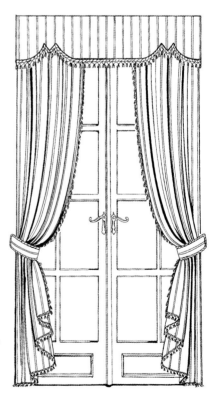

(COR104) Vertically striped drapery panels coordinate well with a matching, upholstered cornice and horizontally-striped fabric tiebacks crafted from the same fabric.

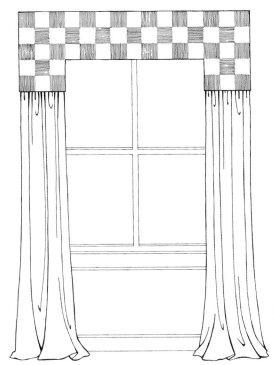

(COR105) Sometimes the fabric pattern will help in choosing the cornice box design. Note the checkered pattern is lined up with the dropping sides of this custom shaped cornice. Stationary drapery panels puddle slightly on the floor.

(COR106) A padded, upholstered cornice with unique detailing is the perfect foil for double drapery panels.

(COR107) Lambrequin with welt edge over Roman shade.

(COR108) Shirred lambrequin over pleated drapery.

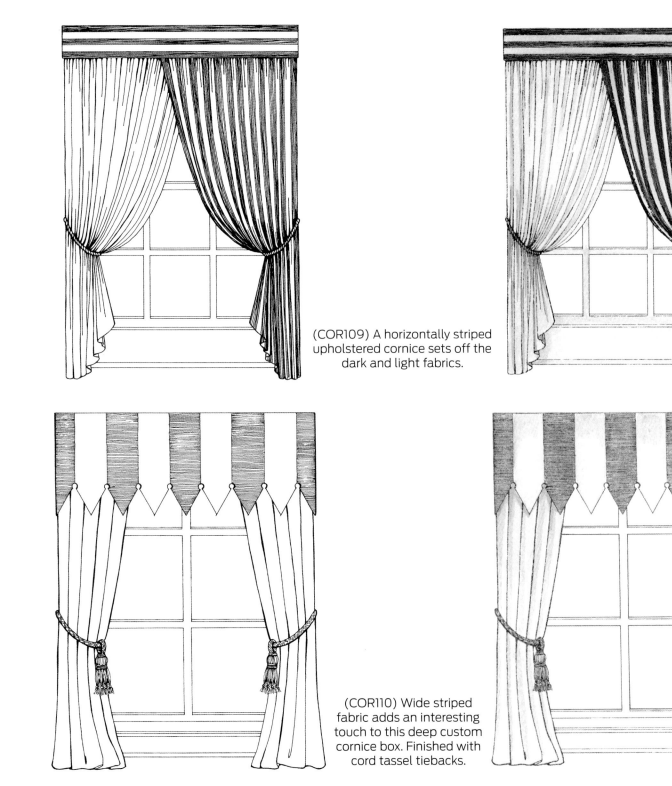

(COR109) A horizontally striped upholstered cornice sets off the dark and light fabrics.

(COR110) Wide striped fabric adds an interesting touch to this deep custom cornice box. Finished with cord tassel tiebacks.

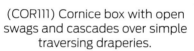

(COR111) Cornice box with open swags and cascades over simple traversing draperies.

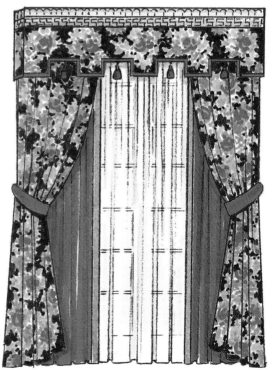

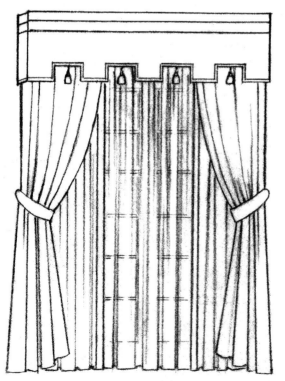

(COR112) Gold leaf wood moulding tops this designer cornice box. Draperies with banding over sheers make a stunning four layer treatment.

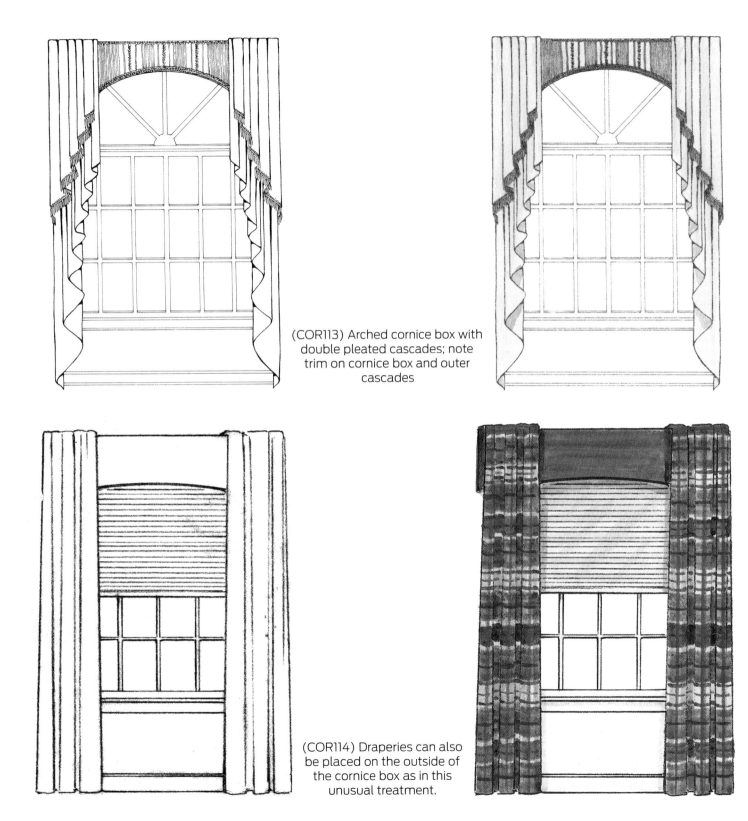

(COR113) Arched cornice box with double pleated cascades; note trim on cornice box and outer cascades

(COR114) Draperies can also be placed on the outside of the cornice box as in this unusual treatment.

(COR115) A large arched upholstered cornice with matching trillian cornices showcase this enormous window as well as hold small swags and Bishop sleeve drapery panels.

(COR116) Upholstered trillian cornices accentuate the view; swagged fabric in between vertically softens, puddled drapery enhances.

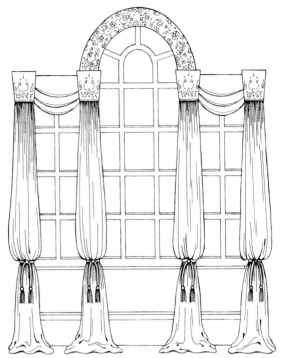

(COR117) A variation of the treatment on the opposing page. Note that by changing a few elements one can have a totally custom window covering.

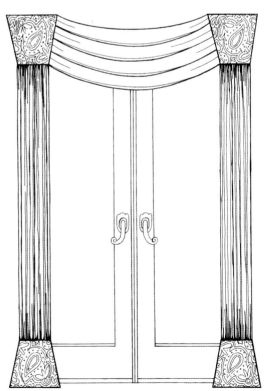

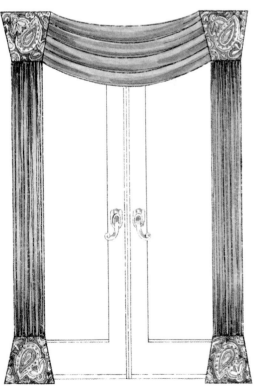

(COR118) Trillian cornices at top and bottom flank the doorway and hold the single swags at the top and the shirred vertical fabric treatments, too.

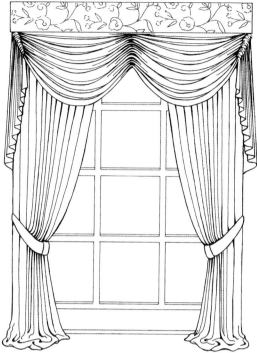

(COR119) A variation of the treatment on the opposing page. Note that by changing a few elements one can have a totally custom window covering.

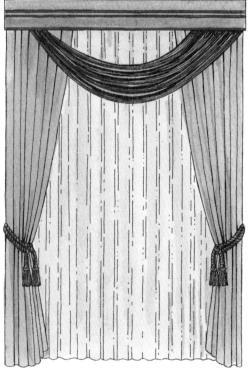

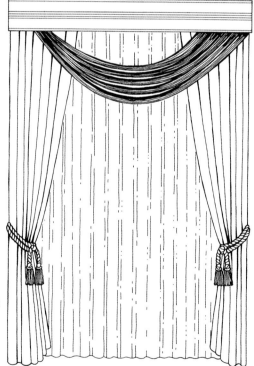

(COR120) A straight cornice with banding and welting houses all the hardware needed for hanging the sheer underdrapery, side panels and single swag.

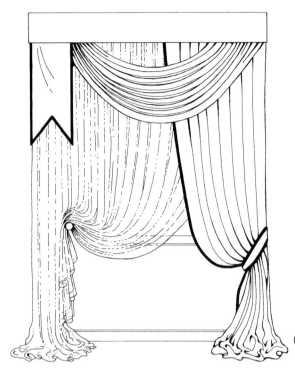

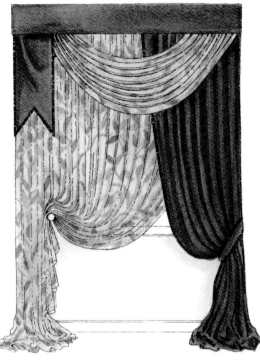

(COR121) To mask an unsightly view, a sheer underdrapery diffuses light, while the swag and tail and right side drapery panel draw the eye away from the view.

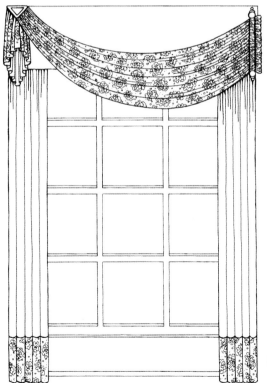

(COR122) This unique treatment turns a rod pocket onits side and then is installed on the outside of an upholstered cornice, finishing in a double cascade. Stationary drapery panels on either side are color blocked to pull the eye.

Based on Patterns Plus Designs: www.patternsplus.com

Cornice shapes, styles & embellishments

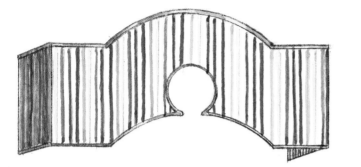
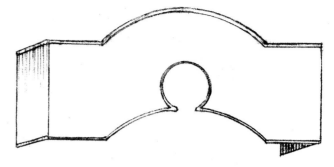

(COR123) Arched cornice with circular center

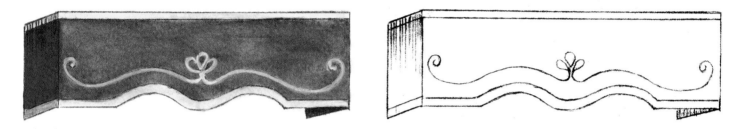

(COR124) Cornice with banding top and appliqué

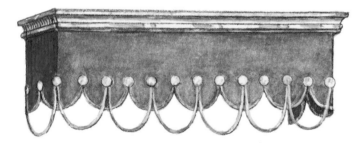
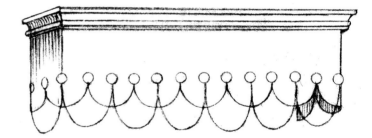

(COR125) Cornice box with gilded top and rope tassels

(COR126) Designer gilded wood top cornice

(COR127) Cornice box with large rope top and appliqué

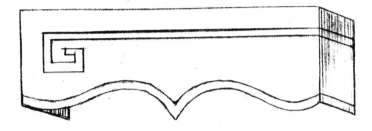

(COR128) Cornice box with appliqué

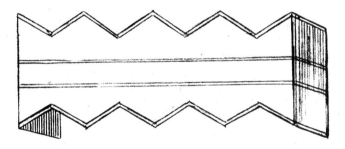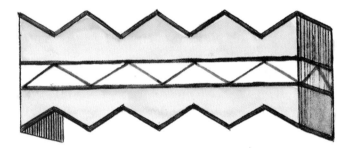

(COR129) Chevron top and bottom cornice

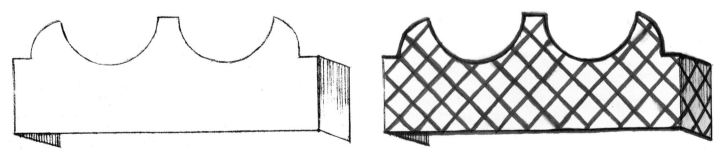

(COR130) Pagoda cornice

(COR131) Arched cornice with fabric ruffles

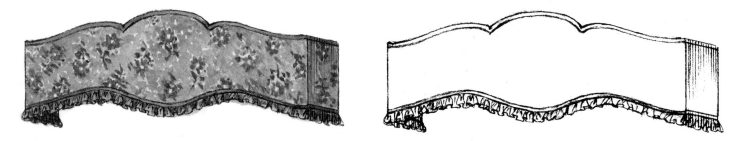

(COR132) Custom design cornice with bottom ruffle

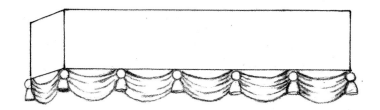

(COR133) Button swagged cornice

(COR134) Shaped crown cornice with gathered valance

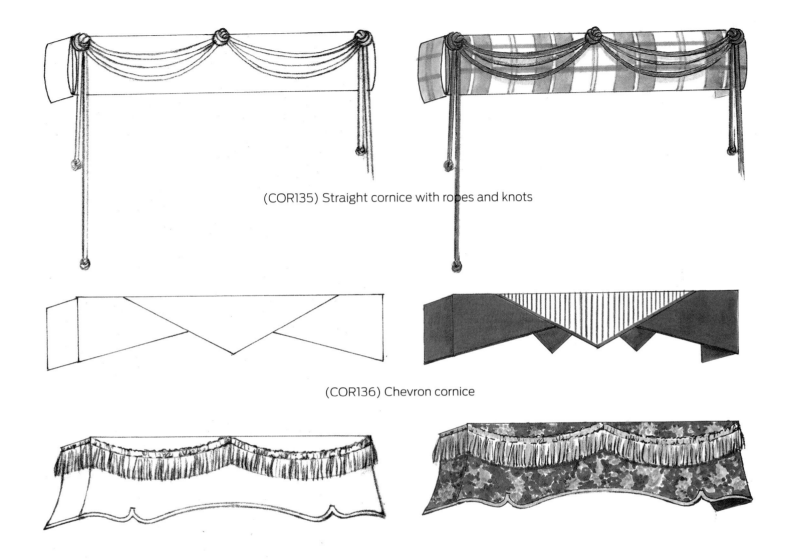

(COR135) Straight cornice with ropes and knots

(COR136) Chevron cornice

(COR137) Pagoda cornice with heavy bullion fringe

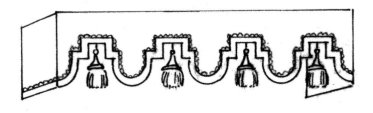

(COR138) Shaped cornice with large tassels

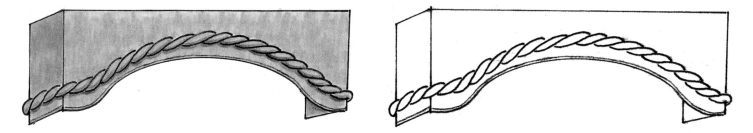

(COR139) Arched cornice with twisted rope

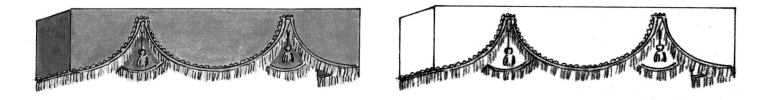

(COR140) Shaped cornice with fringe

(COR141) Box shaped cornice with short side drops

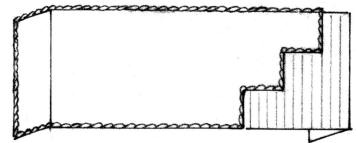

(COR142) Multi-fabric cornice

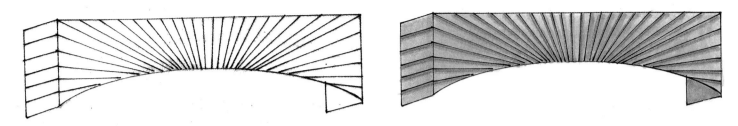

(COR143) Sunburst cornice

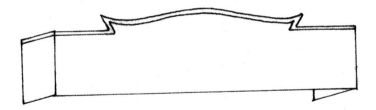
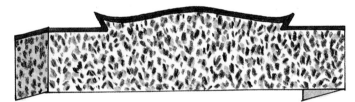

(COR144) Pagoda cornice

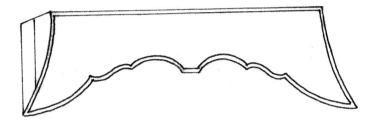
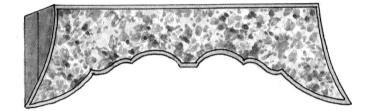

(COR145) Straight cornice with shaped crown

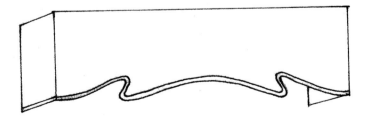
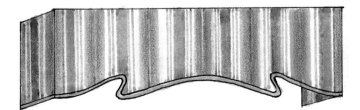

(COR146) Custom shaped cornice

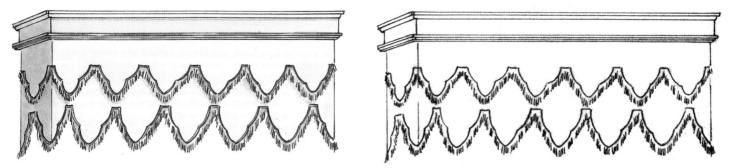

(COR147) Double fringe cornice with wood crown

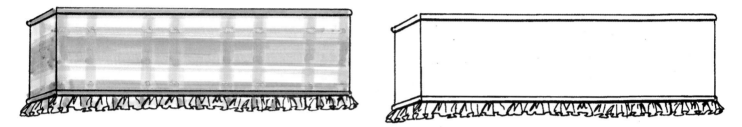

(COR148) Cornice box with ruffle on bottom

(COR149) Cornice box with swag and rosettes

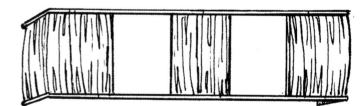

(COR150) Cornice box with shirred and flat panels

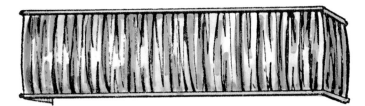

(COR151) Shirred cornice box

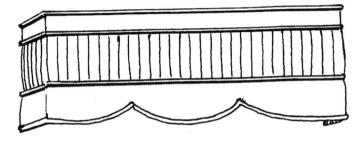

(COR152) Cornice box with pleated fabric in middle

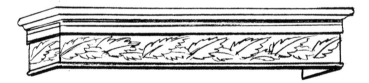

(COR153) Wood cornice with painted leaf design

(COR154) Cornice with wood header and wallpapered front and sides

(COR155) Straight cornice with stenciled design

(COR156) Cornice with over and under swags

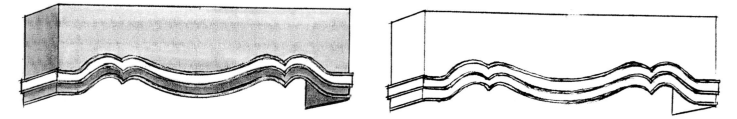

(COR157) Cornice with shaped and raised banding

(COR158) Cornice with pleating

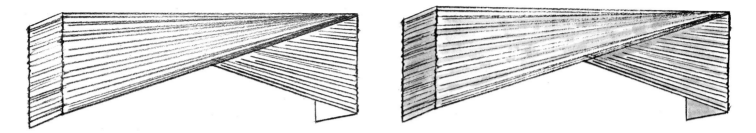

(COR159) Cornice with diagonally arched pleating

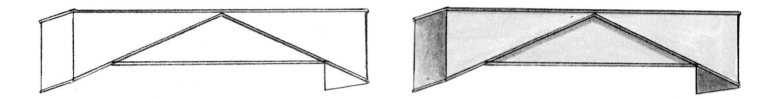

(COR160) Cornice with unique angled top and welting

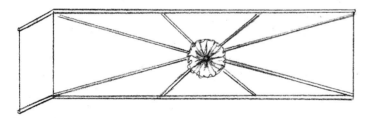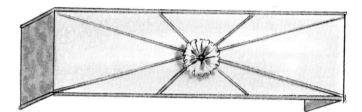

(COR161) Straight cornice with diagonal welts and center rosette

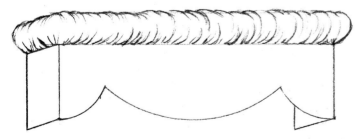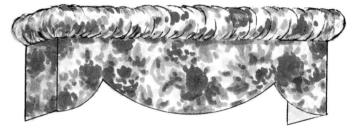

(COR162) Cornice with rounded gathered top and large scalloped bottom

(COR163) Straight cornice with rosettes and jabots

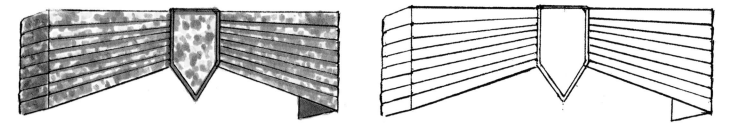

(COR164) Pleated arched cornice with special centerpiece

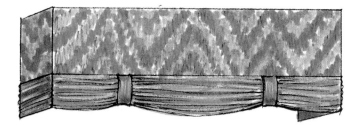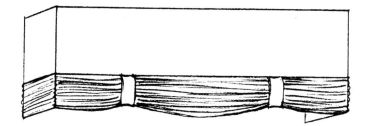

(COR165) Cornice with gathered bottom

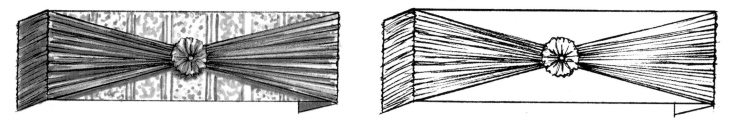

(COR166) Straight cornice with gathered hourglass and rosette accent

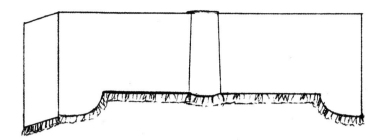

(COR167) Cornice with center jabot

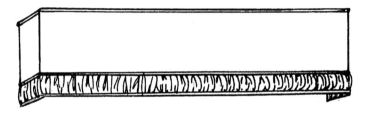
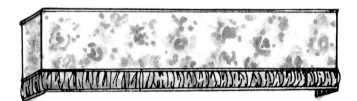

(COR168) Cornice box with shirred bottom band

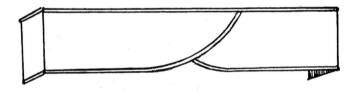
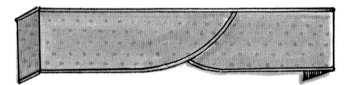

(COR169) Cornice box with special welting

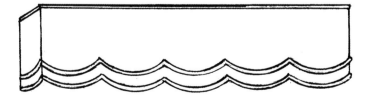
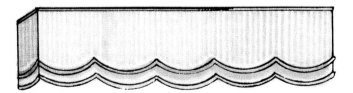

(COR170) Scalloped bottom with banding

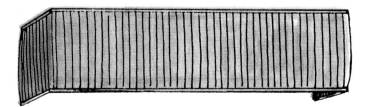
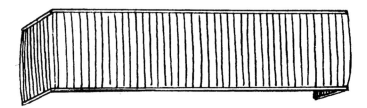

(COR171) Cornice box with one-inch pleats

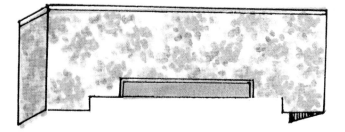
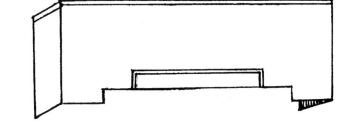

(COR172) Cornice box with fabric inserts

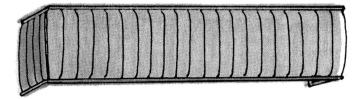
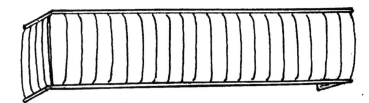

(COR173) Cornice box with two-inch pleats

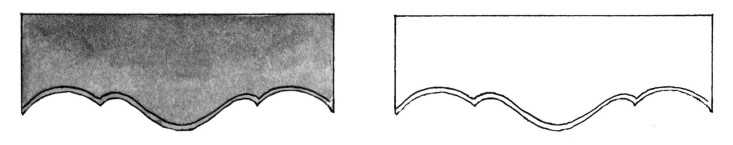

(COR174) Designer specialty cornice box

(LAM101–103)

(LAM104–106)

(LAM107–110)

Cornice box shapes

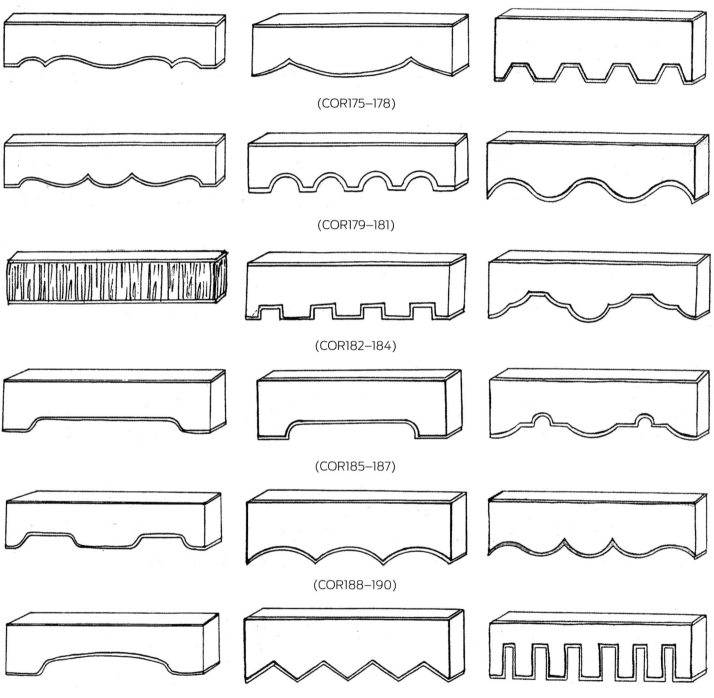

(COR175–178)

(COR179–181)

(COR182–184)

(COR185–187)

(COR188–190)

(COR191–193)

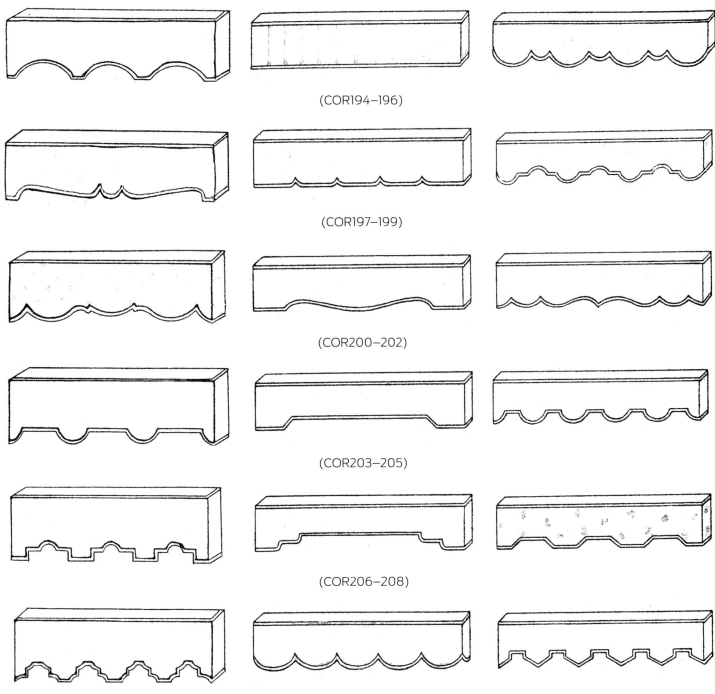

(COR194–196)

(COR197–199)

(COR200–202)

(COR203–205)

(COR206–208)

(COR209–211)

Cornice boxes – information & yardage

General information

Cornices and lambrequins are padded with polyester fiberfill and constructed of wood or chipboard.

Non-directional and solid fabrics should be railroaded to eliminate seams. Matching welting is standard on all cornices and is applied to the top and bottom edges. Coordinating colors for welting has a more dramatic effect.

When ordering to fit tight applications, (i.e., wall to wall, bay windows, for example), be sure to measure at the elevation of this installation. "Exact outside face measurement—wall to wall installation." Allow one inch for clearance.

Measuring

Measure drapery rod from end bracket to end bracket and add four inches for rod clearance and cornice/lambrequin. Six inch returns are needed when mounted over a single rod and eight-inch returns when mounted over a double rod.

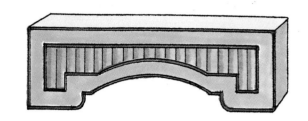

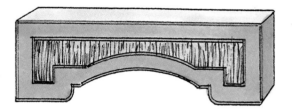

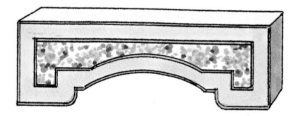

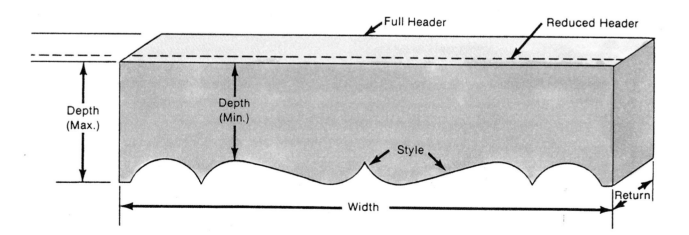

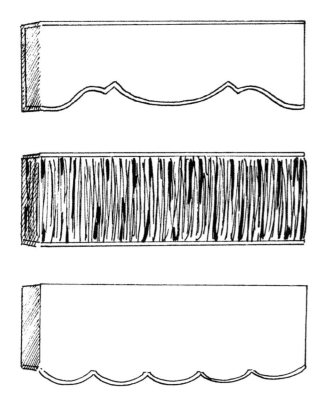

Upholstered cornices provide a classic topping for windows of any size, making an excellent overtreatment for draperies, vertical blinds or Venetian blinds. The cornice is constructed of a wooden frame that is padded and upholstered in a decorative fabric and finished with piping on the top and bottom edges.

Yardage
See box below

Things to consider
- Width
- Length: shortest + longest points
- Return
- Style
- Fabric details
- Color of lining

Special notes
1. A check measure and installation are strongly recommended.
2. Off center prints may create an unbalanced effect, so choose fabric carefully.

Style	Width		
	48" to 84"	84" to 120"	120" to 144"
Tailored	2 yards	3 yards	3½ yards
Square Notch	2 yards	3 yards	3½ yards
Scallop	2 yards	3 yards	3½ yards
Scroll	2 yards	3 yards	3½ yards
Ruched	3 yards	4½ yards	5½ yards

Swags & cascades

As diverse as they are versatile, swags and cascades can assume many roles, taking the lead role in a dramatic and eye-popping capacity—or perhaps just a supporting role or bit part. At its most subtle, a swag and cascade combination can take shape as it winds itself around a pole in a slouchy and casual way; for a more involved installation, look to a swag accompanying drapery panels. No matter how it's installed, however: board mounted, pole mounted, multi-layers or just a single, this time tested top treatment is certain to make a statement.

(SC100) Fabric hangs in shabby chic swag and cascade style, layered over lush, puddled stationary drapery panels. Note how the braid lines the edge of the panels and then is also draped casually among the folds of the swag.

(SC101) Gathered linear swags over traditional overlapping swags with stacking cascades make for an elegant and expensive treatment. Finished with rosettes and tassels.

(SC102) A sheer undertreatment, puddled drapery panels, and swags and cascades top treatment dripping with bullion fringe and braid.

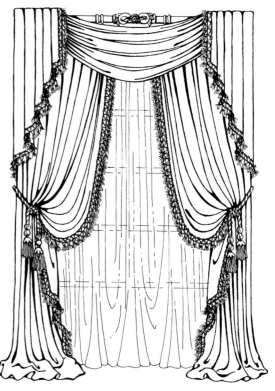

(SC103) Gathered single swag under pleated cascades mounted on designer drapery rod and finished with trim and tassels

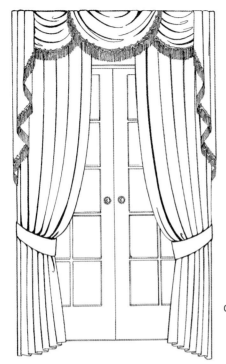

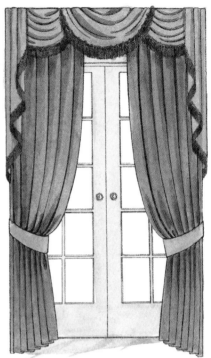

(SC104) Classic (pleated and overlapping) swags and cascades are trimmed in fringe and serves to hide the mechanisms upon which the drapery panels are held in place.

(SC105) An asymmetrical swag treatment is lushly detailed wth bullion, tassels and plenty of thick, drapeable fabric. This treatment consists of three different parts but looks like one continuous piece of fabric.

(SC106) Gathered swags with rope and tassel heading. Raised jabot adds a dramatic touch. Tiebacks with banding finish this formal treatment.

(SC107) A two-layered treatment incorporates a sheer side panel, held back with tassel tieback and asymmetrical pole swag with bullion fringe and tassel tieback. The panel is easily released from its tieback to offer additional sun filtering.

(SC108) Tap top gathered open swags are anchored on decorative wood rod. Since the pleated under draperies cover the entire window the ties can be undone for privacy.

(SC109) A pole swag exhibits large decorative knots, which heightens the treatment visually and draws the eye. Side panels, held back with braided tassel trim, complete the stately, yet casual look.

(SC110) A simple but elegant top treatment, perfect for French doors: A pole swag with lovely detailing draws attention but does not impede egress.

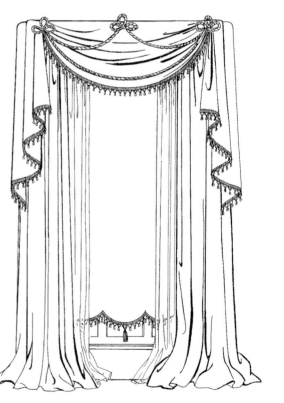

(SC111) Trim on the scalloped fabric shade is echoed in the soft swag and cascade cornice. Note, too, that this is a four part treatment—both sheer and regular drapery panels are employed.

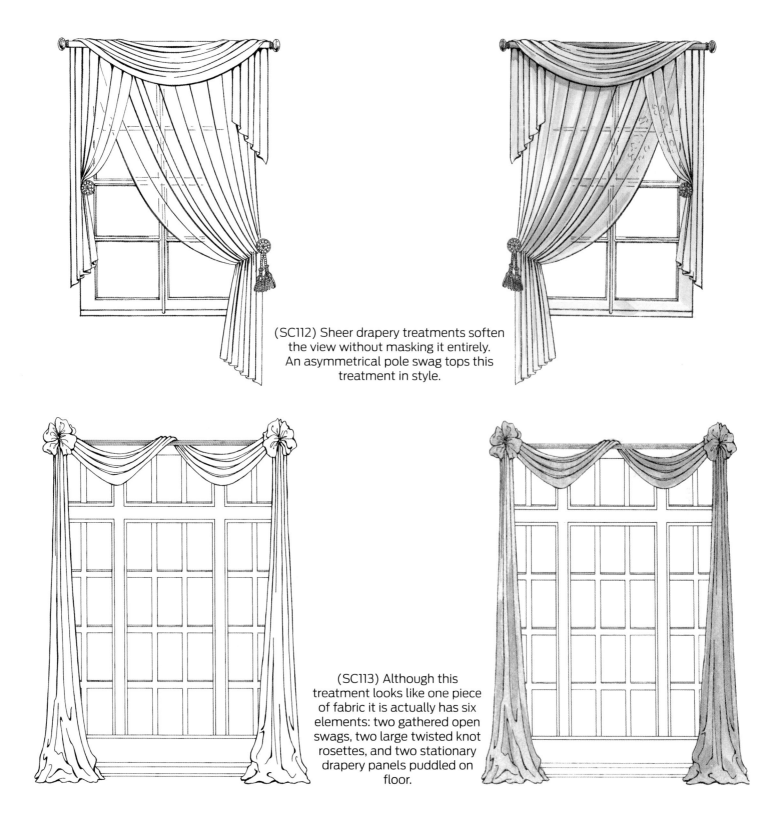

(SC112) Sheer drapery treatments soften the view without masking it entirely. An asymmetrical pole swag tops this treatment in style.

(SC113) Although this treatment looks like one piece of fabric it is actually has six elements: two gathered open swags, two large twisted knot rosettes, and two stationary drapery panels puddled on floor.

(SC114) Two linear swags raised slightly in the middle cover a small flat jabot. Two gathered cascades with contrasting lining match nicely with the stationary banded panels.

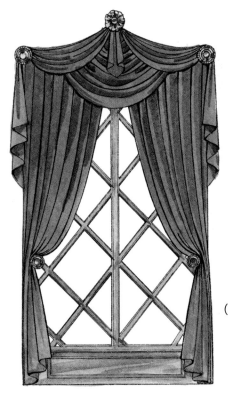 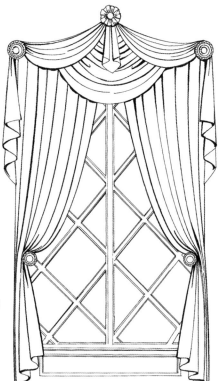

(SC115) This eye-pleasing treatment is achieved by using one large swag topped by two smaller swags and jabot. Medallion holdbacks complement the use of medallions atop the cascades.

(SC116) This treatment is best left to professional drapery workrooms. These swags and jabot are usually board-mounted and a template is recommended. The rod pocket drapery side panels extend to the top of the window and are pulled back as to not obstruct the view are complete with the cascades.

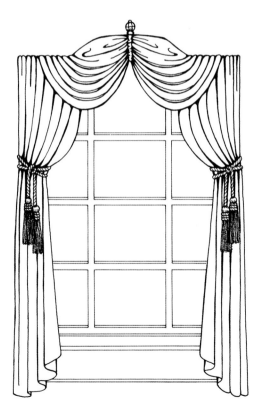

(SC117) Large tassels dangling from braided tiebacks create visual interest in this simple but stunning treatment.

(SC118) A simple but elegant treatment is achieved by adding bullion fringe and rosettes to a gathered swag and stacked extra long stacked cascades.

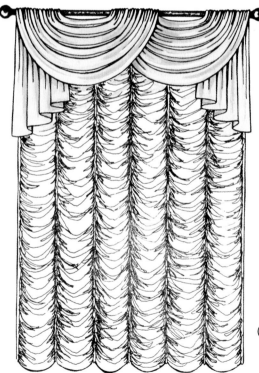

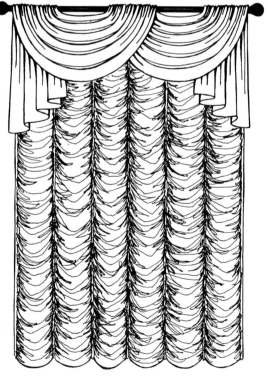

(SC119) An Austrian shade looks lovely under pole swags and cascades.

(SC120) For a creative use of swags this treatment uses two large and one small gathered swags; extra long pleated trimmed cascades add a very custom look to this treatment.

(SC121) Elaborately pleated cascades tumble down the sides of the stationary drapery panels, enhanced by the linear swags above.

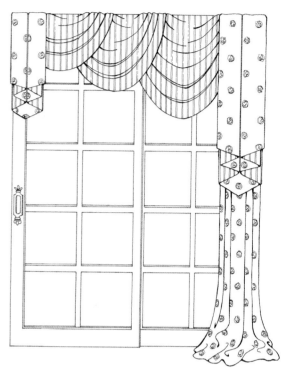

(SC122) Asymmetrical double cascades and three different sized swags create a truly custom treatment. Puddled stationary panel finishes unique statement.

(SC123) This crisp treatment includes swag and pleated cascade, stationary drapery panel, all edged in petite tassel trim, and a fabric covered three-inch pole.

(SC124) This asymmetrical swag and double cascade treatment with side panel accent is a perfect solution for sliding glass doors. Note how the bulk of the treatment resides in the non-egress area of the door.

Based on Patterns Plus Designs: www.patternsplus.com

(SC125) An asymmetrical pole swag edged in bullion fringe and accented with braided tassel is classically beautiful.

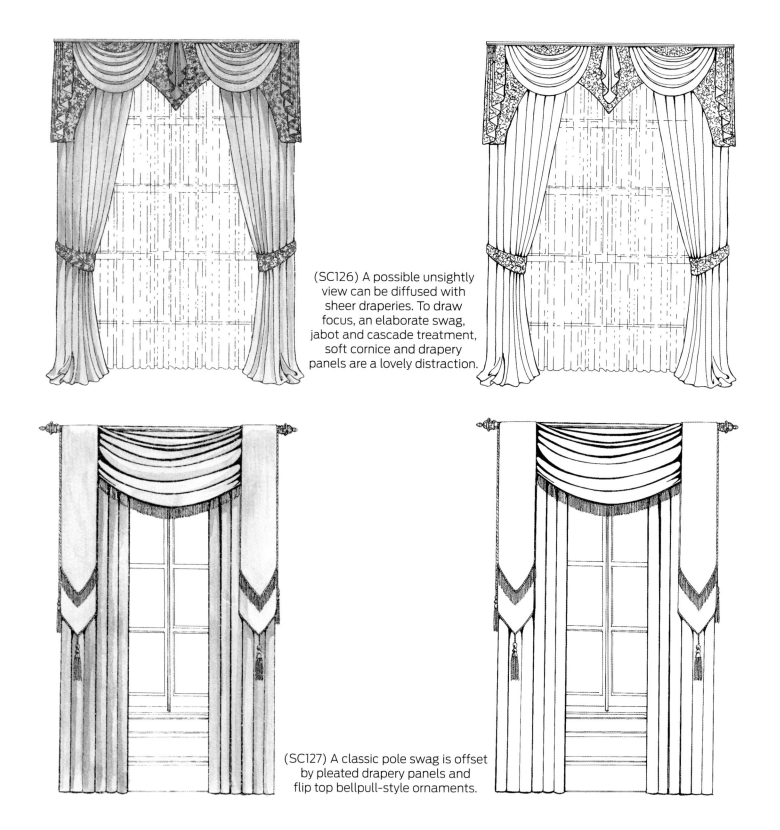

(SC126) A possible unsightly view can be diffused with sheer draperies. To draw focus, an elaborate swag, jabot and cascade treatment, soft cornice and drapery panels are a lovely distraction.

(SC127) A classic pole swag is offset by pleated drapery panels and flip top bellpull-style ornaments.

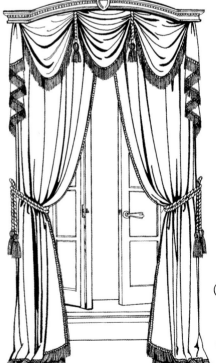

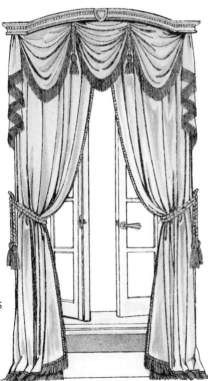

(SC128) Double swags with petite bow accents cap a set of double drapery panels—one patterned, one plain. Lovely tassel tiebacks hold the fabric away from the window until night falls.

(SC129) A detailed wood cornice houses a fringed cascade swag and top treatment, accented with tassel embellishments. Braid follows the leading edge of the drapery panels with bullion fringe brushing the floor.

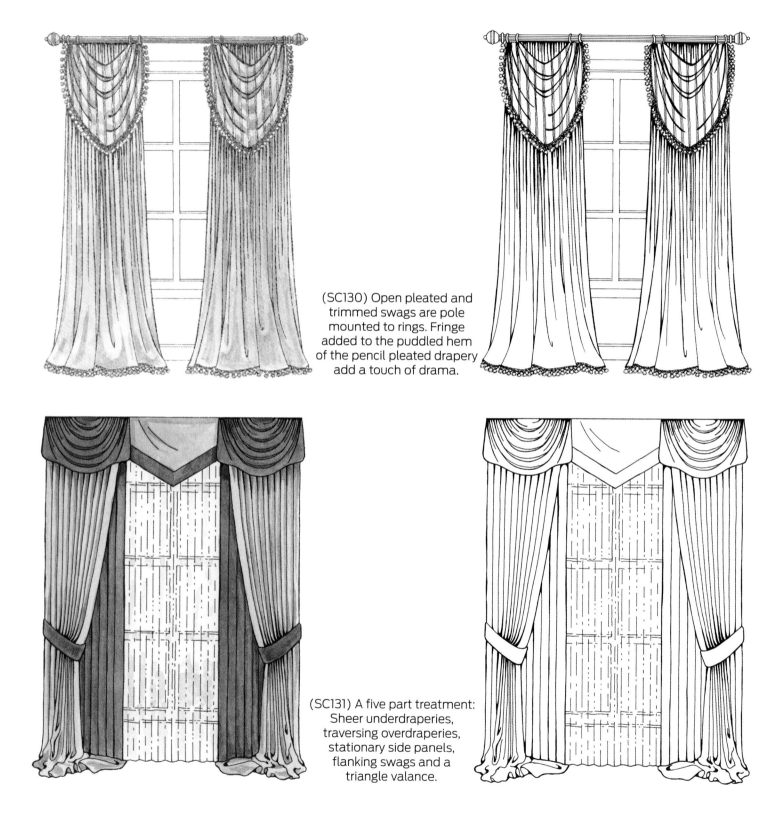

(SC130) Open pleated and trimmed swags are pole mounted to rings. Fringe added to the puddled hem of the pencil pleated drapery add a touch of drama.

(SC131) A five part treatment: Sheer underdraperies, traversing overdraperies, stationary side panels, flanking swags and a triangle valance.

(SC132) A wood cornice with sconce-like embellishments hold scalloped swags, trimmed in fringe and accented with brush fringe. Matching drapery panels are held back with braided tassels.

(SC133) Elaborately styled swags hang gracefully from a small wood cornice, ending in lushly fringed cascades. Underneath, draperies contained by braid fringe and trimmed tiebacks complete the window treatment.

Board mounted

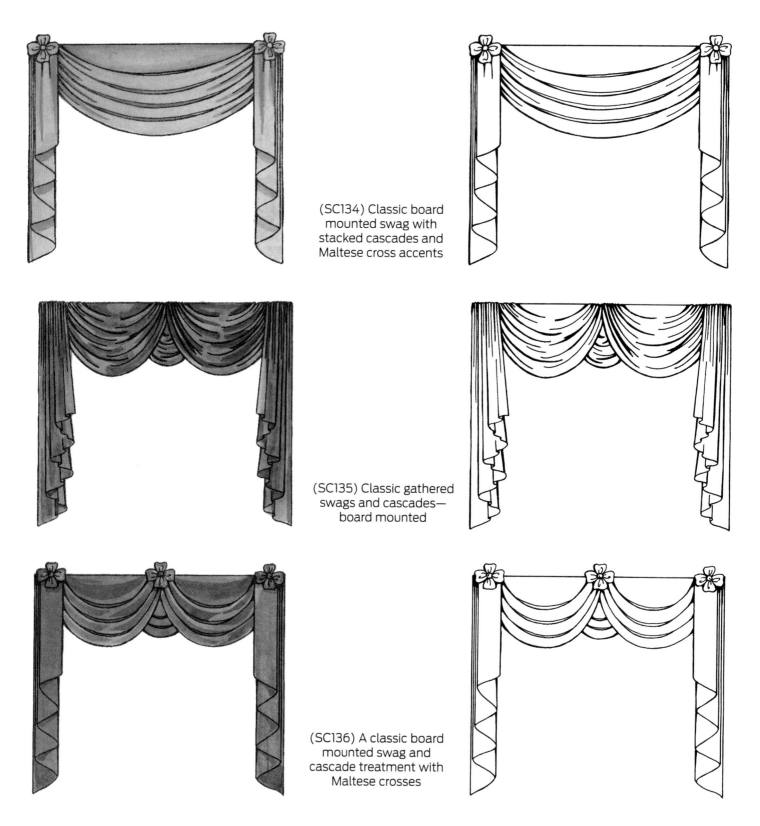

(SC134) Classic board mounted swag with stacked cascades and Maltese cross accents

(SC135) Classic gathered swags and cascades—board mounted

(SC136) A classic board mounted swag and cascade treatment with Maltese crosses

(SC137) Simple board mounted swag and cascade

(SC138) Board mounted swag and cascade top treatment with jabot and Maltese cross accents

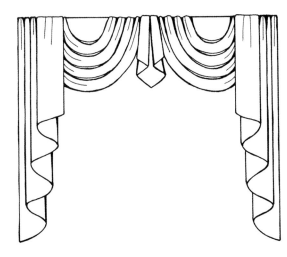

(SC139) A simple board mounted swag, cascade and jabot treatment

(SC140) Gathered swag and cascades with bow tie jabot

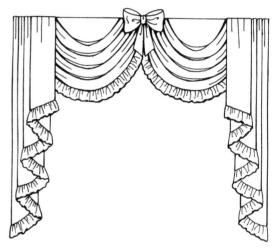

(SC141) Swag and cascade treatment with ruffle trim and bow accent

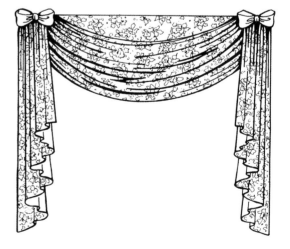

(SC142) Board mounted swag and cascade with contrast underlining and bow accents

(SC143) Pleated swag and stacked cascade with center jabot. Note coordinating buttons

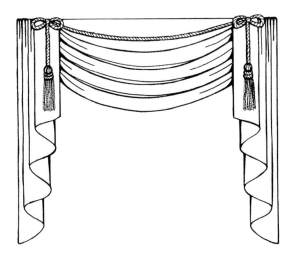

(SC144) Board-mounted swag and cascade with tassel and braid detailing

(SC145) Board-mounted swag with flanking soft cascades and rosette on upper corners

Pole mounted

(SC146) A simple pole swag and cascade with ruffle trim

(SC147) Pole mounted swag and cascades wth contrast underlining and rosette accents

(SC148) Stacked cascades over pleated swags, pole mounted brush fringe and rosette

(SC149) Pole swag and jabot with contrast underlining and center rosette accent

(SC150) Asymmetrical pole swag with bullion fringe

(SC151) Casual pole swag with tied corner detailing

Additional swag & cascade styles

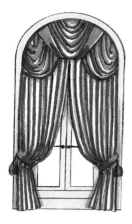

(*Left to right*) Arched swags over pleated draperies; Gathered draperies over single swag;
Arched knotted swag drapery

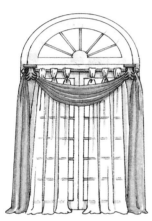

(*Left to right*) Tab draperies under swag; Single swag with rosettes over draperies and horizontal blinds; Knotted
lace swag over lace draperies

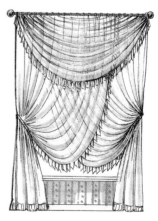

(*Left to right*) Single swag over draperies and café curtain; Swags and cascades over pleated draperies and Roman
shade; Deep swag and full tiebacks

(*Left to right*) Fabric swagged over a pole with cord and tassel trim; Pleated swag over soft cornice with long cascades and gathered jabots; Empire swags over draperies with tassel

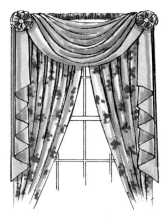

(*Left to right*) Raised swags over tiebacks; Swag and jabot with tassels and rope; Single swag and cascades with rosettes

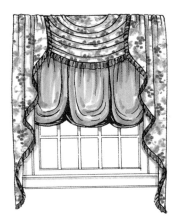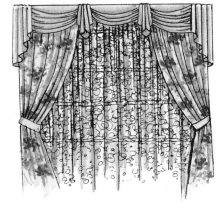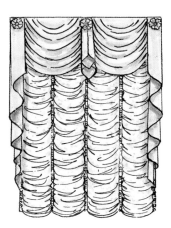

(*Left to right*) Swag and cascades with ruffle over balloon shade; Swags and jabot over lace panels; Swags over Austrian shade

(*Left to right*) Sheer swag with knots; Swags over decorative rod; Swags and cascades with ropes and fringe

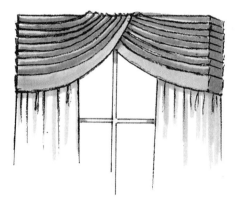

(*Left to right*) Swags and cascades over decorative rod; Turban swags;
Double swags with cascades draped over covered rod

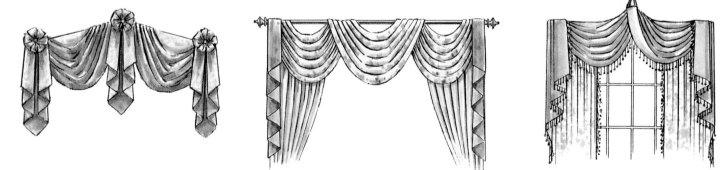

(*Left to right*) Arched double swags and cascades with rosettes; Triple draped swags with cascades on decorative rod; Double cascades and swags joined in the middle to large finial

(Left to right) Board mounted swag and cascades; Fabric swagged through sconces;
Single swag with extra long cascades

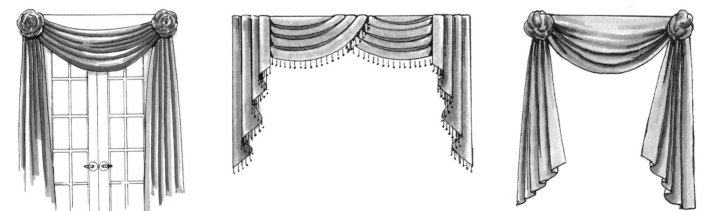

(Left to right) Draped swag with rosettes; Overlapping board mounted swags; Swag with rosettes and cascades

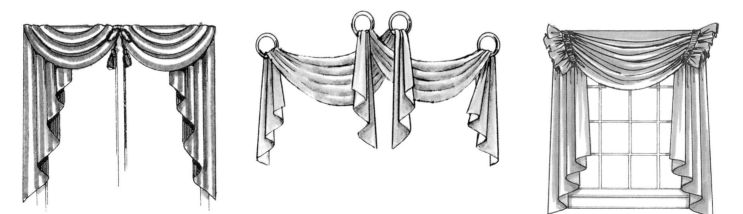

(Left to right) Swags and cascades with bow detail; Double swags crossed in middle with four single cascades on rings; Gathered swag

(*Left to right*) Swag drped over rod; Double swag with rosettes and cascades; Draped swag with contrasting lining

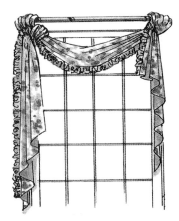

(*Left to right*) Asymmetric swag held by fabric ties; Swag with lifted center and cascading tails;
Double swagged valance

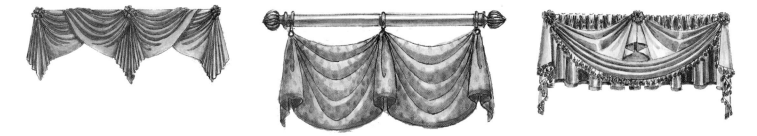

(*Left to right*) Waterfall swag; Open Empire swags; Swag and cascade over pleated valance

(*Left to right*) Gathered fan swag over pleated draperies; Swags and cascades with Maltese Cross; Swags and cascades over decorative rod

(*Left to right*) Lifted swags and cascades with cameo crown and tassels; Swags and cascades with rosettes; Swags and cascades over rod pocket valance

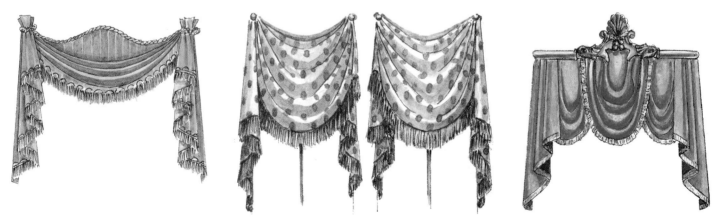

(*Left to right*) Swags and cascades over designer cornice; Empire swags and cascades; Elaborate swags and cascades with gilded heading and shell crown

Swag & cascade arrangement styles

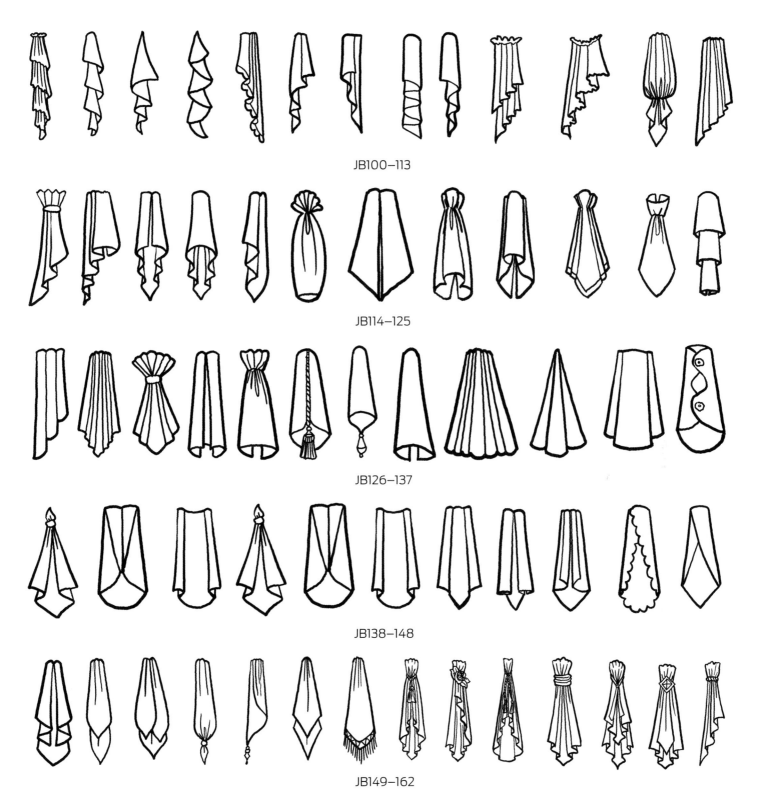

JB100–113

JB114–125

JB126–137

JB138–148

JB149–162

Swag & cascade yardage specifications

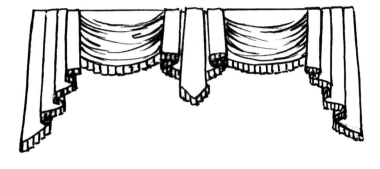

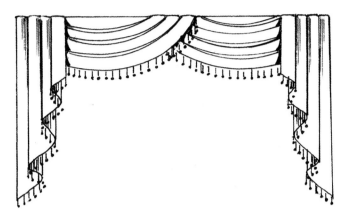

Single or Double, Traditional Cascade Yardage
Please note that the yardages specified below are for a single pair of cascades.

Lined in contrasting fabric
Length: FL (finished length, or long point) + 4" ÷ 36 = yardage.

For double cascades, double the yardage after the calculations.

Self-lined
Length: FL (finished length, or long point) x 2 + 4" ÷ 36 = yardage.

Yardage — Jabots
Allow approximately one third yard of fabric for each jabot.

Special note
1. See page 85 for detailed calculating terms

Overlapping swags are draped gracefully across a window, making an elegant and formal statement. A section of draped fabric at the top of the window that typically resembles a sideways "C" shape, a swag is sometimes coupled with a vertical cascade or "tail" which hangs gracefully on either side.

Yardage: Traditional swag & cascade
Swags, plain fabric – 1.5 yards for contrast lined swags up to 40" and 3 yards if self-lined. Two yards for swags between 40" and 60" and 4 yards if self-lined. For swags over 60" consult a professional drapery workroom as these swags may need to be "railroaded" and yardage calculations can be complex.

Things to consider
• Swag type: pleated, gathered or boxed
• Color of lining or self-lined
• Window sizes in relation to swags in the same room
• Clearance for French doors
• Returns

Special notes
1. Swags look best between 30" and 40" wide
2. A re-measure by the workroom is strongly recommended
3. Linear swags are a better choice for bay windows
4. See page 85 for detailed calculating terms

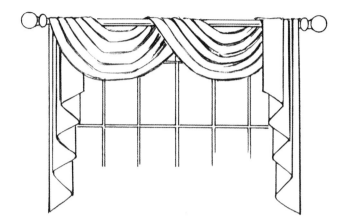 

Swags are draped across the window on a decorative pole and constructed to appear as if the fabric is thrown casually over the rod or constructed as one large swag that is mounted on wood, wrought iron, or medallions.

Yardage: Contemporary swag
One swag
Width of area to be covered + 30% ÷ 36 = yardage
More than one swag:
Width of area to be covered x 1.5 ÷ 36 = yardage

Things to consider
- Color of lining
- Width and drop of swags
- Number of swags
- Mounting on medallions, wrought iron or poles

Special notes
1. These swags are usually cut on the straight grain of the fabric. Any fabric with an obvious directional print is not suitable.
2. Proportions are important for this type of swag
3. A check measure by the workroom is highly recommended.
4. For bay windows consult a professional
5. See page 85 for detailed calculating terms

These swags are butted together, without overlapping; therefore, they most often require cascades, jabots and/ or rosettes to conceal molding, drapery headings, or unsightly hardware. Linear swags are a good choice for bay windows, where overlapping swags are difficult and inappropriate. Linear swags need not "touch" each other; they can be separated by a few inches, thus saving on yardage and labor, if double cascades are used (see above).

Yardage: linear swag
Swags, plain fabric – 1.5 yards for contrast lined swags up to 40" and 3 yards if self-lined. Two yards for swags between 40" and 60" and 4 yards if self-lined. For swags over 60" consult a professional drapery workroom as these swags may need to be "railroaded" and yardage calculations can be complex.

Things to consider
- Color of lining, or self lined
- Contrast or self lined jabots, cascades
- Width and length in relations to other windows in the same room
- Number and type of swags
- Returns, if any

Special notes
1. To achieve proper proportions, consult with workroom.
2. See page 85 for detailed calculating terms

Fabric shades

From Victorian to Art Deco to modern, fabric shades are a fitting contribution to almost every decorating style. Their simplicity allows them to accompany other window treatments while their classic lines allow them to individually grace a window. For an especially appropriate choice, a fabric shade can be a splendid addition to oddly shaped windows, such as a bay or bow. In a child's room, a fabric shade will ensure rooms are dark and cozy, and in kitchens, their lack of interlining will keep odors from lingering in the fabric.

   To determine the shade that suits your interior best, consider each style, as well as its lifting mechanisms, carefully.

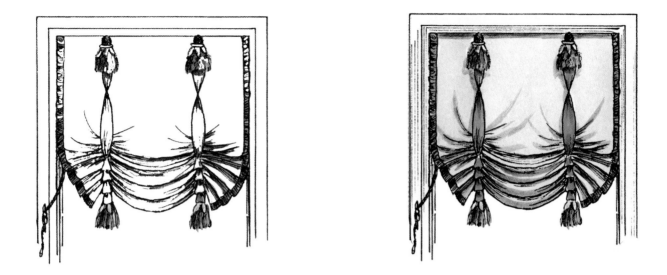

(*above*) (FS100) Balloon shade with side ruffles and tassels; (*below*) (FS101) Cathedral A-frame cloud shade

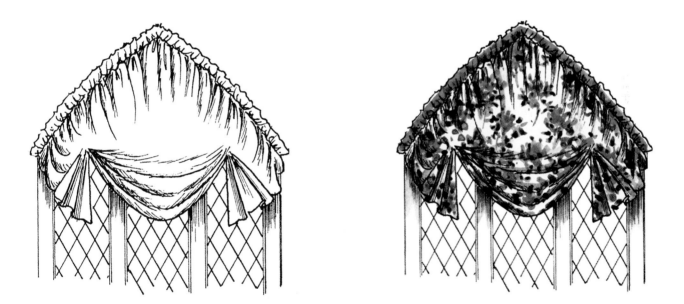

For example, Austrian shades are gathered both horizontally and vertically for a full look. When lowered, they offer the swagged effect of a curtain, and when raised appear much like a valance.

Roman shades present a more modern silhouette. With their bold lines and clean, tailored edges, this type of shade makes an attractive solitary window treatment. Its simplicity is also complementary to a more dramatic drapery or valance. Roller shades are economical, practical and simple to use. Often, the leading edge of the shade is embellished with fringe, pull tassels and other pretty details. So many choices!

(FS102) London Shade:
Flat panel shade pulls
up into graceful folds

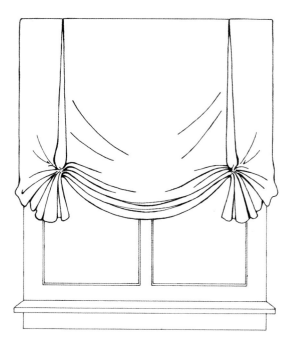

(FS103) London Shade:
Same style as above
but with pleats

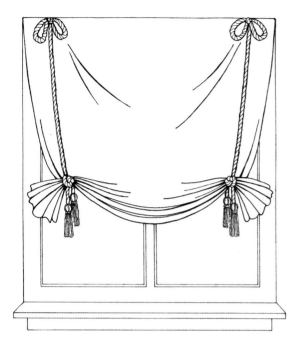

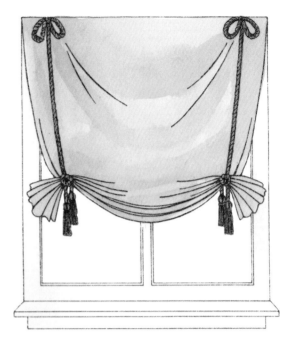

(FS104) London shade
with rope

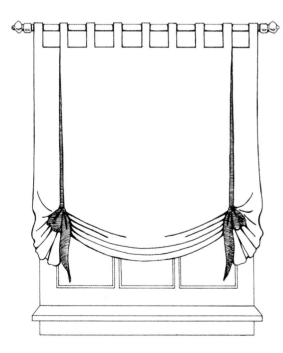

(FS105) Tab top London
shade with pleats and
contrasting fabric

(FS106) Scalloped gathered valance with ruffled over a flat Roman shade with visible drawing mechanism

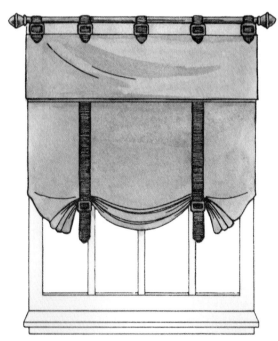

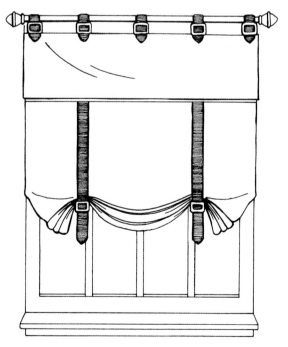

(FS107) Flat Roman shade held in place with leather straps. Note, too, the unique buckle top tabs

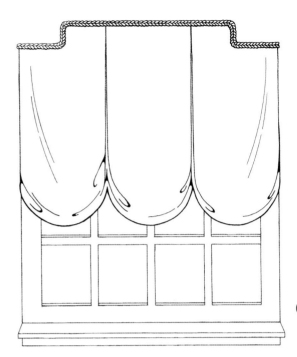

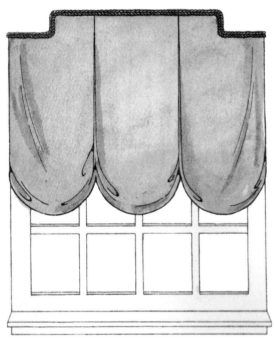

(FS108) Cut out corners on this balloon shade are a unique draw for the eye

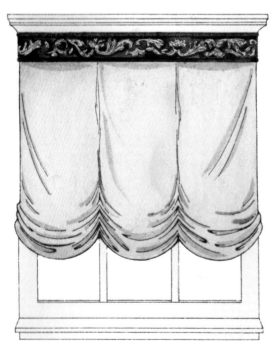

(FS109) A wood cornice with wallpaper insert offers seamless installation for the shirred balloon shade

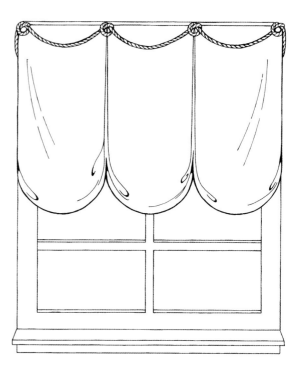

(FS110) Pleated balloon shade with braid trim accent

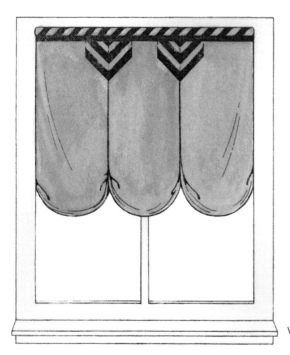

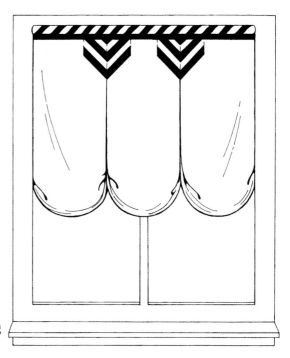

(FS111) Triangle accents draw the eye toward the window and accompanying balloon shade

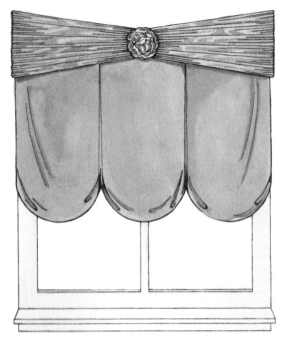

(FS112) Shirred hourglass cornice atop a classic balloon shade

(FS113) Classic simple lines balloon shade

(FS114) Rod pocket swagged cloud shade

(FS115) A shirred cloud shade exhibits a matching blouson valance

(FS116) Wide swag inside mount cloud shade

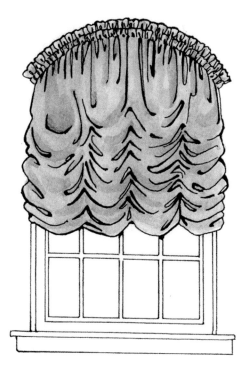

(FS117) Arched top cloud shade

(FS118) Double rod pocket
cloud shade with bottom ruffle

(FS119) Cloud shade with
ruffled bottom

(FS120) An overlapping triangle valance is a fine accompaniment to a patterned Roman shade

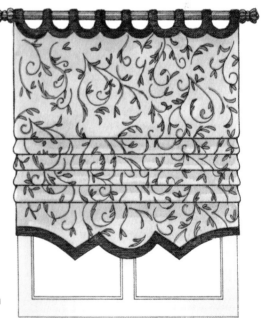

(FS121) Tab top scalloped roman shade with contrasting banding

Fabric Shades   **237**

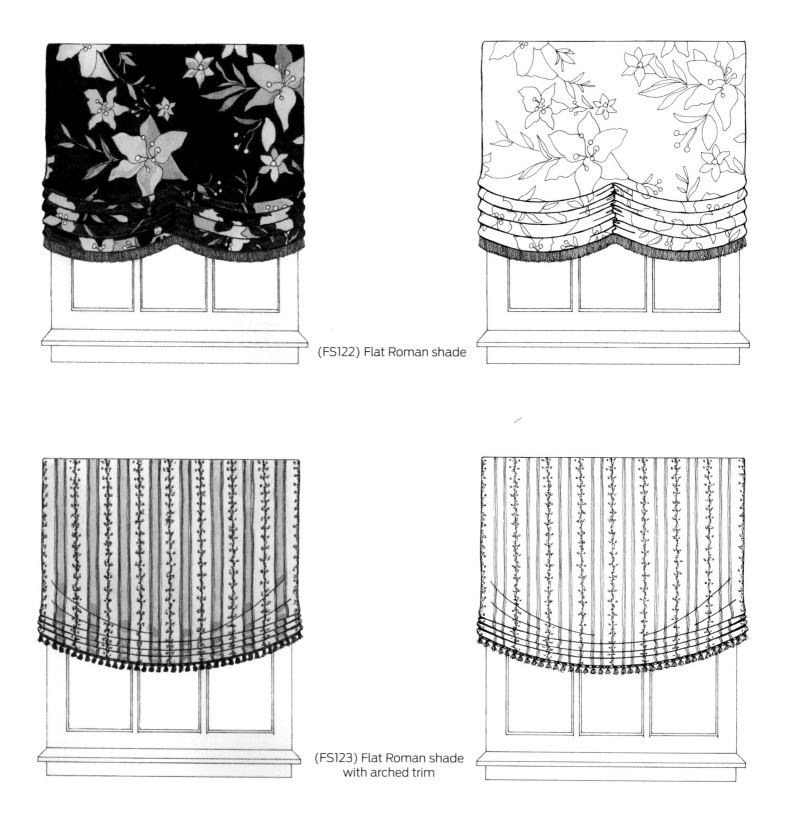

(FS122) Flat Roman shade

(FS123) Flat Roman shade
with arched trim

(FS124) Stagecoach shade with contrast strips

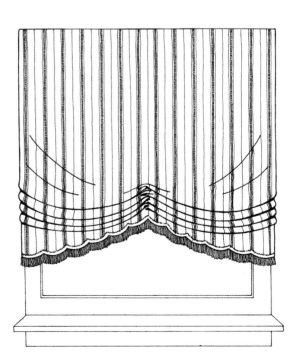

(FS125) Flat Roman shade with trim

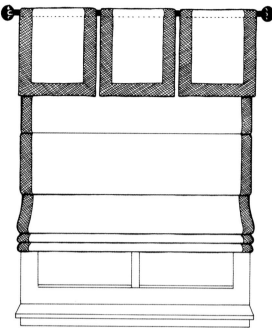

(FS126) A flat, simple Roman shade draws up into graceful folds. Rod pocket flags decorate the front for additional interest

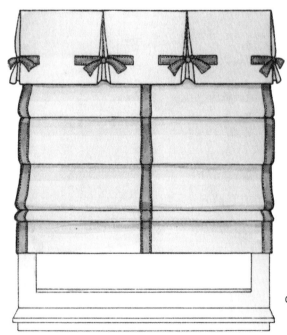

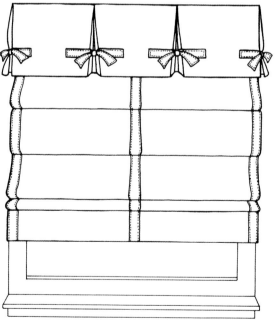

(FS127) Roman shade with contrast stripes and inverted pleat valance decorated with bows

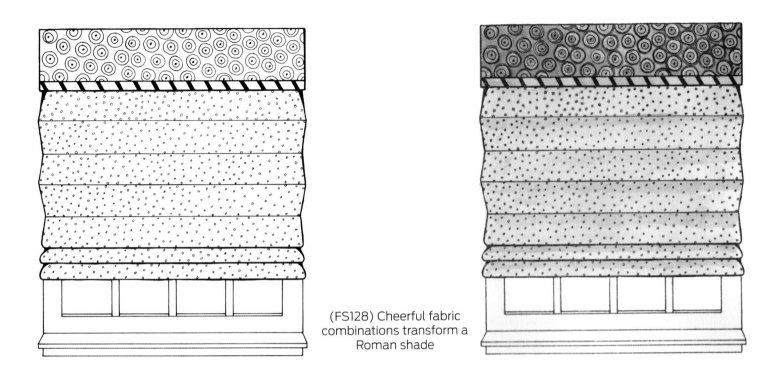

(FS128) Cheerful fabric combinations transform a Roman shade

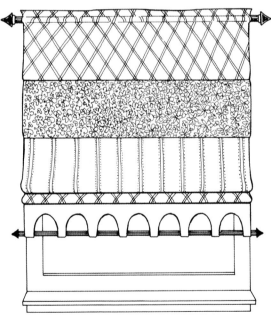

(FS129) Rod pocket top and inverted tabbed bottom with contrasting fabric combinations

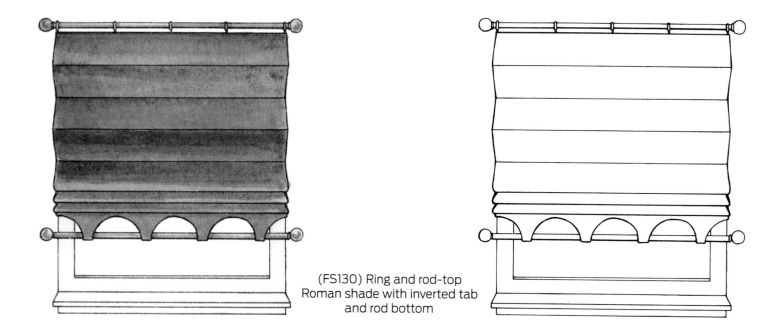

(FS130) Ring and rod-top
Roman shade with inverted tab
and rod bottom

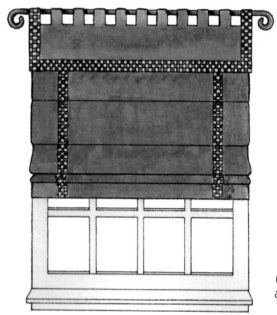
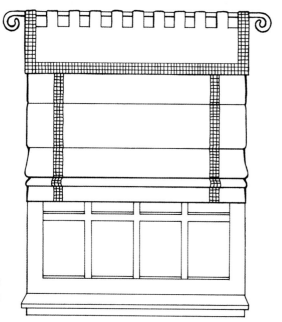

(FS131) With a unique tab top
and contrast trim, this Roman
shade delights

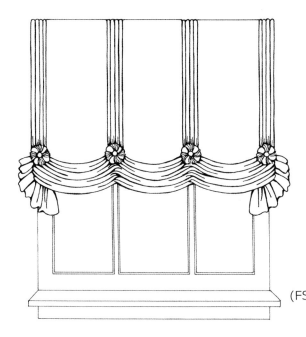

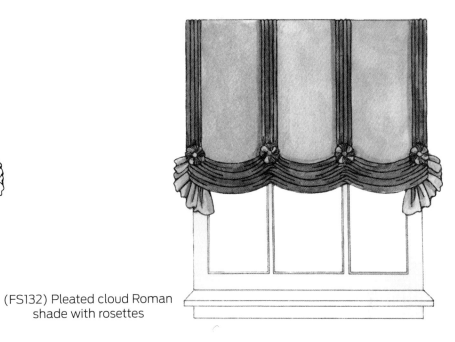

(FS132) Pleated cloud Roman
shade with rosettes

(FS133) Rod pocket soft
specialty shade

(FS134) Invisibly
mounted cloud shade

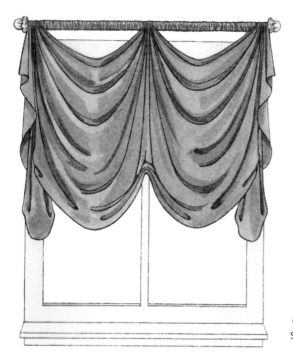

(FS135) Soft swag-style
shade with shirred fabric
covered rod

Patterns Plus designs: www.patternsplus.com

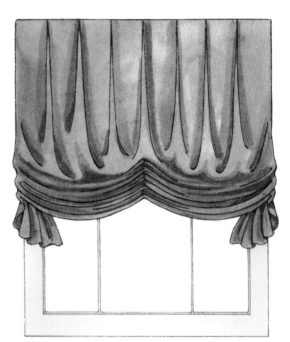

(FS136) Inverted box
pleated Roman shade

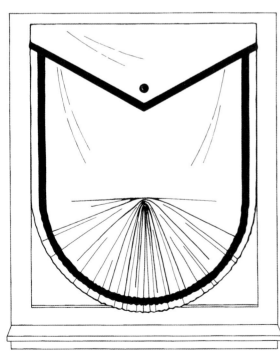

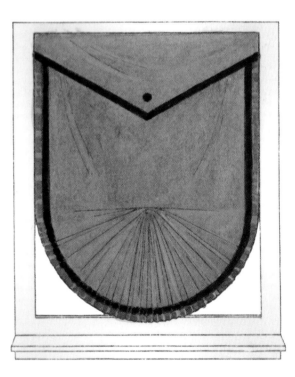

(FS137) Specialty fan
shade with triangle
valance top

Patterns Plus designs: www.patternsplus.com

Additional fabric shade styles

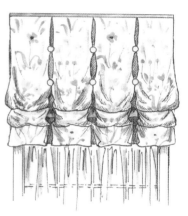

(*Left to right*) Pleated cloud shade; Arched balloon shade with ruffles on the bottom;
Balloon shade with button accents

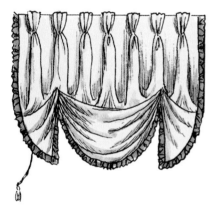

(*Left to right*) French pleated cloud shade; Roman shade with fan bottom; Balloon shade with ruffles under
cornice box

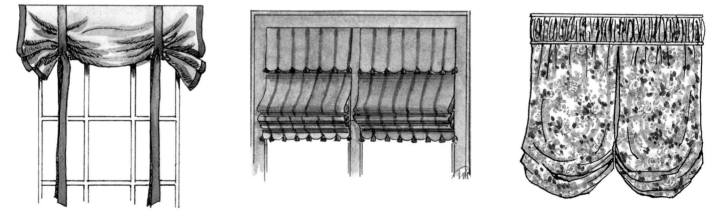

(*Left to right*) Flat Roman shade with ties; Roman shades; Balloon shade with shirred cornice box

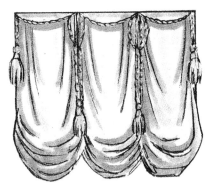

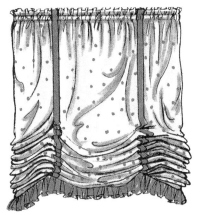
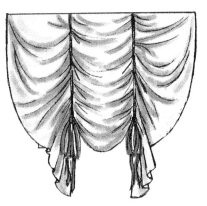
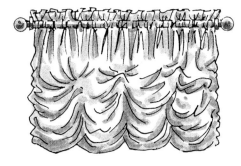
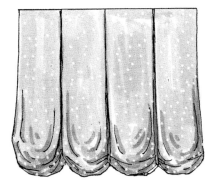

(*Left to right*) Balloon shade under chevron valance; Roman shade under valance; Cloud shade under cornice box

(*Left to right*) Balloon shade with rope tassels; Suspender balloon shade; Specialty soft shade

(*Left to right*) Cloud shade gathered on a pole with ruffled upper edge; Traditional balloon shade; Cloud shade with bows at top

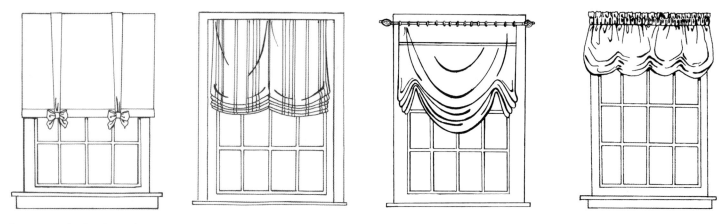

Stagecoach shade with ties; Wide pleated balloon shade; Designer cloud shade; Cloud shade gathered on a pole with ruffle at the top

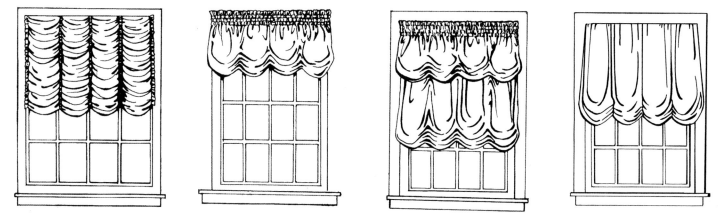

Triple fullness Austrian shade with scalloped panels; Cloud shade with four-inch shirring; Shirred cloud shade with matching valance; Balloon shade with inverted pleats and pouffed bottom edge

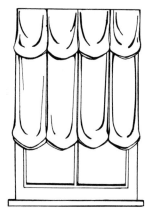
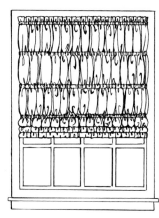

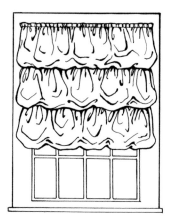

Pleated balloon shade with matching valance; Triple fullness shade gathered on horizontal rods; Bottom arched balloon shade; Tiered cloud shade

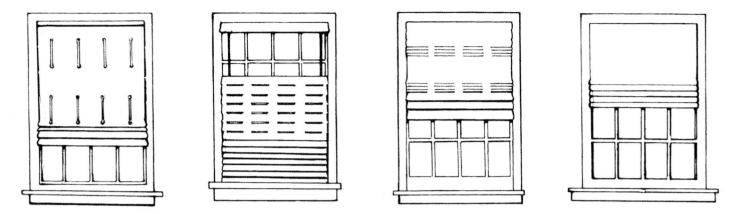

Flat Roman shade with brass grommets and front cording; Top down Roman shade; Roman shade with mini-pleats; Flat Roman shade

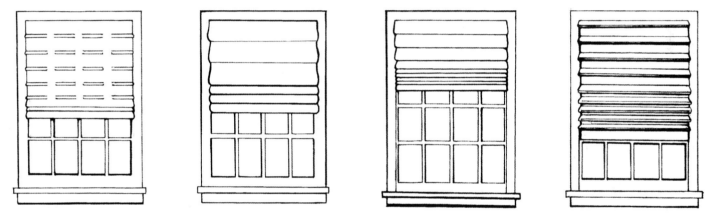

Roman shade with alternating large and small pleats; Flat fold Roman shade with horizontal pleats; Roman shade with overlapping folds; Soft mini fold Roman shade

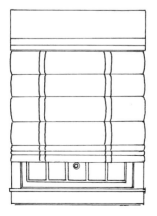
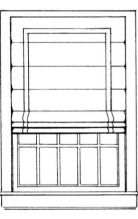

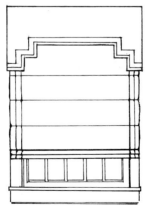

Roman shade with banding on shade and valance; Roman shade with coordinating banding; Rod pocket cloud shade with ruffled hem; Cloud under cornice box with coordinating banding

Shade specifications

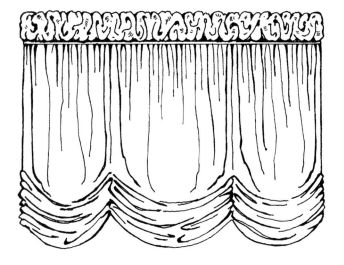

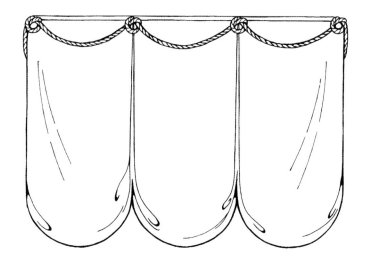

A fully functional shade with a gathered heading that falls into soft poufs that can be finished with or without a skirt.

Yardage: Cloud shade
Step 1 – Width of area to be covered + returns x 2.5 ÷ width of fabric = number of widths (whole numbers only)
Step 2a – Number of widths x (length of shade + 20") ÷ 36 = yardage without pattern repeat
—or—
Step 2b – Length of shade + 20" ÷ pattern repeat = number of repeats required (round upward to nearest whole number)
Step 2c – Number of repeats required x pattern repeat = cut length
Step 2d – Number of widths x cut length ÷ 36 = yardage with pattern repeat

Things to consider
• Width
• Length
• Color of lining
• Inside or outside mount
• Skirt or no skirt
• Size of returns or size of board
• Ceiling or wall mount
• Right or left pull

A fully functional shade with large inverted pleats for a more tailored look that is softened by billowing poufs.

Yardage: Balloon shade
Step 1 – Width of area to be covered + returns x 3 ÷ width of fabric = number of widths (whole numbers only)
Step 2a – Number of widths x (length of shade + 20) ÷ 36 = yardage without pattern repeat
—or—
Step 2b – Length of shade + 20" ÷ pattern repeat = number of repeats required (round upward to nearest whole number)
Step 2c – Number of repeats required x pattern repeat = cut length
Step 2d – Number of widths x cut length ÷ 36 = yardage with pattern repeat

Things to consider
• Width
• Length
• Color of lining
• Inside or outside mount
• Skirt or no skirt
• Size of returns or size of board
• Ceiling or wall mount
• Right or left pull

 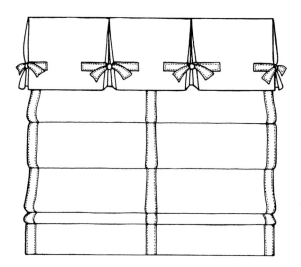

A versatile shade that hangs straight and collapses into folds as it is raised. The Roman shade fits many different décors, from contemporary to traditional to formal. To add interest to the shade, use contrast bands, a scalloped edge or a single permanent pleat at the bottom.

Yardage: Flat Roman shade

Step 1 – Width of area to be covered + 5" ÷ width of fabric = number of widths (whole numbers only)

Step 2a – Number of widths x (length of area + 12") ÷ 36 = yardage without pattern repeat

—or—

Step 2b – Length of shade + 12" ÷ pattern repeat = number of repeats required (round upward to nearest whole number)

Step 2c – Number of repeats required x pattern repeat = cut length

Step 2d – Number of widths x cut length ÷ 36 = yardage with pattern repeat

Things to consider

- Width
- Length
- Color of lining
- Inside or outside mount
- Right or left pull

Special note

1. Roman shades are not recommended wider or longer than 84".
2. Cannot be made with returns.

A folded Roman shade is designed with overlapping folds cascading down the full length of the shade.

Yardage: Folded Roman shade

Step 1 – Width of area to be covered + 5" ÷ width of fabric = number of widths (whole numbers only)

Step 2a – Number of widths x (length of area x 2.5) ÷ 36 = yardage without pattern repeat

—or—

Step 2b – Length of shade x 2.5 ÷ pattern repeat = number of repeats required (round upward to nearest whole number)

Step 2c – Number of repeats required x pattern repeat = cut length

Step 2d – Number of widths x cut length ÷ 36 = yardage with pattern repeat

Things to consider

- Width
- Length
- Color of lining
- Inside or outside mount
- Right or left pull

Special note

1. Folded Roman shades larger than 60" in width or 84" in length are not recommended.
2. Due to the nature of the fabric, the folds do not hang evenly, therefore they are not recommended for an application where two or more blinds are side by side.
3. Cannot be made with returns.

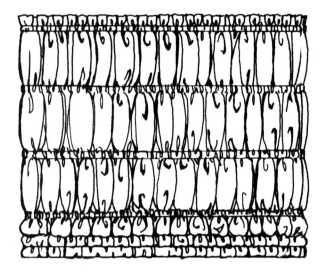

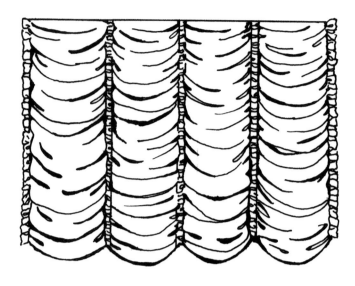

Fabric is shirred onto rods to create this very elegant yet functional shade that adds romance to the look of a traditional Roman shade.

Yardage: Shirred Roman shade
Step 1 – Width of area to be covered x 3 ÷ width of fabric = number of widths (whole numbers only)
Step 2a – Length of shade x 1.25 x number of widths ÷ 36 = yardage without pattern repeat
—or—
Step 2b – Length of shade x 1.25 ÷ pattern repeat = number of repeats required (round upward to nearest whole number)
Step 2c – Number of repeats required x pattern repeat = cut length
Step 2d – Number of widths x cut length ÷ 36 = yardage with pattern repeat

Things to consider
• Width
• Length
• Right or left cord pull
• Inside or outside mount
• Lining color (if applicable)

Special note
1. Use only soft, drapeable fabrics for optimum effect.
2. This treatment cannot be made with returns and therefore is intended to be used alone or as an undertreatment.
3. Not recommended wider than 60".

A soft, formal treatment created by vertical shirring between scallops.

Yardage: Austrian shade
Step 1 – Width of area to be covered x 1.5 ÷ width of fabric = number of widths (whole numbers only)
Step 2a – Number of widths x (length of area x 3) ÷ 36 = yardage without pattern repeat
—or—
Step 2b – Length of area x 3 ÷ pattern repeat = number of repeats required (round upward to nearest whole number)
Step 2c – Number of repeats required x pattern repeat = cut length
Step 2d – Number of widths x cut length ÷ 36 = yardage with pattern repeat

Things to consider
• Width
• Length
• Color of lining (if applicable)
• Inside or outside mount
• Right or left cord pull

Special note
1. This treatment has a tendency to pull in on the sides. It should not be used where this will cause a problem.
2. Use heavier fabric for privacy or sheer or lace fabric for a more decorative look.
3. It can be used as a single treatment or in combination with draperies or valances.

Fabric shade measuring instructions & footage chart

Outside or wall mount
Width – Measure exact width of the area to be covered. It is recommended that shades extend past actual window opening by two inches on each side. Furnish finished shade width, no allowances will be made.

Length – Measure length of area to be covered, allowing a minimum of 2½" at top of window to accommodate headerboard and brackets. At this time you may want to take into consideration stackage of shades and allow for this in your length measurement. Furnish finished shade length, no allowance will be made.

Inside or recessed mount
Width – Measure width of window at the top, center and bottom of window. Use the narrowest measurement when ordering. Specify on order form if outside clearance has been made. If no clearance has been allowed, the factory will deduct ¼" from the overall width.

Length – Measure the height of the window from top of opening to top of sill, no allowance is made for length.

All installations:
- Specify right or left cord position. If no cord position is indicated, cords will be corded to right hand side.
- Specify cord length (length of cord needed for easy reach, when shade is completely down). If no specification is made, cord will be approximately one-third the length of the shade.
- For pole cloud, cloud and balloon shades, specify if length given is high or low point of pouf.

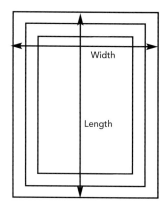

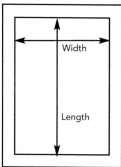

Fabric shade square footage chart

shade width in inches

	24	30	36	42	48	54	60	66	72	78	84	90	96	102	108	114	120	126	132	138	144
30	10	10	10	10	10	11¼	12½	13¾	15	16¼	17½	18¾	20	21¼	22½	23¾	25	26¼	27½	28¾	30
36	10	10	10	10½	12	13½	15	16½	18	19½	21	22½	24	25½	27	28½	30	31½	33	34½	36
42	10	10	10½	12¼	14	15¾	17½	19¼	21	22¾	24½	26¼	28	29¾	31½	33¼	35	36¾	38½	40¼	42
48	10	10	12	14	16	18	20	22	24	26	28	30	32	34	36	38	40	42	44	46	48
54	10	11¼	13½	15¾	18	20¼	22½	24¾	27	29¼	31½	33¾	36	38¼	40½	42¾	45	47¼	49½	51¾	54
60	10	12½	15	17½	20	22½	25	27½	30	32½	35	37½	40	42½	45	47½	50	52½	55	57½	60
66	11	13¾	16½	19¼	22	24¾	27½	30¼	33	35¾	38½	41¼	44	46¾	49½	52¼	55	57¾	60½	63¼	66
72	12	15	18	21	24	27	30	33	36	39	42	45	48	51	54	57	60	63	66	69	72
78	13	16¼	19½	22¾	26	29¼	32½	35¾	39	42¼	45½	48¾	52	55¼	58½	61¾	65	68¼	71½	74¾	78
84	14	17½	21	24½	28	31½	35	38½	42	45¼4	49	52½	56	59½	63	66½	70	73½	77	80½	84
90	15	18¾	22½	26¼	30	33¾	37½	41¼	45	8¾	52½	56¼	60	63¾	67½	71¼	75	78¾	82½	86¼	90
96	16	20	24	28	32	36	40	44	48	52	56	60	64	68	72	76	80	84	88	92	96
102	17	21¼	25½	29¾	34	38¼	42½	46¾	51	55¼	59½	63¾	68	72¼	76½	80¾	85	89¼	93½	97¾	102
108	18	22½	27	31½	36	40½	45	49½	54	58½	63	67½	72	76½	81	85½	90	94½	99	103½	108
114	19	23¾	28½	33¼	38	42¾	47½	52¼	57	61¾	66½	71¼	76	80¾	85½	90¼	95	99¾	104½	109¼	114
120	20	25	30	35	40	45	50	55	60	65	70	75	80	85	90	95	100	105	110	115	120
126	21	26¼	31½	36¾	42	47¼	52½	57¾	63	68¼	73½	78¾	84	89¼	94½	99¾	105	110¼	115½	120¾	126
132	22	27½	33	38½	44	49½	55	60½	66	71½	77	82½	88	93½	99	104½	110	115½	121	126½	132
138	23	28¾	34½	40¼	46	51¾	57½	63¼	69	74¾	80½	86¼	92	97¾	103½	109¼	115	120¾	126½	132¼	138
144	24	30	36	42	48	54	60	66	72	78	84	90	96	102	108	114	120	126	132	138	144

shade length in inches

Shades, shutters & blinds

This book has thus far been a celebration of all things fabric: draperies, fabric shades, curtains, valances. And yet, the practical good looks of a "hard" window treatment such as a blind or shutter need not be considered unimaginative. There are many charismatic options for those who prefer a more streamlined look at the window.

There are simple, vinyl roller shades for kitchen windows and woven wood shades that will beautifully complement a living room. There are stained wood Venetian blinds for the window above your desk and modest vertical blinds which fit nicely across sliding glass doors. Consider panel shutters for a bay window. No matter what type of hard window covering you decide upon, it is certain that your shades, blinds or shutters will fulfill your needs for visual impact and light control while they provide you with a calming sense of privacy.

(Above) Drapery folded over decorative rod, over pleated shade; Fabric draped over pleated shade; Box pleated valance over pleated shade (Below) Flat panels pulled back over pleated shade; Gathered swag and cascade over pleated shade

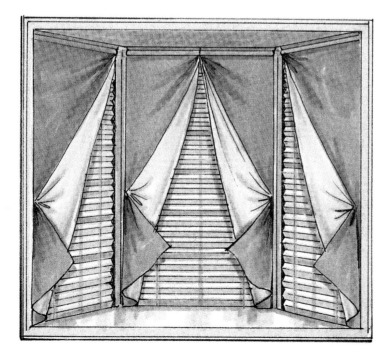

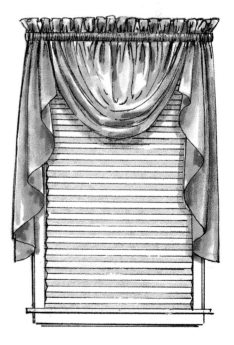

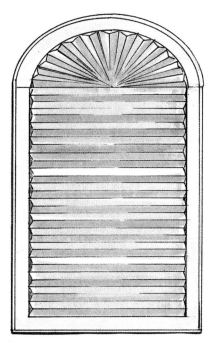
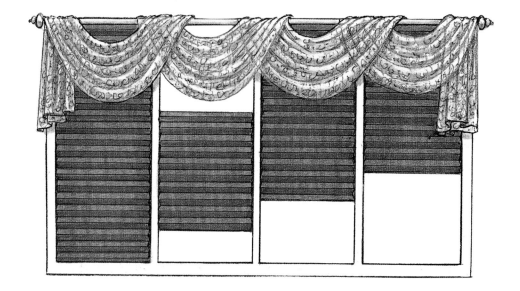

(Above) Pleated shade with arched pleated shade at top; Multiple lace fabric swags on decorative rod
(Below) Fabric draped over pleated shade; Cloud valance over mini blind

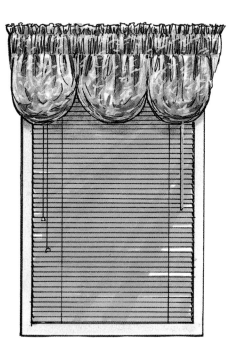

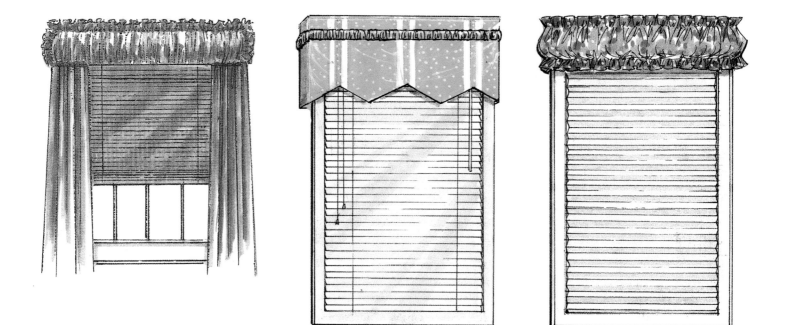

(Above) Shirred valance with ruffle over gathered side draperies and wood blind; Unique geometric valance over mini blind; Puffed and ruffled valance over pleated shade; (Below) Lace tiebacks on decorative rod over mini blind; Full gathered valance on double rods; Scalloped awning valance over mini blind

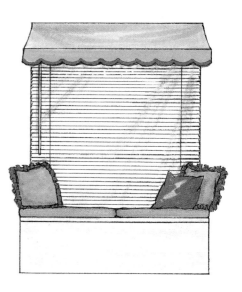

Roller shades

(Above) Gathered valance with bows over shade with appliqued bottom; Fringed scalloped roller shade with valance; Banded roller shade with valance; (Below) Rod pocket valance over roller shade; Traditional shutters on tall windows; Tab top curtain on decorative rod over roller shade

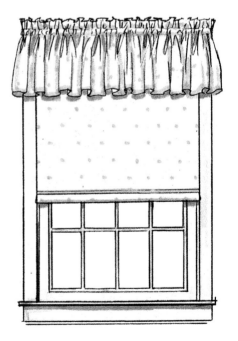

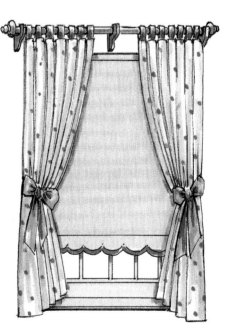

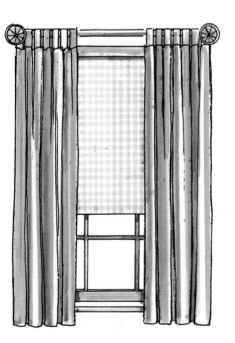

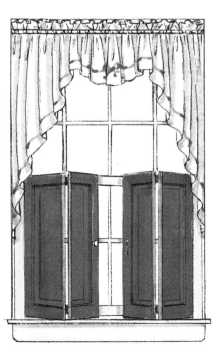

(Above) Ruffled swags over café shutters; Cathedral window with custom fitted shutters; Two tone swag over full/ shutters (Below) Shutter with shirred fabric inserts; Gathered valance over louvered shutters; Rod pocket valance over solid wood shutters

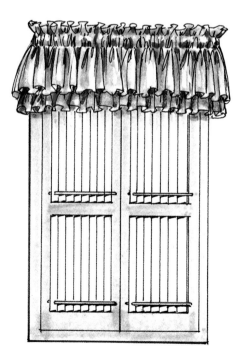

(Above) Leaded glass over wide blade shutters; Fabric insert shutters; Draperies over traditional shutters
(Below) Louvered and solid shutters with valance; Fabric insert shutters; Draperies over tranditional shutters

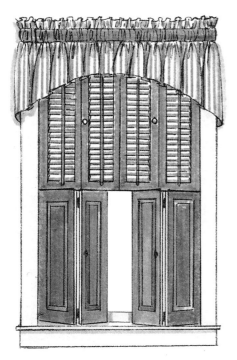  

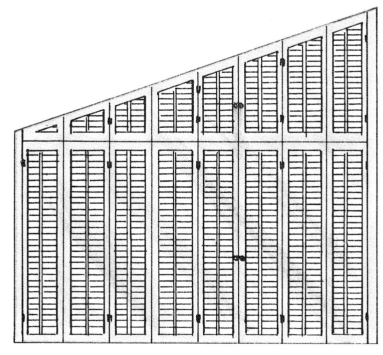

(Above) ;Arched shutters; Shutters custom fitted to slanted clerestory windows
(Below) Cornice box with rope and tassels over shutters

Verticals

(Above) Simple shirred cornice over vertical blinds; Slanted windows with custom cut vertical blinds; Scalloped pleated valance over vertical blinds (Below) Swag with ruffled side drops over vertical blinds; Shirred cloud valance over vertical blinds; Floor length fabric swagged on shirred rod over vertical blinds

(Above) Vertical blinds with cornice cap; Decorative stencil design on vertical blinds; Double gathered cornice over vertical blind (Below) Vertical blinds with stagecoach valance; Double brass ros over vertical blinds with brass trim at bottom; Fabric or wallpaper inserts in vertical blinds

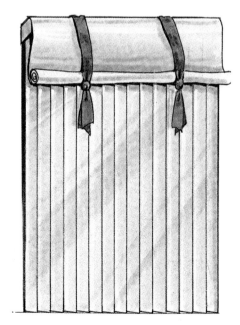
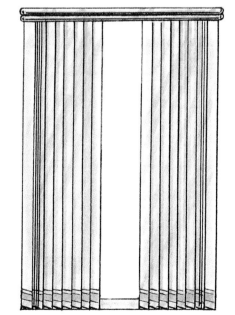
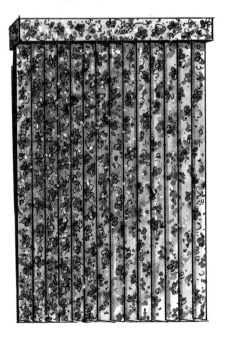

(Above) Vertical blinds in a bay window; Slant top vertical blinds (Below) Bay window with Bishop sleeve effect over vertial blinds

(Above) Swag with tassels and fringe; Cornice box over white wood blinds with wide tapes; Lace tiebacks over wood blinds (Below) Tabbed valance on decorative rod and over wood blind

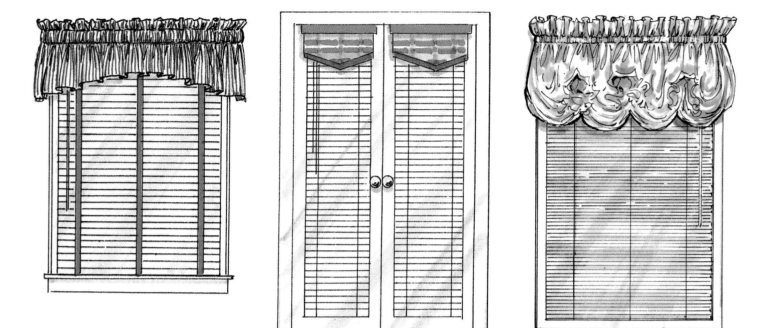

(Above) Arched gathered valance over wood Venetian blinds; French doors with wood blinds and chevron valances; One inch wood blind in natural finish with cloud valance (Below) Bishop sleeve draperies over wood blind; Box pleated valance over wood blind

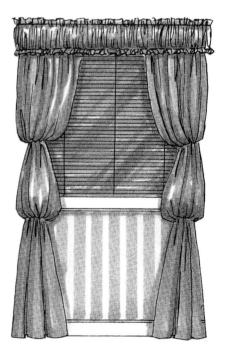

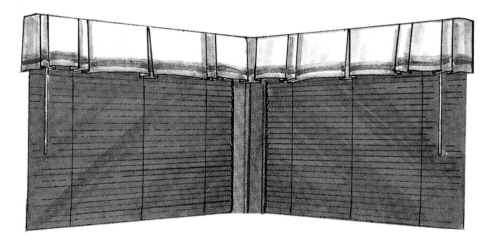

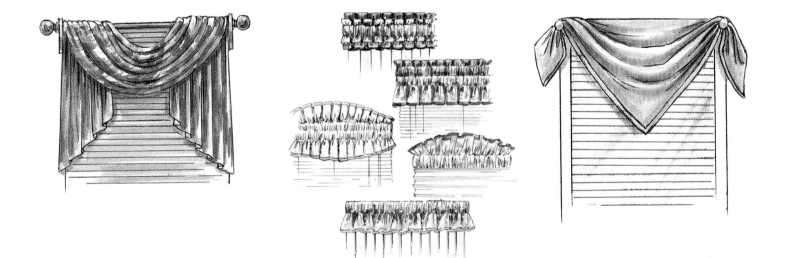

(Above) Gathered swag on decorative rod; Additional valance styles over blind varieties; Handkerchief tie over pleated blinds (Below) Balloon valance over wood blind; Fabric swag with side drop over wood blind; Fabric draped swag over blinds

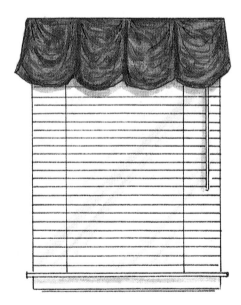

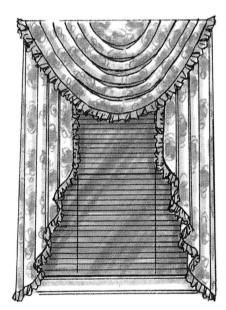

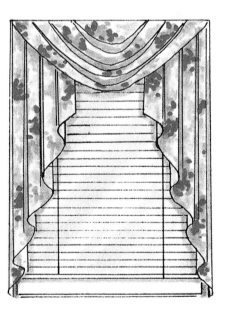

Bed coverings

For some, the bedroom is merely a place to sleep. For others, it is a playroom, a reading room or a quiet place to catch up on work. Yet, no matter how much time one spends in the bedroom, the look and feel of the space is of utmost importance. And thankfully, it is space with boundless options that extend well beyond the decision between draperies and shutters. When beginning to design in the bedroom, there are an infinite number of starting points. But whether choosing the window, the floor or the walls, eventually you will come to the bedding. A well-chosen bedspread can quietly blend with a complex color scheme, or can easily become the room's focal point. Surrounded by an exotic

(B100) Soft scalloped cornice with brush fringe; lush drapery panels and box pleated bed skirt. Matching fabric on the bolsters.

(B101) Gathered valance showcases an elaborate fabric bed ceiling with matching dust ruffle and draperies.

swag and cascade combination or sophisticated floral draperies, a light blue bedspread that complements one of the many colors in the room may be just enough. For a more augmented involvement, a pink and gray gingham bedspread may find its place in a room with a perfectly-matched valance, surrounded by simple walls and pale pink pillows. And when a bedspread is ready to become the centerpiece of a bedroom, the fabric can become as vivacious as reality will allow, as window treatments, armoires and carpeting fall into place to complement the ingenuity.

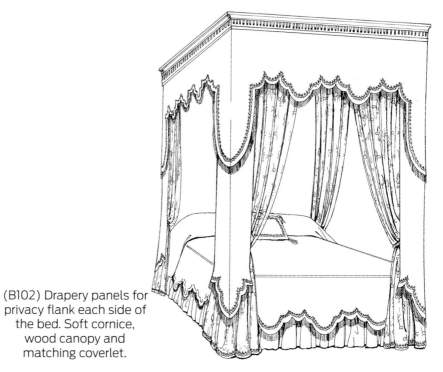

(B102) Drapery panels for privacy flank each side of the bed. Soft cornice, wood canopy and matching coverlet.

(B103) Pencil pleated top treatment with matching side panels and bed skirt trimmed in tassel fringe; upholstered headboard.

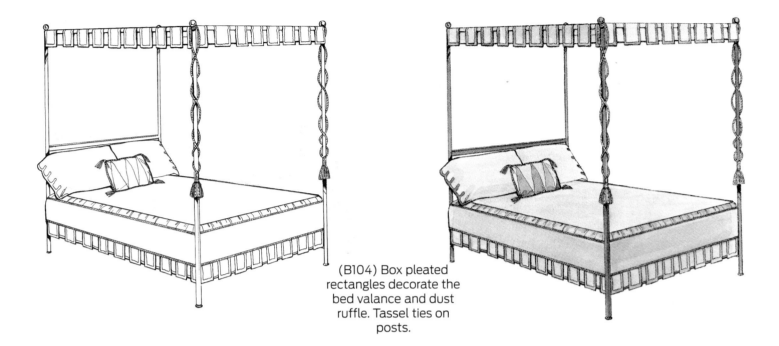

(B104) Box pleated rectangles decorate the bed valance and dust ruffle. Tassel ties on posts.

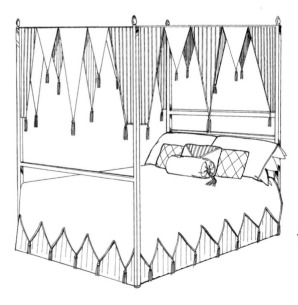

(B105) Triangle valance flags with tassel accents are mirrored in the matching coverlet and pillow cases.

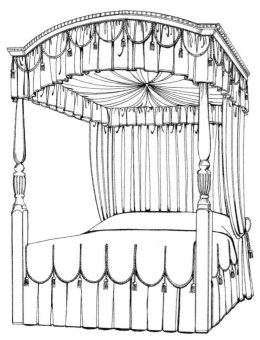

(B106) Box pleated, curved valance with shirred fabric ceiling, scalloped coverlet with box pleated duster.

(B107) Upholstered headboard matches the gathered bed skirt, swags, jabots and drapery panels; swags cap the top.

(B108) Unusual fabric scarves cascade down each side of the bed; scalloped coverlet with brush fringe; gathered bedskirt; matching headboard and pillows.

(B109) Scarf swags with small knotted cascade; matching upholstered headboard and pleated bedskirt.

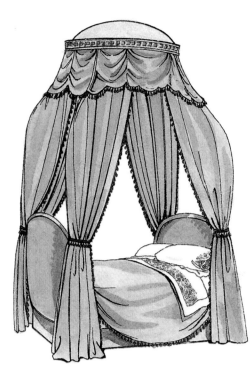

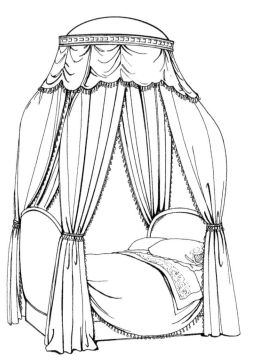

(B110) An oval corona with lush drapery panels and tassel and fringe decorated coverlet.

(B111) Crown corona with double Bishop-sleeve panels, oversized tassel accents and matching coverlet.

(B112) Crown corona with cascade and bow accents, ruched upholstered headboard and scalloped gathered bedskirt.

(B113) Pleated bedskirt with swag and rosette accent; fabric draped headboard with bow accents.

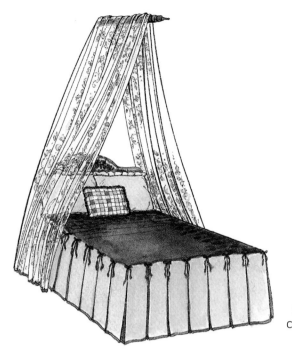

(B114) Fabric draped over a decorative pole; box pleated coverlet with tassel accenting.

(B115) Ruched fabric is seen on the headboard, corona and bed's lower edge. Pleated drapery panels are held in place with decorative hardware and matching coverlet.

(B116) Banner-style canopy is hung from decorative rods, suspended inches from the ceiling with braided straps. Matching upholstered head and footboard with scalloped brush fringe-trimmed dust ruffle.

(B117) Scalloped box-pleated valance with pleated drapery panels and small scalloped edging to soften. Deeply pleated bedskirt.

(B118) A half round corona with swag and jabot; decorative knobs extend from the wall to hold draperies in place; swagged coverlet over the box pleated dust ruffle and coordinated bolster.

(B119) Fabric draped over a decorative pole and secured with large tassel tiebacks; scalloped dust ruffle with bolster pillows on the bed.

(B120) Box pleated bedskirt with braid-trimmed coverlet; floral drapery panels with matching tiebacks and goblet pleated top treatments with back curtain. Matching pillows.

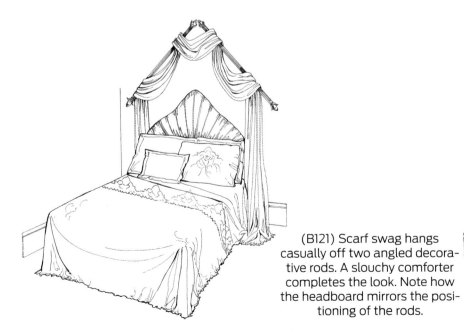

(B121) Scarf swag hangs casually off two angled decorative rods. A slouchy comforter completes the look. Note how the headboard mirrors the positioning of the rods.

(B122) A wood cornice holds pleated fabric valance and drapery panels; matching dust ruffle; scalloped coverlet.

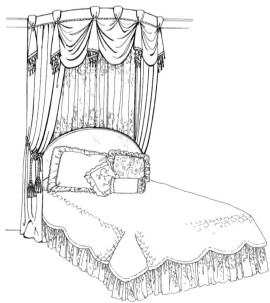

(B123) Horizontally arched Kingston valance with draperies and tassel tiebacks; pleated dust ruffle with pillows to match.

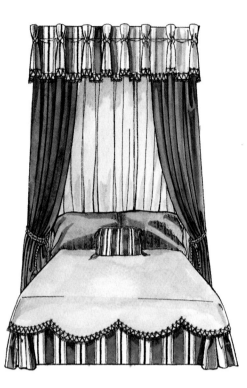

(B124) Goblet pleated valance with unusually trimmed edge; lush draperies and matching dust ruffle and pillow.

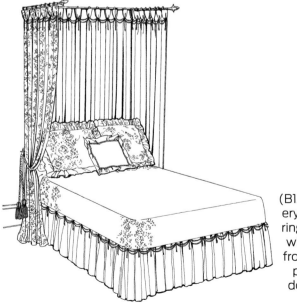

(B125) Goblet pleated drapery panels are attached via rings off of decorative rods, which extend horizontally from the wall. Inverted box pleated dust ruffle with double braid and tassels.

(B126) Bishop sleeve panels are set off by an elaborately swagged cornice, matching pleated dust ruffle and coordinating pillows.

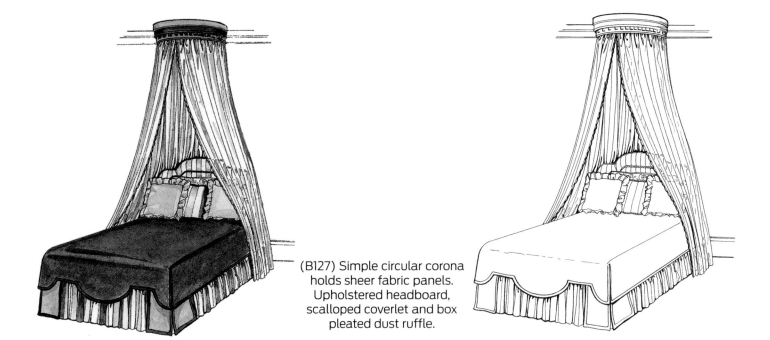

(B127) Simple circular corona holds sheer fabric panels. Upholstered headboard, scalloped coverlet and box pleated dust ruffle.

(B128) A boxy cornice with shell motif holds a pretty swag and cascade top treatment as well as full, pleated drapery panels with braided tassel tiebacks. Coordinated coverlet; upholstered headboard.

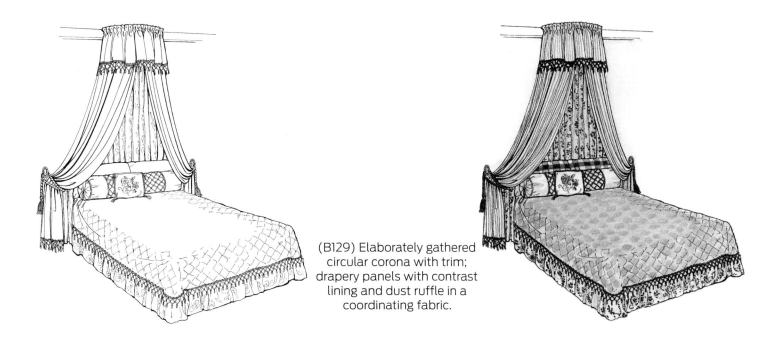

(B129) Elaborately gathered circular corona with trim; drapery panels with contrast lining and dust ruffle in a coordinating fabric.

(B130) Swag draped corona with lushly edged pleated draperies contained by decorative rosettes; pleated dust ruffle; matching coverlet.

(B131) Soft cornice lined in welt houses wide drapery panels; simple box pleated comforter touts the same welt. Ruched, scalloped headboard.

(B132) Goblet pleated valance with a slight curve; jabot and braided tassel accents and inverted box pleat dust ruffle with coordinating pillows.

(B133) Criss-crossing lattice work passementerie on the canopy, overlapping triangles on the coverlet and a gathered dust ruffle make for an elegant bed.

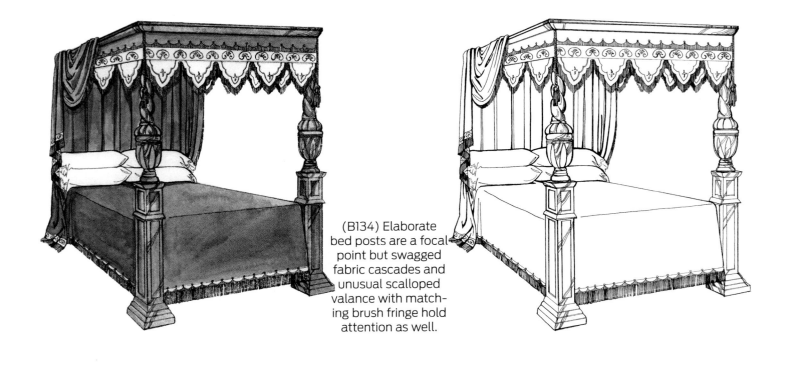

(B134) Elaborate bed posts are a focal point but swagged fabric cascades and unusual scalloped valance with matching brush fringe hold attention as well.

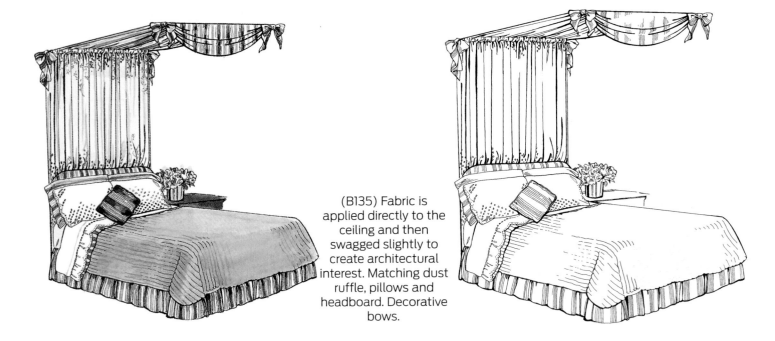

(B135) Fabric is applied directly to the ceiling and then swagged slightly to create architectural interest. Matching dust ruffle, pillows and headboard. Decorative bows.

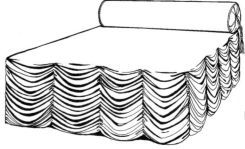

(B136) Fabric is swagged off all four sides of the canopy, punctuated with braid and tassels. Elaborate Austrian-style coverlet adds drama.

(B137) Swags and jabots with tassel trim decorate both the top and bottom of this bed ensemble; a box pleated valance and dust ruffle complete it.

(B138) Flouncy drapery panels edged in lace with matching bedskirt and pillows; note the gathered fabric ceiling: very feminine.

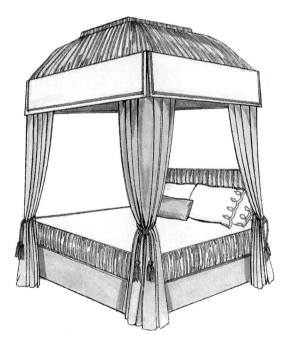

(B139) Crisp box pleated with ruched fabric on the upper canopy, headboard and bedspread are nicely tailored.

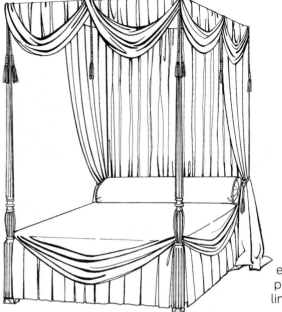

(B140) Tailored bed ensemble displays the box pleating with the horizontal lines of a soft swag both top and bottom. Decorative tassels add a designer touch.

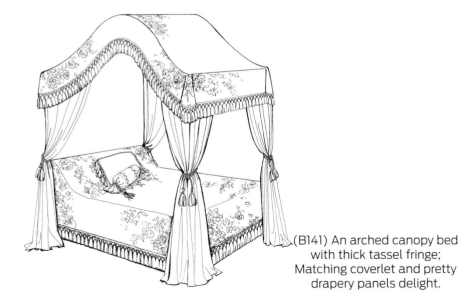

(B141) An arched canopy bed with thick tassel fringe; Matching coverlet and pretty drapery panels delight.

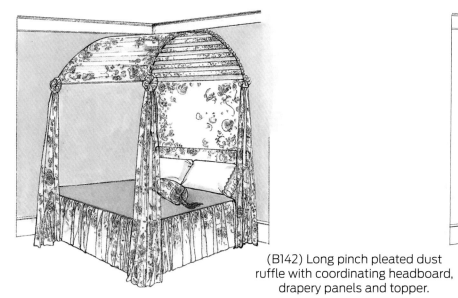

(B142) Long pinch pleated dust ruffle with coordinating headboard, drapery panels and topper.

(B143) Tent top-like canopy with matching dust ruffle, bedding and pillows.

(B144) Deep drooping swags and jabots with contrast banding are used in conjunction with a simple coverlet and pleated dust ruffle.

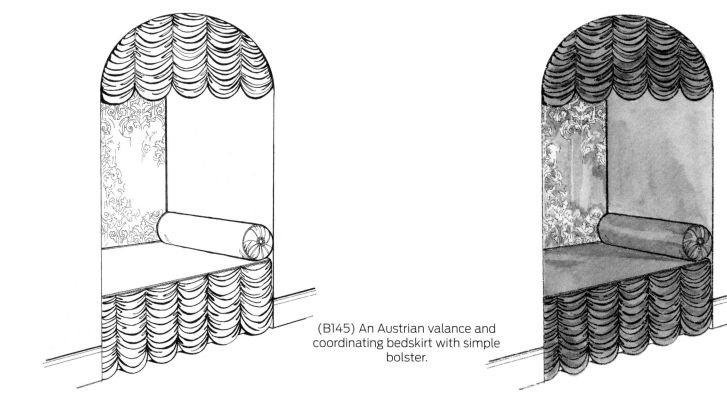

(B145) An Austrian valance and coordinating bedskirt with simple bolster.

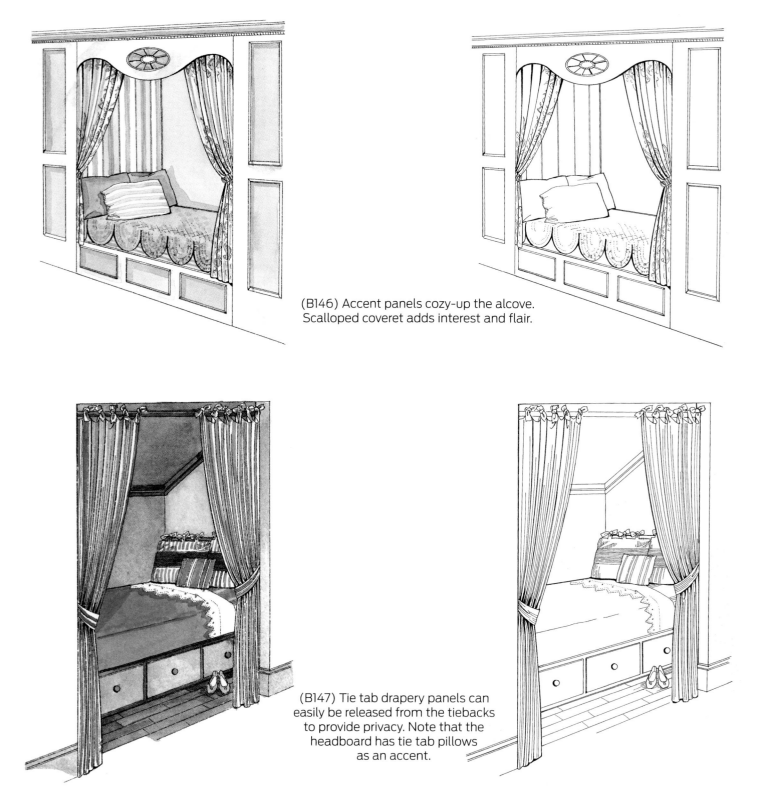

(B146) Accent panels cozy-up the alcove.
Scalloped coveret adds interest and flair.

(B147) Tie tab drapery panels can
easily be released from the tiebacks
to provide privacy. Note that the
headboard has tie tab pillows
as an accent.

(B148) Cuffed draperies with a tab top are gathered smartly into an hourglass shape with matching fabric tiebacks. Coordinating dust ruffle and pillow trim finish this treatment.

(B149) Elaborately trimmed fabric is installed just slightly above the bedposts and then wrapped organically. Coordinating pillows and bedding complete.

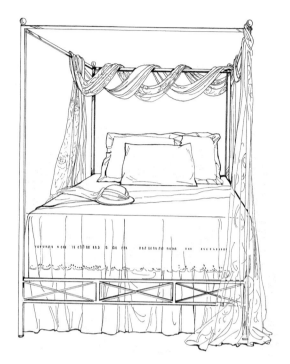

(B150) A sheer scarf swag loops around the metal bed hardware in an almost asymmetrical style. A sheer coverlet offers a lovely accent.

(B151) Romantic country florals with ruffle accent cover this small area beautifully.

(B152) A scarf swag with large center jabot echoes the wall angles. A second swag with cascades hangs across the window. Coordinating bedskirt and fabric covered box at the foot of the bed complete the look.

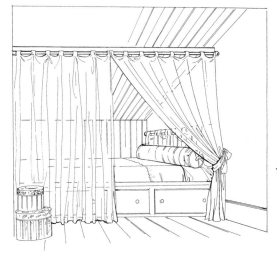

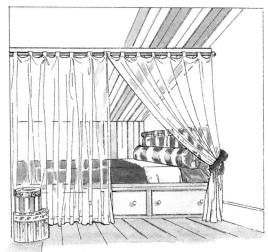

(B153) Wide tab top draperies hang on a decorative rod, shower curtain style, andccover the sleeping area completely when released from the tieback. Note the tab detailing on the headboard, too.

(B154) Soft embellished cornice with coordinating bed coverlet; fabric panel inserted between the bed and wall to soften; draperies for pivacy are a finishing touch.

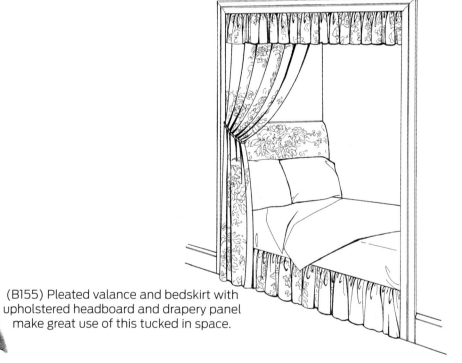

(B155) Pleated valance and bedskirt with upholstered headboard and drapery panel make great use of this tucked in space.

(B156) Smart swags with rosette accents at the top and bottom; Bishop sleeve panels and upholstered sideboard.

(B157) Drapery panels are hung into the sloped ceiling and held back with casual fabric bows. Headboard and pillows have matchig fabric. Contrast comforter.

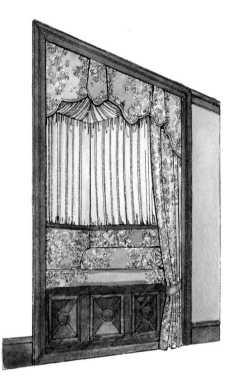

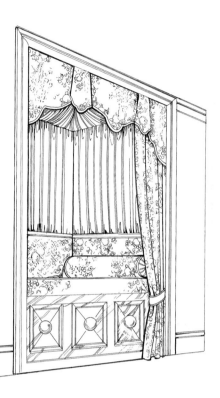

(B158) A tiny daybed area with upholstered walls and ceiling; pleated panels and soft cornice with jabot accents.

(B159) Arched goblet pleated valance with matching drapries accent a sleigh bed; pleated coverlet with coordinating pillows; tassel tiebacks with decorative hardware.

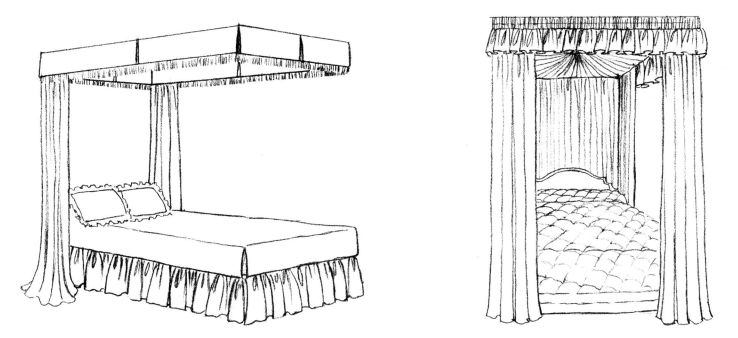

Ceiling mounted valance over box pleated coverlet; Ceiling mounted rod pocket valance over quilted bedspread

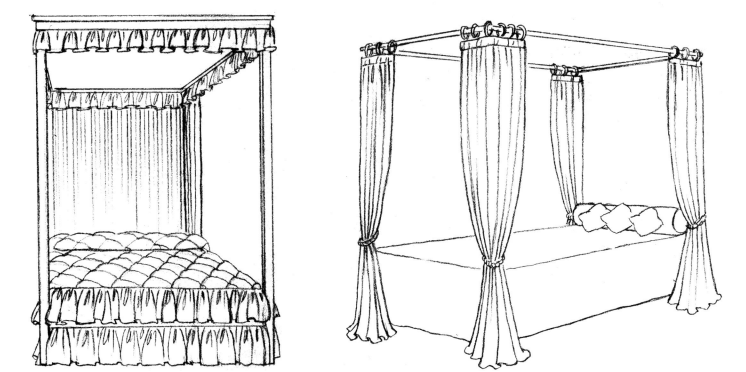

Quilted top double ruffled drop bedspread; Plain bedspread wth side panels

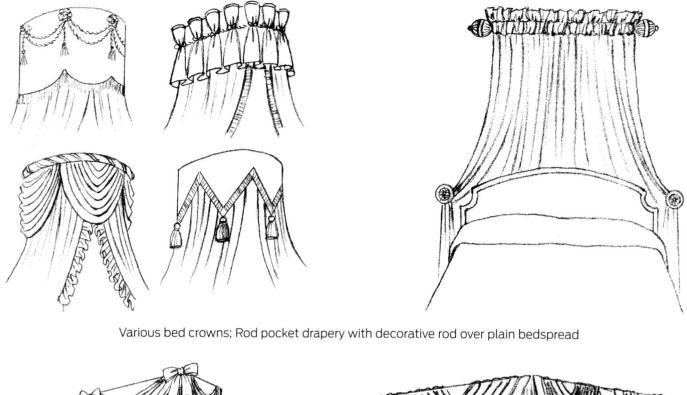

Various bed crowns; Rod pocket drapery with decorative rod over plain bedspread

Swags and jabots with Maltese Cross over plain bedspread; Swags and cascades over plain bedspread
with upholstered headboard

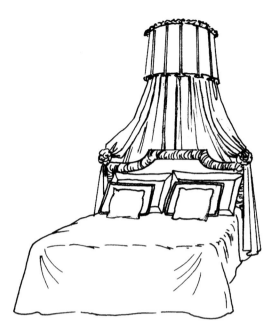 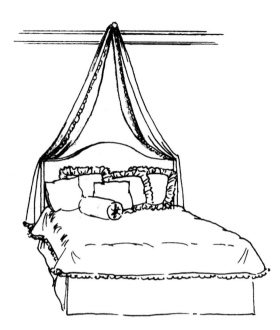

Half-round box pleated valance with draped fabric held by rosettes and upholstered headboard with throw spread;
Fabric draped over decorative pole and coverlet with tailored dust ruffle

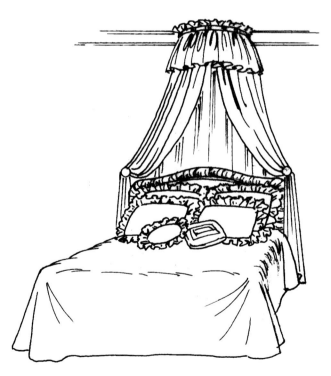 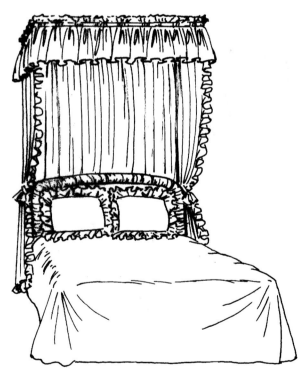

Half-round ruffled valance with fabric draped over hold backs with upholstered headboard and throw spread; Rod pocket
valance with ruffled tiebacks, upholstered headboard and throw spread

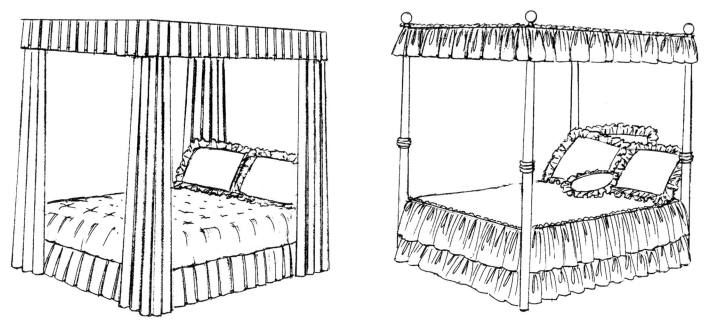

Box pleated canopy valance with stationary draperies, quilted coverlet over box pleated dust ruffle; Gathered canopy valance with ruffled bedspread over gathered dust ruffle

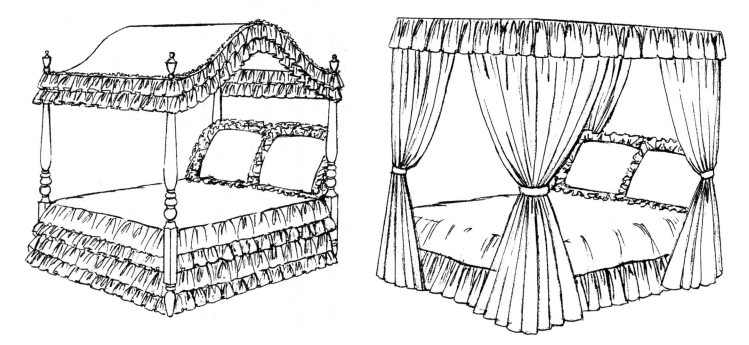

Arched canopy with ruffles, ruffled bedspread and dust ruffle; Gathered canopy valance over tiebacks with coverlet over gathered dust ruffle

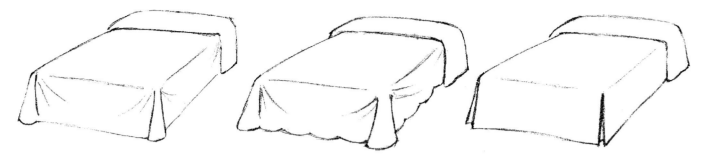

Throw spread; Throw with scalloped edge; Fitted throw

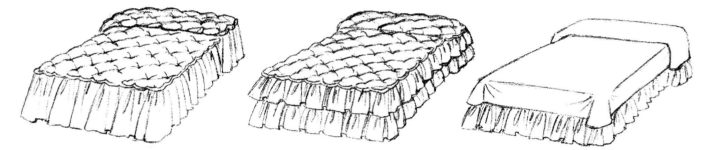

Scalloped quilted top with shirred drop; Scalloped quilted top with double shirred drop; Throw with ruffled bottom

Plain coveret over shirred dust ruffle; Quilted coverlet over shirred dust ruffle; Throw with one-inch welt

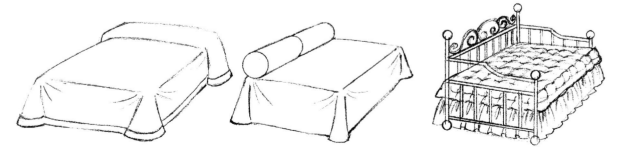

Throw with two-inch welt; Studio couch cover with bolsters; Tufted daybed comforter over shirred dust ruffle

Upholstered benches, bolsters & shams

Plain covered bench

Cylindrical bolster with welt trim; Wedge bolster with welt trim; Rectangular bolster with welt trim

Covered scalloped bench

Sham with three-inch ruffle; Plain sham with ¼" welt

Double bench with shirred skirt

Quilted sham with 2½" flange; Plain sham with double ruffle

Plain bench with upholstered legs and top

Sham with ¼" welt and ruffle; Double ruffle sham with ½" welt

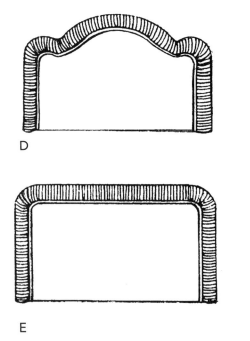

D

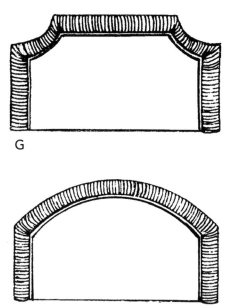

G

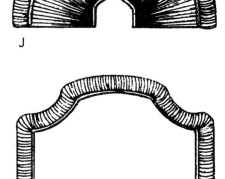

J

E

H

F

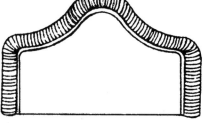

I

Upholstered headboards
Sumptuous and luxurious, the upholstered headboard is not only stylish but also offers extreme comfort for those individuals who like to read in bed, yet loathe leaning against a wood or iron headboard. Plus, the shape of the headboard and the colors and fabric patterns make headboards perfect for those who want to exhibit individual style in their most private home area.

Dimensions
Style D, I, F, G
Twin = 41" wide x 51" high
Full = 56" wide x 53" high
Queen = 62" w x 55" high
King = 81" wide x 56" high

Style J
Twin = 41" wide x 53" high
Full = 56" wide x 55" high
Queen = 62" w x 57" high
King = 81" wide x 57" high

Style E & H
Twin = 41" wide x 49" high
Full = 56" wide x 49" high
Queen = 62" w x 51" high
King = 81" wide x 53" high

Dusters

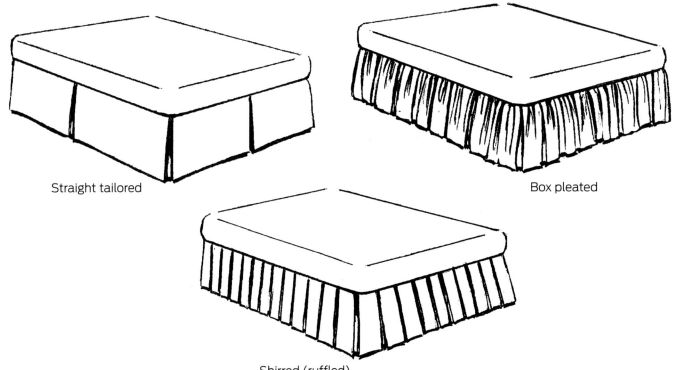

Straight tailored

Box pleated

Shirred (ruffled)

Dusters

A duster, which fits in between the mattress and the boxspring, is a clever way to not only provide your bed with a finished appearance, effectively hiding the more unsightly but necessary box spring, but also covers the distance between the boxspring and the floor. There are three popular styles: straight tailored, shirred (or ruffled) and box pleated.

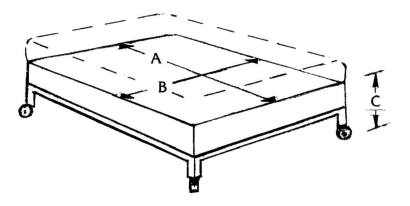

How to measure

Exact measurements are necessary.

A. Measure the length of the boxspring
B. Measure the width of the boxspring
C. Measure the drop from the top of the boxspring to the floor

Spreads

	36"	48"	54"
Twin	12 yards	8 yards	8 yards
Full	12 yards	12 yards	12 yards
Queen	15 yards	12 yards	12 yards
King	15 yards	12 yards	12 yards

Additional yardage requirements:
For prints—Add 1 yard
Additional yardage optional features:
For reverse sham—add 3 yards; For jumbo cord—add 2 yards

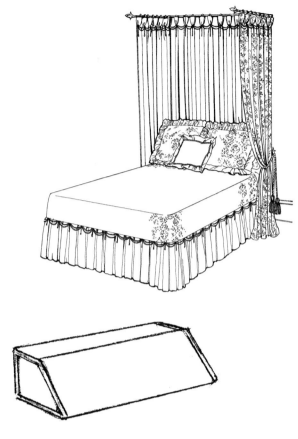

Bolsters

	36"	45"	54"
36"	1½ yards	1½ yards	1 yards
39"	2 yards	1½ yards	1 yards
60"	2 yards	2 yards	2 yards
72"	2½ yards	2 yards	2 yards

Add one repeat of pattern for prints

Dusters

	36" fabric		45" or wider	
	Tailored	Shirred or 4" box pleat	Tailored	Shirred or 4" box pleat
Twin	3¾ yards	8½ yards	2¾ yards	6½ yards
Full	3¾ yards	8½ yards	2¾ yards	7 yards
Queen	4½ yards	10 yards	3 yards	7½ yards
King	4½ yards	10 yards	3 yards	7½ yards

Comforter yardage
Twin, Full, Queen = 7 yards/side; King = 11 yards/side

Pillow shams
1½ yards; Ruffles, add 1½ yards

General information
Bedspreads are made to fit the following standard bed sizes: Twin: 39 x 75; Full: 54 x 75; Queen: 60 x 80; King: 72 x 84. Standard drops: Bedspread: 21"; Coverlet: 12"; Duster: 14"; Pillow tuck: 15"

Throw pillows & cushions

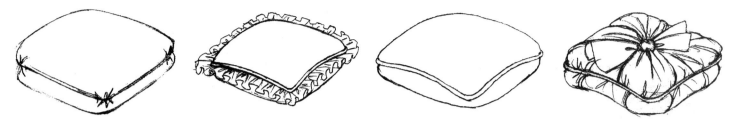

Turkish corners; Three-inch ruffle with welt; Knife edge with ¼" welt; Shirred welt

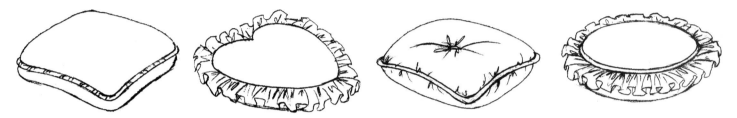

Square knot; Heart shaped with ruffle; Round with welt and ruffle; Square with plain welt and button

Round with plain welt and button; Rope welt on knife edge; Square with welt, tassel accents; Scalloped ruffle with welt edge

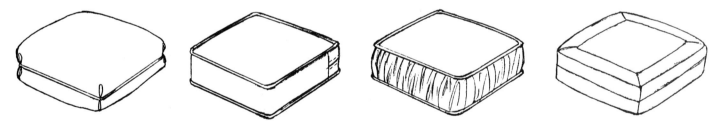

Soft box cushion with welt; Boxed cushion with welt; Box cushion with shirred boxing; Soft box cushion with applique top

Round cushion with welt; Neck roll with ruffle; Shirred neck roll; Tootsie roll neck roll

A

A-frame window: Very contemporary house structures some times form an "A" shape. When draperies are used, they hang from the crossbeam of the "A," or they can be fabricated and installed to conform to the shape of the window.

A La Duchesse: A type of bed supported with a canopy suspension from the ceiling rather than posts. It is also known as an angel bed.

Accordion pleat: Single large pleats which are often used as a method of fan folding in pleated draperies before installing, or can be used in contract draperies by snapping onto channel slides.

Allowance: A customary variation from an "exact" measurement, taken for the purpose of anticipated needs.

Appliqué: The application of a second, decorated layer of fabric onto a base piece of cloth.

Apron: A piece of wood trim beneath the windowsill.

Architectural rodding: Used for contract draperies, a sturdy, sleek or traverse channel.

Architrave: The molding around an arch or wooden surrounding to a window or door frame.

Art glass: Glass which is cut at an angle (other than a right angle), stained and etched, and used for hard window treatments.

Art Nouveau: An historical design movement of the Victorian Era, dating from 1890 to 1910. The motifs are based on flowing plant forms.

Asymmetrical balance: A type of design in which the entire arrangement has a balance, but each side of a central point is different.

Austrian shade: A shade having ruche down the whole side length, creating billows when the shade is raised.

Automated exterior rolling shutters: A treatment used for insulation and privacy purposes, in which the exterior of a window has metal panels, which roll down mechanically over the glass.

Awning window: A type of window that can swing out due to a hinged top.

B

Backstitch: A reverse-stitch used to keep the stitches from coming undone at the ends. Several stitches are sewn at the beginning and end of any seam.

Balloon shade: Shades with vertical rows of horizontally gathered fabric, which can be drawn up to form strips of pleated or gathered trim.

Balloon tiebacks: Curtains which, when tied back, form a rounded sort of cloud shape.

Bamboo shade: A natural light-softening shade, drawn by hand using a cord and made of woven panels of split bamboo. Also called a Bali blind.

Baroque: An elaborate interior design period dating from 1643 to 1730 in France and 1660 to 1714 in England.

Bar tack: A sewing machine operation of repeated stitches concentrated to secure the lowest portion of drapery pleats.

Basement windows: Opposite of awning windows, these windows swing inward due to a hinged bottom.

Basting: A technique used in sewing to temporarily fasten layers of fabric using long, loose stitches.

Baton: A rod or wand used to hand draw traverse draperies.

Bay window: A large projecting type of window made of a group of windows set at angles to each other and joined to each other on some sides.

Bell valance: A gathered or pleated valance that has a number of bell-like shapes at bottom hemline.

Bias binding: A strip of fabric used for added strength when binding edges of fabric and closing piping. The fabric is cut in a slanted manner from selvage to selvage.

Bishop's sleeve curtains: Tie-back curtains which have been bloused at least two times.

Blind: A hard treatment for a window, consisting of a series of horizontal panels.

Bottom hem: The turned part forming a finished edge at bottom of a drapery.

Bow window: A large projecting type of window that is curved or semi-circular.

Box pleat: A fold of cloth sewn into place to create fullness in a drapery. Box pleats are evenly spaced and stitched.

Bracket: Metal piece attached to the wall or casing to support a drapery or curtain rod.

Braid: A woven ribbon that may be used for trimming or can be added to edges of draperies and accessories.

Bull's-eye window: A circular window glazed with flat or arched glass.

Butterfly pleat: A two-part pleat that flares out at the top and is bar-tacked at the bottom.

C

Café curtain: A traversing or non-traversing drapery, designed as a tier. The heading can be various styles. They can be set at a variety of heights to control ventilation, view and light.

Café rod: A small, round decorative rod that comes in white, brass or woodgrain finish, used to mount café curtains that do not have a rod pocket. Café rods are meant to be seen and add an additional decorative touch to the curtain treatment.

Canopy: A fabric window topper created by sewing pockets into fabric panels and inserting a rod with a small projection at the top of the panel, a rod with a larger projection at the bottom.

Cantonniere: A three-sided shaped or straight cornice that frames a window across the top and down the two sides. Made of a hardboard, padded and covered with fabric.

Cape Cod curtain: A café curtain decorated by a ruffle around the bottom and sides. This is also called a ruffle-round curtain.

Carriers: Small runners installed in a traverse rod which hold a drapery pin or hook.

Cartridge pleat: A fold of cloth sewn into place to create fullness in a drapery. This is a round pleat 2 to 2 1/2 inches in depth. Roundness is created by stuffing crinoline or paper (removed for cleaning).

Cascade: A fall of fabric that descends in a zigzag line from a drapery heading or top treatment.

Cased heading: A curtain heading with a simple, hemmed top, in which a rod is inserted.

Casement: (1) A cloth drapery that is of an open-weave material but more opaque than a sheer. (2) A type of vertically hinged window, whose panes open by sliding sideways or cranking outward.

Casing (window): Wooden frame around a window.

Catchstitch: A stitch used for hemming raw edges, and then covered by a piece of fabric.

Cathedral window: A window which points upward, and is formed at an angle.

Center draw: One pair of draperies that draw open and close exactly at a window's center point.

Center support: A metal grip which is used to support a traverse rod from above and prevents rod form sagging in the middle, but does not interfere with rod operation.

Clerestory windows: A series of small windows that let in light and air. These are placed high on the wall to allow complete privacy.

Colonial: A design period common prior to the revolutionary war in America. It is typically dated from 1608 to 1790.

Corbel bay: A second story bay window.

Cord: A cable yarn that can be made from either cotton or synthetic materials. It is used for various reasons including holding blinds and shades together, and as a means for drawing traverse draperies, shades and blinds.

Corner window: A window that wraps a corner of the building at right angles.

Cornice: A shallow, box-like structure, usually made of wood, fastened across the top of a window to conceal the drapery hardware.

Cornice board: A horizontal board used as support for a cornice or as foundation for swags and tails.

Cornice pole: A curtain pole having rings and used for heavy curtains.

Corona drape: A drapery that is hung at the top of a bed from a semi-circular bracket or a pole.

Cottage curtains: A term used to describe curtains displayed in a casual or informal manner.

Country curtains: A casual curtain treatment with ruffles at valance, bottom, sides and ties. The curtain is shirred a maximum of five times in fullness and is usually made with plain or tiny-printed fabric.

Coverage: A term used to describe the fullness of fabric used on a window.

Crown glass: A particular type of glass consisting of hand-blown crowns, measuring about one meter in diameter.

Curtain: A window covering either hung from rings, or made with a casing so that it slips over a rod. Curtains are informal window coverings.

Custom glazing: Unusual sized or oddly shaped window glass, which is custom made and installed.

Custom-made draperies: Draperies made to order in a workroom or decorator shop.

Cut length: The length after allowances have been made for heading and hem.

Cut width: The width that the fabric should be cut after allowances have been made.

D

Decorator rods: Hardware used for the purpose of decorating, that is meant to be seen in the open. Usually made from chrome, wood, brass or antique wrought iron.

Diaphanous sheers: Drapery used for the purpose of day-time privacy. The finely woven transparent fabrics filter out glare. Also know as glass curtains.

Dormer window: An upright window which breaks the surface of a sloping roof.

Double hung: May be several items: Double-hung window, double-hung shutters or double-hung draperies (two sets of draperies, usually sheer fabric under opaque fabric, both operating independently).

Drapability: How well a fabric can flow or fall into folds in an attractive manner.

Drapery: A window covering that is usually hung from a traverse rod. Draperies most often have pleated headings that may be lined or unlined.

Draw draperies: Panels of fabric, featuring pleated headings.

Dress curtains: Curtains used for the sole purpose of decorating. They are not meant to be drawn.

E

Ease: Refers to extra fabric allowance given in order to make the finished length more accurate. Sometimes fabric that was not calculated into the final length will be lost when stitching double-fold hems, headings or rod pockets, or when gathering a treatment onto a rod. It is a good idea to add 1/2" ease to the length before cutting to ensure a more accurate finish.

Elements of design: The elements which make up a design, including: texture, light, color, space, form, shape, pattern and ornament.

Empire: A design period dating from 1804 to 1820 in France and 1820 to 1860 in America.

End bracket: The two supporting metal grips that hold a drapery rod to the wall or ceiling. They control the amount of projection.

End housing: Refers to the box parts at the extreme ends of a traverse drapery rod. They enclose the mechanism through which the cords run.

End pleat: The final pleat in a drapery, hooked into the end bracket.

English sash window: A sliding frame consisting of a number of rectangular shaped glass panels. Also called Renaissance sash.

F

Fabric finishes: Treatments used to give the fabric more durability, decoration and usefulness. These can be chemical or mechanical.

Fabric sliding panels: Panels of fabric that are drawn with a baton. They are flat, overlapping and installed on a track rod.

Face fabric: The primary fabric on draperies or curtains. This is the fabric that faces the interior of the room.

Facing: A strip of fabric over the main fabric, with the purpose of hiding raw edges and unlined curtains or draperies.

Factory-made treatments: Custom specifications in hard window treatments ordered from a manufacturer or factory. These include shades, shutters, blinds and screens.

Fan folding: Fan folding helps to obliterate wrinkling, set the folds and provide better drapeability. This is done by folding pleated draperies into a thin band.

Fascia: A rectangular-shaped board set horizontally with the purpose of covering a curtain heading or shade fixture.

Federal Period: A design period dating from 1790 to 1820. Also called Neoclassic.

Fenestration: Location and proportion of windows in relationship to solid wall areas.

Festoon: A decorative drapery treatment of folded fabric that hangs in a graceful curve and frames the top of a window. Also called Parisian shade.

Finial: Decorative end piece on café rods or decorative traverse rods. Also referred to as pole ends.

Finished length: The length after draperies have been made, using the extra allowances in hem and heading.

Finished width: The width after draperies have been made. Found by measuring the length of the mounting board or rod and then adding in the depth of any returns.

Fixed glass: Term used to describe windows that are not made to open or close.

Flat curtain rod: A curtain rod that differs from a traverse rod in that it does not use a pulley and cord to operate.

Flemish heading: A goblet type of heading where each of the pleats are connected along their base using a hand-sewn cord.

Flounce: A technique adding an extra long heading sewn at the top of a rod pocket and having the curtain fall over the rod pocket to create the appearance of a short, attached valance.

French door draw: A swinging door or casement window with one-way traverse rods attached.

French doors: Doors in a pair, which are lengthwise, mostly made up of glass panes.

French pleats: A three-fold pleat; one of the most used pleats in draperies.

French seam: A seam most often used when the seam will be visible, or when using lightweight fabrics.

Fringe: An edging with hanging tassels or threads, used as decoration.

Fullness: The proportion of the finished width of the valance or curtain to the length of the mounting board or rod.

G

Gathered heading: A heading for a curtain or valance in

which the heading is gathered by means of gathering tape.

Gathering tape: A tape stitched to the top of a curtain to create a gathered effect by pulling on cords which run through the tape.

Gathers: Folding and puckering formed when pulling on loosely-stitched thread.

Georgian Period: A design period which dates from 1700 to 1790.

Glue-baste: A technique using glue to secure two pieces of fabric together before sewing.

Goblet heading: A curtain heading having a series of hand-sewn tubes, in which each of the tops are stuffed with padding or contrast fabric.

Goblet pleats: Similar to pinch pleats, except that the top edge is padded and pushed out in a goblet type of shape.

Greenhouse window: A window that generally extends at a 90-degree angle from the wall, has a glass top and sides and two accompanying shelves for plants.

Group pleat: A set of pleats, generally three, with space between each one.

H

Half-canopy: A canopy above a bed in a rectangular shape, which extends only partially from the headboard down the bed.

Heading: The hemmed, usually stiffened, portion across the top of a curtain or drapery.

Hem: Refers to finished sides and bottom edges of a drapery.

Holdback: A decorative piece of hardware that holds draperies to each side of the window.

I

Insert pulley: An auxiliary traverse rod part, over which the cords operate.

Inside mount: A treatment installed inside of a window frame.

Installation: A process which undergoes the various aspects of placing and setting a window treatment.

Interlining: A soft fabric, sewn in between the curtain and the back lining to improve bulk, insulation and overall drapability.

Inverted pleat: A pleat formed the opposite way of a traditional box pleat, in which the edges of the pleat meet in the middle right side of the fabric. Also know as the kick pleat.

J

Jabot: A decorative piece of fabric that is hung over seams or between swags on a valance. Jabots may be rounded, tie- or cone-shaped on the bottom.

Jalousie window: A window made from a number of horizontal slants, delivering good ventilation properties.

Jamb: Interior sides of a door or window frame.

K

Keystone arch: An arch used as part of a wooden molding for decoration, rounded and Roman in style.

Knife pleats: Narrow, finely pressed and closely spaced pleats which all go in the same direction.

L

Lambrequin: A cornice that completely frames the window. Sometimes used interchangeably with valance or cantonniere.

Laminated weights: Weight covered on both sides to avoid rust marks on draperies.

Lanai: A type of window covering made of a series of hinged, rigid plastic panels, hung from a traverse track.

Lapped seam: A seam, which is most useful for matching patterns together on the right sides of two separate pieces of fabric.

Lining: A fabric backing for a drapery.

Lintel: Wood, steel or reinforced concrete beams placed over both window and door openings to hold up the wall and roof above.

Lit a la Polonnaise: A drape set made to fall from a center point above a bed.

Lock stitch: A stitch purposely made loose, to give way for a little movement. An excellent stitch when used for holding together fabrics, linings and interlinings.

Louvers: Slats, generally made from metal, wood or plastic. These can be horizontal or vertical and are used for blinds and shutters.

M

Master carrier: Two arms that overlap in the center of a rod when draperies are closed, allowing them to close completely.

Milium: Trade name for a thermal lining.

Miniblinds: A series of one-inch, horizontal metal or plastic slats, which are held together with a cord. They can be tilted and lifted. Micro-miniblinds are similar except that the slats are only a half inch.

Miter: A technique in folding the fabric so as to keep excess fabric out of sight, eliminating bulk.

Mitered corner: The formation of the bottom edge of a drapery with a 45-degree angle on hem side.

Modern Period: A design period dating from 1900 to present.

Mullion: The vertical wood or masonry sections between a series of window frames.

Multi-draw: The simultaneous opening and closing of several draperies on one rod at one time.

Muntin: The horizontal wooden strips that separate panes of glass in windows.

N

Neoclassic Period: A design period dating from 1760 to 1789 in France, 1770 to 1820 in England and 1790 to 1820 in America.

Notch: A tiny cut, usually in a V-shape, at the edge of a fabric.

O

Off-center: A window not centered on a wall, but draperies still meet at its center point.

One-way draw: Drapery designed to draw only one way, in one panel.

Opacity: A degree measuring the amount to which solid material blocks view and light.

Open cuff: On the backside of a drapery and at top. Open cuffs make one of the strongest type headings on any drapery. This results when you carry both fabrics to the top and make a turn with the crinoline.

Oriel bay: Similar to a corbel bay window, but having the second story window descend down to the first floor.

Orientation: A term used to describe the direction in which a window faces: north, east, south or west.

Outside mount: A treatment installed over and to the side of a window frame on the wall.

Overdraperies: A layer of drapery fabric which is installed over an existing layer of drapery.

Overlap: The part of a drapery panel, which rides the master carrier of a traverse rod, and overlaps in the center when draperies are drawn closed, usually 3½" on each side.

P

Padded edge: A fabric border rolled and stuffed to form a long, round shape.

Palladian window: A window consisting of a high, rounded, middle section and two lower squared sections at each side. Also know as a Venetian window.

Panel: One half of a pair of draperies or curtains.

Passementerie: This term is used to describe the vast range of trimmings and decorative edges.

Pattern repeat: The distance between any given point in a design to where that exact point is repeated again.

Pelmet: A upholstered wood cornice or stiffened and shaped valance.

Pencil-pleat heading: Formed by a certain type of tape that, when pulled together, creates a column of tightly-packed folds.

Period window treatment: Refers to historically designed treatments from any specific design period.

Picture window: A type of window with a large center glass area with two smaller glass areas on each side.

Pinch pleats: A drapery heading where the basic pleat is divided into two or three smaller, equal pleats, sewn together at the bottom edge on the right side of the fabric.

Pin-on-hook: A metal pin to fasten draperies to a rod. It pins into drapery pleats and hooks to traverse carrier or café rod.

Piping: Cords used at the edges of a curtain for added effects, usually fabric covered and put in through a seam.

Pivot: This technique requires the machine to be stopped with the needle down in the fabric, which is turned at the corner before continuing to stitch.

Plate glass: A design which was popular in France from the seventeenth century to the nineteenth century. Molten glass is ironed smooth after being poured onto a table, and is then made into large sheets.

Pleat: A fold of cloth sewn into place to create fullness.

Pleat to: The finished width of the fabric after it has been pleated. Example: A width of 48" fabric has been pleated to 18", i.e., "Pleat To" 18".

Pleater tape: Pocketed heading material designed to be used with pleating hooks.

Polonnaise: A bed set against the wall lengthwise, having a small, ascending dome.

Portiere: A term used to describe a doorway treatment, either a hung curtain or drapery.

Pouf shade: Shades or valances with a soft looking fabric and a gathered hem.

Pressing: An important part of sewing technique. With an iron selected to the appropriate setting for a particular fabric, a steaming method is used by lifting the iron up and pressing it down, instead of sliding it across the fabric.

Principles of design: The theory of design made possible by manipulating the elements of design to create proper balance, emphasis, proportion and scale.

Priscilla curtains: Curtains with ruffled valance, sides, bottom, hem and ties. They are usually made from sheer or opaque fabrics and sometimes they meet or cross in the center.

Projection: Refers to a jutting out, an extension. On a curtain or drapery rod, it is that part which returns to the wall from the front of the rod.

Protractor: A drapery tool by which exact angles are measured (as in bay windows).

R

Railroading: Some decorator fabrics use railroading in correspondence to widths for floor-length treatments. In this technique the lengthwise grain runs in a horizontal manner across the window treatment, making vertical seams unnecessary.

Ready-mades: Standard size draperies, factory-made and available at local stores or through mail order sources.

Renaissance Period: A design period dating from 1400 to 1600 in Italy, 1589 to 1643 in France and 1558 to 1649 in England. An era rich in art, literature, architecture and science.

Repeat: The space from one design motif to the next on a patterned fabric.

Return: The distance from the face of the rod to the wall of the casing where the bracket is attached.

Reveals: Sides to a window opening, with right angles facing the wall and window.

Rococo Period: A French design period dating from 1730 to 1760, where decorations were curved, asymmetrical and ornamental.

Rod: A metal or plastic device from which curtains are hung, an alternative to a pole. Double rods are used for two layers of fabric.

Rod pocket: A hollow sleeve in the top—and sometimes the bottom—of a curtain or drapery through which a rod is inserted. The rod is then attached to a solid wall surface.

Rod width: Measures the width between the end of a bracket to the end of the other bracket including the stackback and window width.

Roller shade: A shade operated by a device with a spring.

When the spring is let loose, the shade coils itself around the device's cylinder.

Roman shade: A corded shade with rods set horizontally in back to give the shade a number of neat sideset pleats or folds when raised.

Ruching: A thin area of pleated or gathered fabric, often used for trimming or tiebacks.

Ruffle: A decorative trimming consisting of a strip of gathered fabric.

R-Value: A window treatment, ceiling or wall's capacity to keep heat in or out.

S

Sash: A wooden frame used to hold the glass of swinging and sliding windows.

Sash curtain: Any sheer material hung close to the window glass. Usually hung from spring tension rods or sash rods mounted inside the window casing.

Sash rod: A small rod, either decorative or plain, usually mounted inside a window frame on the sash.

Scalloped heading: A popular top treatment for café curtains featuring semi-circular spaces between curtain rings.

Seam: Stitching two pieces of fabric together at the right sides, leaving the stitches hidden on the other side of the fabric, for a clean, finished look on the right side.

Seam allowance: A slim, extra allowance in the fabric between the line for stitching and the raw edge of the fabric.

Selvedge: The tightly woven edge on a width of fabric to hold the fabric together.

Shade: A window covering usually made from cloth or vinyl that covers the glass, and rolls up or down off of the window.

Shirring: A rod that is smaller than the fabric width is slid through a rod pocket to create a gathered effect in the fabric.

Shoji screen: An oriental design with paper attached to a wooden grid, forming a translucent effect with sliding or stationary panels.

Shutters: A series of folding wooden panels, which are hung by a side hinge.

Side hem: The turned part forming a finished edge at the side of the drapery.

Sill: The horizontal "ledge-like" portion of a window casing.

Skylight: A window set into a ceiling or roof, made from glass or plastic.

Slides: Small runners installed in a traverse rod which hold a drapery pin or hook.

Slip stitch: Matching colored thread is used to stitch the folded edge of a lining to the base fabric.

Smocked heading: A curtain heading consisting of a honeycomb effect. A heading full of pencil pleats hooked together at specific spacing give this effect.

Spacing: Refers to the flat space between pleats; the fuller the drapery, the less the spacing.

Spanish arch: A rounded arch designed in Spanish fashion.

Stacking: The area required for draperies when they are completely open. Also referred to as stackback.

Swag: A section of draped fabric above a window.

T

Tails: Shaped and stiffened or free falling, hanging trails of fabric from the end of swags.

Tambour curtains: Curtains that originally were used as folk craft in Scandinavia, they are lightweight or sheer embroidered fabrics.

Tape-gathered heading: A gathered effect for curtain headings, using thin threaded tape sewn onto the top of a curtain and then pulled by the parallel threads.

Tension pulley: The pulley attachment through which the traverse cords move for one continuous smooth operation when a drapery is drawn. May be mounted on a baseboard, casing or wall, on one or both sides.

Tester: A canopy supported by a bed with tall corner posts.

Tie: A thin strip of fabric which is used with tiebacks to secure a drapery to a wall. The tie can be decorated or shaped.

Tiebacks: Decorative pieces of hardware, sometimes called holdbacks. Available in many forms and designed to hold draperies back from the window to allow light passage or add an additional decorative touch to the window treatment.

Tier: Curtain layers arranged one above the other with a normal overlap of 4". Upper tiers project from the wall at a greater distance than lower panels to allow each curtain to hang free.

Traverse: To draw across. A traverse drapery is one that opens or closes across a window by means of the traverse rod from which it is hung.

Traverse rod: A rod which is operated by a cord and pulley.

Turkish bed: A thin bed set back into a draped alcove.

U

Under draperies: A lightweight drapery, usually a sheer, closest to the window glass. It hangs beneath a heavier over-drapery.

V

Valance: A horizontal decorative fabric treatment used at the top of draperies to screen hardware and cords.

Victorian Period: A design period dating from 1837 to 1910 in England and 1840 to 1920 in America.

W

Wall fasteners: Window treatments are fastened to hollow walls using toggle bolts or molly bolts.

Weave: The act of interlacing when forming a piece of fabric.

Weights: Lead weights are sewn into the vertical seams and corners of a drapery panel. Chain weights are small beads, strung in a line along the bottom hemline of sheers, to ensure an even hemline and straight hanging.

Width: A word to describe a single width of fabric. Several widths of fabric are sewn together to make a panel of drapery.

Z

Zigzag stitch: One of various sewing machine settings. In this stitch, the needle moves back and forth, at the desired length and width, in a zigzag pattern. This stitch is often used for finishing seams.

Glossary of fabric terms

A

Acetate: Used to make many persuasive artificial silks. It has similar draping and finish qualities to silk but is less likely to rot or fade.

Acrylic: A soft lightweight fabric made from a synthetic longchain polymer, primarily made of acrylonitrile.

Aluminum-coated: A lining used to help exclude light, heat and cold. It is not visible, as it faces inside the fabric, while the outside of the fabric shows woven cream cotton.

Antique satin: One of the most common drapery fabrics sold. Characterized by a lustrous effect, normally composed of rayon/acetate blends.

B

Baize: Similar to flannel and dyed green or red. Mostly used for card tables or lining silverware drawers. Its texture and color make it convenient for improvised shades or curtains. Fades in sunlight.

Basketweave: Plain under- and over-weave; primarily in draperies.

Batik: A dyeing technique developed in Java, where dye is applied and then washed, leaving bold patterns.

Batiste: A soft finished fabric, which has a high count of fine yarns. It is more opaque than voiles. Usually composed of 100% polyester or a polyester blend.

Batting: A man-made fluffy fiber, used for padding edges.

Bias: A diagonal line which intersects the crosswise and lengthwise grain of any fabric. Woven fabrics, which do not stretch at the crosswise or lengthwise grains, do stretch at the bias.

Blackout: A heavy interlining in which a layer of opaque material is placed between two pieces of cotton to block out any light. Improves the drapability qualities. It is most often white or cream.

Boucle: French for curled, indicates a curled or looped surface.

Broadcloth: (1) A medium to heavyweight twill blend or worsted wool fabric which is napped and felted. (2) A cotton fabric similar to muslin, due to its fine crosswise cords.

Brocade: Rich jacquard-woven fabric with all-over interwoven design of raised figures or flowers. Brocade has a raised surface in contrast to felt damask, and is generally made of silk, rayon and nylon yarns with or without metallic treatment.

Brocatelle: Usually made of silk or wool, similar to brocades.

Bump: Interlining imported from England, heavy weight, cotton, and available bleached or unbleached. Similar to table felt and reinforcement felt, but slightly stiffer. Cotton flannel is often used instead of bump.

Burlap: Coarse, canvas-like fabric made of jute, hemp or cotton. Also called Gunny.

C

Canvas: A heavy woven cotton and linen blend, similar to cotton duck.

Casements: Open-weave casual fabric, characterized by its instability.

Challis: One of the softest fabrics made. Normally made of rayon and sometimes combined with cotton.

Cheesecloth: Cheap and loosely woven, this fabric will easily fade, wrinkle and shrink. Similar to muslin.

Chiffon: A transparent sheer fabric with a soft finish.

Chintz: Glazed cotton fabric often printed with bright colors or large, floral designs. Some glazes will wash out in laundering. The only durable glaze is a resin finish which will withstand washing or dry cleaning. Unglazed chintz is called cretonne.

Corduroy: A cut-filling pile cloth with narrow to wide wales which run in the warp direction of the goods and made possible by the use of an extra set of filling yarns in the construction. The back is of plain or twill weave, the latter affording the better construction. Washable types are available and stretch and durable press garments of corduroy are very popular. Usually an all-cotton cloth, some corduroy is now made with nylon or rayon pile effect on a cotton backing fabric or with polyester-cotton blends.

Cotton: An inexpensive, versatile fiber which can be printed, dyed and finished in numerous ways. It also has the ability to be made colorfast and withstand light and heat. It is popular among furnishing fabrics when used alone or as a cotton blend. Its shortcomings include crushing and mildewing.

Cotton duck: A cotton varying in weight from 7 to 15 oz. per yard. Heavier types are ideal for no-sew curtains as lining is unnecessary and the edges can be glued or pinked.

Cotton lawn: Finely woven cotton, given an extremely smooth finish.

Crash: A coarse fabric having a rough, irregular surface obtained by weaving thick, uneven yarns. Usually cotton or linen, sometimes spun rayon or blends.

Cretonne: A cotton fabric usually having printed floral or angular shapes. It is a plain weave, unglazed and coarser than chintz.

Crewelwork: Indian Cotton, wool or linen fabric adorned with wool chain stitching. Most often on a cream background. Used as early American and English bed hangings.

Crinoline: A heavily-sized, stiff fabric used as a foundation to support the edge of a hem or puffed sleeve. Can be used as interlining. Also referred to as Buckram.

Crosswise grain: Crosswise grain runs perpendicular to the selvages on woven fabric.

D

Dacron: A synthetic fiber with good filling and padding qualities.

Damask: Firm, glossy jacquard-patterned fabric. Similar to brocade but flatter and reversible. Can be made from linen, cotton, rayon or silk, or a combination of fibers.

Denim: A sturdy fabric, mostly in dark blue, twill weave.

Domette: A lightweight cotton interlining imported from England. Similar to American needle-punched fleece. It is used with light shades, curtains and swags.

Dotted Swiss: A sheer fabric with opaque dots, sometimes given a raised texture.

Double knit: A fabric knitted with a double stitch on a double needle frame to provide a double thickness and is the same on both sides. Has excellent body and stability.

Dupion: Textured, real or synthetic silk. It is lightweight, which gives this fabric the tendency to rot or fade. Synthetic dupion is made from viscose and acetate and real silk dupion is typically imported from India.

E

Eyelet: Embroidered white cotton fabric often used for unlined shades or light curtains.

F

Faille: Plain weave (flat-rib); with filling yarns heavier than warp.

Figured material: A fabric whose pattern is created from the structure of the weave.

Foamback: Term used to denote that a fabric has been laminated to a backing of polyurethane foam.

Fusible buckram: A strip of white cotton filled with glue and used as a stiffener. Good for use inside of hand-pleated headings to avoid the visibility of machine stitching. It is fused to the fabric with a hot iron.

Fusible heavyweight buckram: An open-weave stiffener, made from jute and filled with glue. It is used for the base of a cornice. A hot iron will fuse it in place, releasing the glue.

G

Gauze: A sheer but coarse fabric, available in a variety of thread thicknesses.

Gimp: A wind of fabric which can be stiffened with wire or cord.

Gingham: A cheap, classic cotton fabric with a checkered pattern. The checkers come in a variety of sizes and mostly primary colors.

Glassing: Thin finish provides luster, sheen, shine or polish to some fabrics. Chintz is an example of a glazed fabric.

Grosgrain: A silk fabric with a ribbed texture on surface.

H

Hand, handle: The reaction of the sense of touch when fabrics are held in the hand. There are many factors which give "character or individuality" to a material observed through handling.

Herringbone: A versatile medium weight fabric with a zigzag pattern, named after the spine of the herring fish. It is a novelty twill weave, available mostly in neutral colors. Also called Chevron.

Holland: A linen or cotton medium-weight fabric, fade resistant and sturdy, also stiffened with oil or shellac. Standard for valances and roller shades due to its non-fraying edges.

I

Ikat: Chinese cotton or silk fabric with faint geometric patterns as a result of tie dying.

Inherent flame frees: Fabric woven of from unprocessed, flame-resistant material and flame-free for the life of the fabric.

Interfacing: A fabric stiffener used to give support and hold the shape of the fabric.

J

Jacquard: A loom which can produce woven patterns in a variety of colors. The patterns are known for being intricate and large.

Jute: An inexpensive, easily available and long lasting fabric. Comes in a neutral color but can be dyed. Like linen, it is one of the most important fabrics.

K

Khaki: A beige or earth toned, plain or twill weave fabric with a wide range of uses.

L

Lace: Openwork fabric, generally made from cotton, created by twisting and knotting threads against a net-like background to form the desired design. Lace has an endless variety of designs and is convenient for glass curtains.

Lengthwise grain: Runs parallel to the selvages on woven fabric. Fabrics are typically stronger along the lengthwise grain.

Linen: A product of the flax plant. Linen possesses rapid moisture absorption, a neutral luster and stiffness and will not soil quickly.

Linen union: A cotton-linen blend fabric, durable and reasonably priced.

M

Madras cotton: Inexpensive Indian cotton, woven in a checkered, plaid or striped fashion and brightly colored. Sometimes referred to as sari fabric.

Marquisette: An open mesh, thin fabric. Usually made from synthetic fibers.

Matelasse: Appearance of a quilted weave; figured pattern with a raised, bubbly surface.

Mesh: A term used to describe textiles or open-weave fabrics having a net-like structure.

Modacrylic: A modified fiber in which the fiber-forming substance of any long-chain synthetic polymer is composed of less than 85%, but at least 25%, acrylonitrile units.

Mohair: Comes from the Angora goat. It is lighter weight drapery fabric with a slightly brushed or hairy finish.

Moiré: A finish-given cotton, silk, acetate, rayon, nylon, etc., where bright and dim effects are observed. This is achieved by passing the fabric between engraved rollers which press the particular motif into the fabric.

Moreen: A heavyweight fabric in a wool or wool and cotton blend fabric, usually having a watered pattern.

Muslin: Usually white or off-white in color, this fabric is sheer and delicately woven, but strong.

N

Ninon: A smooth, transparent, high-textured type of voile fabric. Usually made from 100% polyester.

Non-fusible buckram: A medium-weight cotton stiffener, typically sewn into tiebacks.

Non-fusible heavyweight buckram: Two-ply double starched stiffener made from jute; unlike fusible heavyweight buckram, it is sewn onto the cornice instead of being fused. It is also easier to clean than the fusible version.

Nylon: A durable and versatile fabric, made from a long-chain polymer, originating from petroleum, air, natural gas and water. It has remarkable strength and is moderately priced.

O

Olefin: A wax-like fiber, made from petroleum products. It is lightweight but strong, and inexpensive.

Ombre: A graduate or shade effect of color used in a striped motif. Usually ranges from light to dark tones. Also called jaspe or strie.

Organdy: Very light and thin, transparent, stiff and wiry cotton cloth. Its crispness will withstand repeated launderings Organdy is a true, durable finish cloth.

P

Padding: A soft and bulky fabric used for stuffing or filling.

Paisley: A timeless motif, this fine woolen cloth has detailed pine, floral or scroll-type designs printed or woven onto it.

Plaid: A fabric which can be printed or woven with rectangular and square shapes in a variety of colors.

Plush: A favorite of the Victorian era, this fabric is an old-fashioned form of velvet made from wool, mohair, and less often cotton, with a deeper but more thinly scattered pile. Now in modern times, it is man made.

Polyester: A stable fabric which displays excellent drapability. This fabric can be woven or knit.

Poplin: Sometimes printed decoratively, this is a plain weave with raised, circular weft cords created with large filling threads. Can be cotton, blend or synthetic and has a variety of uses.

R

Raw edge: The edge of fabric which is cut, having neither selvage nor hem.

Rayon: Displays a texture similar to silk in touch and visibility. Rayon is available in a vast range of textures and types.

Repp: A fabric having ribbed qualities or appearance.

S

Saran: A plastic, vinyl fiber, durable and colorfast.

Sateen: A firmly woven, strong cotton or cotton blend fabric, usually having stripes or bright solid colors. The finish is smooth and shiny.

Satin weave: One of the three basic weaves, the others being plain and twill. The surface of satin weave cloth is made almost entirely of warp or filling floats since, in the repeat of the weave, each yarn of one system passes or floats over or under all but one yarn of the opposite system. Satin weaves have a host of uses including brocade, brocatelle and damask.

Selvage: Each side edge of a woven fabric and an actual part of the warp in the goods. Other names for it are listing, self edge, and raw edge.

Shantung: An inconsistently textured raw silk, once hand-woven in China's Shantung Province.

Silk: The only natural fiber that comes in a filament form, reeled from the cocoon, cultivated or wild.

Slub yarn: Yarn of any type which is irregular in diameter. May be caused by error, or may purposely be made with slubs to bring out a desired effect.

Suede cloth: A fabric made to be similar to suede leather in visibility and touch.

T

Taffeta: A fine, plain weave fabric that is smooth on both sides, usually with a sheen on its surface.

Tapestry: A heavy, well insulating fabric, once made in replication of hand-sewn tapestries, but now produced on a jacquard loom.

Tartan: A cloth fabric made of a specific checkered pattern, having particular colors of a certain Scottish clan. This fabric has great insulating qualities.

Terry cloth: This cloth fabric has uncut loops on both sides of the cloth. Terry is also made on a jacquard loom to form interesting motifs.

Texture: (1) The actual number of warp threads and filling picks per inch in any cloth that has been woven. (2) The finish and appearance of cloth.

Thread count: (1) The actual number of warp ends and filling picks per inch in a woven cloth, also known as texture. (2) In knitted fabric, thread count implies the number of wales or ribs, and the courses per inch.

Ticking: A striped cotton fabric, traditionally made of only black and white, but now comes in a wide variety of colors.

It is used for covering mattresses or cushion pads, or can be made into curtains or shades.

Tricot: Usually made from nylon, this soft and thin fabric is made with crosswise elastic ribs in the back and non-elastic on top. It is seldom used for draperies due to its lack of body, but is beneficial for custom sheeting.

Tussah silk: A raw, typically Indian silk, in a yellowish-brown color, difficult to dye.

V

Velour: (1) A term loosely applied to cut pile cloths in general, but also to fabrics with a fine, raised finish. (2) A cut pile cotton fabric comparable with cotton velvet but with a greater and denser pile. (3) A stable, high-grade woolen fabric which has a close, fine, dense, erect and even nap which provides a soft, pleasing hand.

Velvet: A warp pile cloth in which a succession of rows of short cut pile stand close together so as to give an even, uniform surface. When the pile is more than one-eighth of an inch high, the cloth is usually called Plus.

Viscose (Rayon): The most ancient of man-made fibers. Well known for its distinctive sheen used in highlighting patterns and its ability to add luster and strength to cotton and silk blends.

Voile: A thin, open-mesh cloth made by a variation of plain weave. Most voiles are made of polyester. Similar to ninon, but with a much finer denier of yarn with a soft, drapable hand.

W

Warp: The yarns which run vertically or lengthwise in woven fabric.

Weft: The yarns which run horizontally in woven fabric.

Wool: An expensive versatile fabric which comes from the fleece of domesticated sheep. It has excellent insulating uses and is wrinkle and flame resistant.

Worsted: Fabric made of twisted yarn, of a wool type.

Textile fibers & their properties

Man-made fibers

Rayon

Blended with other fibers: cotton, acetate and linen.

- Drapability: good hang, soft hand
- Color fastness: good to excellent (solution dyed)
- Sun resistance: good, but not as good as cotton or linen
- Abrasion resistance: good, but not as good as cotton or nylon
- Sagging: poor, stretches in loose yarns, but OK in tightly woven fabrics
- Resiliency: good, does not pack, wrinkles less than cotton or linen
- Care: dry clean and iron at medium temperature

Acetate

Blends well with other fibers, including rayon and nylon.

- Drapability: good hand, soft hand
- Color fastness: good (solution dyed)
- Sun resistance: good, but not as good as cotton or linen
- Abrasion resistance: good, but not as good as cotton or nylon
- Sagging: poor, stretches in loose yarns, but OK in tightly woven fabrics
- Resiliency: good, does not pack, wrinkles less than cotton or linen
- Care: dry clean and iron at low temperature

Polyester

An excellent fabric for most drapery applications. Blends well with other fibers. In polyester cotton blends, the fabric will wrinkle less.

- Drapability: excellent hang, very soft hand
- Color fastness: good to excellent
- Sun resistance: excellent
- Abrasion resistance: good, sheers must be handled with care as fabric can bruise.
- Sagging: excellent, does not stretch or shrink

- Resiliency: good to excellent, does not pack, wrinkle-free
- Care: wash or dry clean and iron at low temperature

Nylon

Not widely used in drapery fabric.

- Drapability: good, soft to stiff hand, not as soft as polyesters
- Color fastness: good to excellent
- Sun resistance: poor
- Abrasion resistance: excellent
- Sagging: excellent, does not sag
- Resiliency: good to excellent, does not pack, wrinkle-free
- Care: dry clean and iron at low temperature

Acrylic

Hangs well and does not sag. Can be blended with polyester. Modacrylics are flame-resistant.

- Drapability: excellent, very soft hand
- Color fastness: excellent, if solution dyed
- Sun resistance: excellent, good as cotton or linen
- Abrasion resistance: good
- Sagging: very good, does not stretch
- Resiliency: very good, does not pack, wrinkle-free
- Care: dry clean and iron at low temperature, 50 degrees

Dynel

- Drapability: excellent, soft hand like acrylic
- Color fastness: excellent
- Sun resistance: good to excellent
- Abrasion resistance: excellent
- Sagging: excellent, compared to rayon or acetate
- Resiliency: very good, does not pack, wrinkle-free
- Low flammability
- Care: wash only, ironing does not affect it much, use low heat

Natural fibers

Cotton

Generally wears excellently in drapery (print or plains).

- Drapability: excellent hang, soft hand
- Color fastness: good, vat dyes best
- Sun resistance: excellent, sun does not rot
- Abrasion resistance: excellent
- Sagging: does not stretch, except when wet
- Resiliency: poor, packs easily, wrinkles easily, very absorbent, burns
- Care: wash or dry clean and iron at high temperature

Linen or flax

Excellent in plain and casement fabric and good in prints.

- Drapability: good hang, not as soft as cotton
- Color fastness: good to poor, prints do not hold their color as well as plain fabrics
- Sun resistance: excellent, sun does not rot
- Abrasion resistance: excellent
- Sagging: strong, does not stretch
- Resiliency: poor, packs badly, does wrinkle
- Care: dry clean and iron at high temperature

Silk

Rarely used due to sun rot and cost.

- Drapability: good hang, medium to soft hand
- Color fastness: good
- Sun resistance: poor, rots in short time, lining helps
- Abrasion resistance: good
- Sagging: strong, does not sag
- Resiliency: good, does not pack badly
- Care: dry clean and iron at medium temperature

Wool

Virtually unused as drapery fabric.